Daniel's Son of Man in Mark

Daniel's Son of Man in Mark

A Redefinition of the Jerusalem Temple and the Formation of a New Covenant Community

Robert S. Snow

◥PICKWICK *Publications* • Eugene, Oregon

DANIEL'S SON OF MAN IN MARK
A Redefinition of the Jerusalem Temple and the Formation of a New Covenant Community

Copyright © 2016 Robert S. Snow. All rights reserved. Except for brief quotations in critical publications or reviews, no part of this book may be reproduced in any manner without prior written permission from the publisher. Write: Permissions, Wipf and Stock Publishers, 199 W. 8th Ave., Suite 3, Eugene, OR 97401.

Pickwick Publications
An Imprint of Wipf and Stock Publishers
199 W. 8th Ave., Suite 3
Eugene, OR 97401

www.wipfandstock.com

PAPERBACK ISBN: 978-1-4982-7894-2
HARDCOVER ISBN: 978-1-4982-7896-6
EBOOK ISBN: 978-1-4982-7895-9

Cataloguing-in-Publication data:

Names: Snow, Robert S.

Title: Daniel's Son of Man in Mark : A Redefinition of the Jerusalem Temple and the Formation of a New Covenant Community / Robert S. Snow.

Description: Eugene, OR: Pickwick Publications, 2016 | Includes bibliographical references and index.

Identifiers: ISBN 978-1-4982-7894-2 (paperback) | ISBN 978-1-4982-7896-6 (hardcover) | ISBN 978-1-4982-7895-9 (ebook)

Subjects: LSCH: Bible. Mark—Criticism, interpretation, etc. | Bible. Daniel—Criticism, interpretation, etc. | Son of Man. | subject

Classification: BT232 S6 2016 (print) | BT232 (ebook)

Manufactured in the U.S.A.   10/20/16

To Jen, with all my love

Contents

Acknowledgments | ix

Chapter 1: Introduction | 1
    A Brief Survey of Research on the Son of Man | 2
    A Narrative and Intertextual Approach | 6
    Chapter Outline | 14

Chapter 2: Daniel's "One Like a Son of Man" | 16
    Introduction | 16
    Historical Context | 17
    Literary Context | 24
    Judgement from the Heavenly Temple | 28
    The Danielic Son of Man and Faithful Israel | 37
    Conclusion | 42

Chapter 3: The Son of Man in 1 Enoch 37–71 and 4 Ezra 13 | 44
    Introduction | 44
    The Son of Man in the *Parables* | 45
    The Son of Man in *4 Ezra* | 57
    Conclusion | 64

Chapter 4: The Son of Man's Divine Authority on Earth | 67
    Introduction | 67
    Literary Context of Mark 2:1–12 and 2:23–28 | 68

CONTENTS

  The Son of Man's Authority to Forgive Sins | 72
  The Son of Man's Authority Over the Sabbath | 80
  Conclusion | 90

Chapter 5: The Son of Man's Suffering and Death | 92
  Introduction | 92
  Predictions of the Son of Man's Suffering,
  Death, and Resurrection | 94
  The Purpose of the Son of Man's Suffering and Death | 115
  Conclusion | 123

Chapter 6: The Coming of the Son of Man
     in the Heavenly Temple | 126
  Introduction | 126
  The Coming of the Son of Man in 8:38 | 127
  The Coming of the Son of Man in 13:26–27 | 137
  The Coming of the Son of Man in 14:62 | 153
  Initial Fulfilment: Rending of the Temple Veil
  and Going to Galilee | 167
  Conclusion | 170

Chapter 7: Conclusion | 174

Bibliography | 181
Author Index | 201
Subject Index | 205
Ancient Document Index | 211

Acknowledgments

THIS WORK IS A substantially revised version of my PhD thesis which I completed at the University of Manchester in 2008. I began this degree in 2002, and there were a number of individuals that supported me throughout this period. My advisor, Dr. Kent E. Brower, was a continual source of encouragement, offering not only insightful and probing critiques of my work, but also prompt ones at that. I would like to thank my wife, Jen, for her continued support and encouragement during these years, making many sacrifices so that the hope of completion would become reality. I also want to express my gratitude to my mother-in-law, Carol Straiton, for always being available to help Jen with Nathan, our son, while I was studying in Manchester.

In 2013, I undertook a major revision of my thesis to prepare it for publication. The generous sabbatical policy at Ambrose University, where I am Associate Professor of New Testament, made it possible for me to carry out the majority of this revision in a timely manner. Finally, I would like to thank my research assistant, Nikayla Reize, for her assistance in formatting this work to conform it to the house style of Pickwick Publications at Wipf and Stock Publishers.

Chapter 1: Introduction

EVEN A BRIEF SURVEY of scholarship on the Son of Man [SM] reveals that this topic is a near insolvable matter of debate and has been for many years. In 1955, T. W. Manson observed that "the problems raised by the use of this phrase [ὁ υἱὸς τοῦ ἀνθρώπου] are among the most complex and difficult in New Testament study . . . [in which] definite generally accepted conclusions are still few in comparison with the vast amount of labor and learning expended on various problems which have arisen."[1] Typically, the majority of studies analyze the issue from an historical perspective with many different assumptions and methods that produce just as many results and conclusions. This is quite evident in a recently published collection of essays on the SM titled *'Who is This Son of Man?': The Latest Scholarship on a Puzzling Expression of the Historical Jesus*.[2] One of the editors, Larry W. Hurtado, concludes the volume arguing that the use of ὁ υἱὸς τοῦ ἀνθρώπου in the Gospels reflects Jesus' own distinctive use of the phrase which for him, along with the Gospel authors, expresses "some sort of emphasis on him as a particular human being, [but] the expression 'the son of man' has little by way of inherent Christological meaning."[3] Meanwhile, in another essay, Darrell L. Bock contends that Dan 7 had a formative influence on the historical Jesus' use of the phrase which communicates "a full vindication to a status that was inseparably connected to God's throne and rule."[4] The first three essays in the collection are all dedicated critiques of Maurice Casey's scholarship, particularly of his audaciously titled book, *The Solution to the "Son of Man" Problem*, highlighting flaws in both his method and conclusions.[5] Casey, one of the most prolific SM scholars, contends that

1. Manson, *Teaching of Jesus*, 211.
2. Hurtado and Owen, *"Who is This Son of Man?"*
3. Hurtado, "Summary," 167–68.
4. Bock, "Use of Daniel 7," 99.
5. Casey, *Solution*.

the solution to the SM problem is found in appreciating the Aramaic background of ὁ υἱὸς τοῦ ἀνθρώπου, but not all are convinced he has solved the problem, the present author included! Unlike the methodology of most scholarship on the SM that centers on the historical Jesus, to which no resolution seems to be in sight, this study examines the SM's portrayal in the Gospel of Mark from a narrative-critical and intertextual perspective arguing that Dan 7 has a formative influence on the markan figure. In this introductory chapter, I will survey past and current research on the SM explaining in more detail where this study fits within this scholarship and also explain the methodology by which I examine the sayings in Mark. I conclude with a brief outline and summary of the following chapters.

A Brief Survey of Research on the Son of Man

From the beginning of the twentieth century until the end of the 1960s, many scholars argued that the SM was a unified concept in pre-Christian Judaism.[6] According to this view, many Jews expected the heavenly, messianic SM to return at the end of time both to save and judge. The similar functions of the SM in the *Parables* and *4 Ezra*, inspired by Dan 7, form the basis of the "SM concept." For many of the scholars who subscribe to this approach, only the Gospel passages that depict the future coming of the SM are genuine, e.g., Mark 8:38; Luke 17:23–24; Matt 24:37–39.[7] Although many scholars today reject the apocalyptic SM concept,[8] there are common

---

6. Burkett, *Debate*, 43. For a detailed bibliography, see Longenecker, "Self-Designation," 151–58. Some of the seminal works include, Fuller, *Foundations*; Higgins, *Son of Man*; Tödt, *Son of Man*; Hahn, *Titles*.

7. Burkett claims that Rudolf Bultmann was one of the most notable proponents of this view having influenced many other scholars such as Hahn, *Titles*, 23–28 and Fuller, *Foundations*, 121–25 (*Debate*, 38). See Bultmann, *Theology*. See also Colpe, "ὁ υἱὸς τοῦ ἀνθρώπου," 77.

8. One of the first to reject this approach was Leivestad, "Exit," 243–67. His refutation marked a significant change in the landscape of the SM debate. Burkett, *Debate*, 74–76, provides three reasons that led to the demise this theory: 1. the absence of the *Parables* among the fragments of *1 Enoch* at Qumran called into question the pre-Christian origin of the enochic SM; 2. the argument of Norman Perrin and others who challenged the idea of the apocalyptic SM concept (see Perrin, *Rediscovering*, 164–72); and 3. Geza Vermes' investigation of the Aramaic meaning of the SM. One notable exception is Caragounis who argues "that the concept of the Son of Man was current at the time of Jesus and that its *characteristica* were those of a primarily exalted, transcendental being, seated beside the Almighty and with prerogatives and functions identical to his" (*Vision*, 164).

Chapter 1: Introduction

features between the depictions of the figure in the *Parables* and *4 Ezra* that studies of the Gospel SM cannot ignore.⁹

Another line of inquiry gained prominence in the 1970s, when some scholars began to refute the concept, which considered the Aramaic background of ὁ υἱὸς τοῦ ἀνθρώπου. In 1967, Geza Vermes published a highly influential essay titled, "The Use of בר נש/בר נשא in Jewish Aramaic" in which he argued that the Aramaic phrase functions as a circumlocution for "I" in Jewish Aramaic literature.¹⁰ Several years later, Vermes applied these findings to the Synoptic SM and concluded that the term functions as a circumlocution in twenty sayings, for example, Mark 2:10 and 2:28.¹¹ Although a number of scholars accepted this approach¹², the majority rejected it because in the Aramaic sources, בר אנש(א) does not function as a first person circumlocution, but rather generically referring to "man," or indefinitely "a man" or "someone."¹³ Alternatively, Maurice Casey argued that during the time of Jesus בר אנש(א) was a generic phrase for "man" which has two connotations. First, applied to Jesus, the phrase is used to make a general statement, e.g., Mark 14:21, and, second, the general statement communicates something about Jesus himself, e.g., Mark 2:10, 28.¹⁴ Meanwhile, Barnabas Lindars claimed that the idiomatic use of בר אנשא enables the speaker to refer "to a class of persons, with whom he identifies himself."¹⁵ Unlike Casey, who argued that the Aramaic phrase was either

---

9. See Horbury, "Messianic Associations," 34–55; Nickelsburg, "Son of Man," 137–50; Collins, "Son of Man," 448–66; Slater, "One Like," 183–98; and, most recently, Reynolds, *Apocalyptic Son of Man*, 19.

10. Vermes, "Appendix," 310–30. Specifically, the phrase is used "when (a) a speaker wishes to avoid undue or immodest emphasis on himself, or (b) when he is prompted by fear or by a dislike of asserting openly something disagreeable in relation to himself" ("Appendix," 320).

11. Vermes, *Jesus the Jew*, 160–91.

12. Some of these scholars include Dodd, *Founder of Christianity*, 110–13; Müller, "Have You Faith," 291–94; and Kingsbury, "Observations," 283–90.

13. Bowker, "Son of Man," 19–48; Casey, *Son of Man*, 224–26; Lindars, *Son of Man*, 19–24; Chilton, "Son of Man," 203–18. Fitzmyer, review of *Aramaic Approach*, 417–28; Lindars, "Another Approach," 58–68.

14. Casey, "Son of Man Problem," 148. Casey finds this general sense in twelve SM sayings which for him indicates authenticity: Mark 2:10; 2:28; 8:38; 9:12; 10:45; 14:21 (twice); Matt 8:20; 11:19; 12:32; Luke 12:8; 22:22. See also Casey, "General," 21–56 and, of course, his most recent publication, *Solution*.

15. Lindars, *Son of Man*, 24; Ibid., "New Look," 437–62; Ibid., "Jesus as Advocate," 476–97.

absolute or emphatic, Lindars maintained that Jesus used the emphatic בר אנשא which explains the Greek definite form in the Gospels.[16]

Finally, there are those who look to the OT to determine the significance of the SM.[17] Particularly relevant for this examination are studies which consider the relevance of Dan 7.[18] Morna Hooker, in the 1960s, dedicated an entire monograph to the study of Mark's use of the danielic SM and how it contributes to his presentation of Jesus.[19] During the zenith of form criticism, she carried out what might now be considered a literary-critical and intertextual examination of the markan SM. In the opening pages, Hooker stated that "our purpose in this book is . . . not to analyse the various groups or sources [of SM sayings], but to study the problem of the Son of man from another angle: we wish to study the impact which the 'Son of man' sayings make when we look at one gospel—St. Mark's."[20] As is clear from the preceding discussion on the current state of SM scholarship, not much has changed. Scholars still tend to examine possible Aramaic backgrounds of ὁ υἱὸς τοῦ ἀνθρώπου or the use of the term in the Synoptic tradition drawing very different conclusions.[21] In the introduction to her monograph, Hooker concluded that form-critical studies of the SM in the

---

16. Lindars, *Son of Man*, 24. For Casey's response to Lindars's position, see Casey, "General," 27-36. After reviewing the work of Casey and Lindars, Burkett, *Debate*, 92-96, responds that the non-titular idiomatic approach is not helpful as it fails to make sense of all but one of the SM sayings (Mark 3:28-29). Burkett claims that the Greek expression can have two meanings: "Depending on whether the first article is individualizing or generic, the Greek expression could mean 'the son of (the) man,' referring to an individual, or 'the human being' ('man' in a generic sense), but not 'a man'" (*Debate*, 93).

17. Note the following works: Manson, *Teaching of Jesus*, 211-34 [Is; Pss; Dan 7]; Maddox, "Function," 45-74 [Ezek; Dan; 1 En.]; Borsch, *Son of Man*, 314-401 [Gen; Pss; Dan; 1 En.]; Fitzmyer, "New Testament Title," 143-60 [Pss; Dan; DSS]; Mkole, "Mark 14:62," 1119-45 [Pss; Isa].

18. In addition to those who consider Dan 7 in the preceding footnote, see Marshall, "Synoptic Son of Man," 327-51 and Moule, "Neglected," 413-28. More recently, see Kellner, *Traum*; Jennings, "Martyrdom," 229-43; Tuckett, "Son of Man," 371-94; Schröter, "Son of Man," 34-68; Evans, "Daniel in the New Testament," 490-527; Shepherd, "Daniel 7:13," 99-111.

19. Hooker, *Son of Man*.

20. Ibid., 7.

21. The recent work of Reynolds, *Apocalyptic Son of Man*, is a welcomed exception to this long-standing trend. However, Reynolds does not consider how his analysis of John's SM sayings in their respective narrative contexts contributes to the Gospel's larger narrative. See Staley, review of *Apocalyptic Son of Man*, 160-61.

Chapter 1: Introduction

Gospel tradition cannot solve the SM problem.[22] Focusing only on Mark, however, and the intertextual background of Dan 7, a coherent picture emerged. She essentially argued that "the authority, necessity for suffering, and confidence in final vindication, which are all expressed in the Marcan [SM] sayings, can all be traced to Dan. 7."[23] In this work, I utilize her methodology of examining the markan SM in light of Dan 7 and will build upon her conclusions in light of a fresh examination of Dan 7 and its subsequent interpretation in the *Parables* and *4 Ezra*. I will also demonstrate how my analysis contributes to the development of Mark's theology, namely, that Jesus and his faithful followers become a new covenant community founded upon the SM's death thereby marking a shift of the locus of Yahweh's saving presence from the temple cult to the cross.

In this study, I do not take it for granted that the danielic "one like a son of man" is *the* formative background for Mark's SM and so I carefully argue for an allusion to Dan 7 in those passages where one is much less obvious, such as in the so-called "earthly" and "suffering" SM sayings. It is not unusual for some scholars to argue that the danielic SM is evoked in only a few of the sayings. For example, Norman Perrin claims that allusions to Dan 7 are limited to Mark 2:10 and 2:28.[24] About ten years ago, Larry Hurtado endorsed this in his statement that "it is neither necessary nor persuasive to see allusions to Dan 7 in any more than one or two sayings in which 'the son of man' expression appears in the Gospels."[25] Now, in his most recent publication on the subject, to which I referred above, Hurtado implies that Dan 7 does not have any relevance for the Gospel SM. There is also a current trend to ignore completely the OT background in favor of constructing meaning exclusively from its use in Mark. Harry L. Chronis focuses on the narrative function of the SM, as an *incognito* term for "the Son of God," to the exclusion of any OT significance mainly because intertextual analyses are "a path commonly taken but without much result."[26] Likewise, Ulrich Kmiecik, in the only monograph on the SM in Mark to appear in the last thirty years, pays very little attention to the OT.[27] He argues that the SM

---

22. Hooker, *Son of Man*, 5.

23. Ibid., 192.

24. Perrin, *Modern Pilgrimage*, 69–70.

25. Hurtado, *Lord Jesus Christ*, 297 fn. 93. Malbon only considers the danielic background for Mark 8:38, 13:26, and 14:62 ("Narrative Christology," 373–85).

26. Chronis, "Reveal and to Conceal," 465.

27. Kmiecik, *Der Menschensohn*.

is defined by Mark's use of "Messiah" and "Son of God" even disregarding the scriptural background of these titles. Further, there are those who claim that the phrase has absolutely no christological significance within the text of Mark. Douglas Hare comments that the SM self-designation "was apparently innocuous, either because it possessed no recognizable meaning or because its meaning was perceived as no more controversial than the phrase "the Son of the carpenter."[28] Simon Gathercole confirms this brief survey, which demonstrates an aversion to examining the OT background of the SM, and rightly warns that "this is a move which ... should be resisted."[29] This study provides a much needed counterpoint to scholarship which diminishes both the OT background of the SM, namely Dan 7, as well as its contribution to Mark's theology.

A Narrative and Intertextual Approach

Many scholars have long recognized an allusion to Dan 7 in Mark 8:38, 13:26, and 14:62, all of which contain terminology, in addition to "son of man," found in Dan 7:13–14. However, I will also argue that Mark alludes to the danielic figure in those texts where the only allusion is the SM epithet itself, e.g., 8:31; 9:31; 10:33–34; 10:45, and that he evokes aspects of the danielic context of the "one like a son of man" as well. As with any intertextual study, it is absolutely crucial to adopt a sound methodology to ensure that there are adequate controls to guide the examination so that one does not go beyond the data and argue for thematic evocations from an OT text which are simply not there, or propose an allusion when one does not exist. Although Richard B. Hays' influential monograph, *Echoes of Scripture in the Letters of Paul*, is not without its detractors, the guidelines he discusses at the beginning do provide necessary guidance for determining an allusion and what is relevant for the exegesis of the evoking text.[30] Despite the fact that Hays' work focuses on Paul, two recent studies on Mark's use of the OT rely upon his methodology. Timothy Gray argues in his work, *The Temple in the Gospel of Mark*, that Mark does not engage in an atomistic exegesis of OT texts but rather demonstrates an awareness of the wider context of his citations and allusions.[31] However, Gray rightly points out the potential for over-exegeting the

28. Hare, *Tradition*, 210. For a similar view, consult Kingsbury, *Christology*, 162.
29. Gathercole, "Son of Man," 372.
30. Hays, *Echoes of Scripture*, 29–32.
31. Gray, *Temple*, 5. Gray also refers to three recent studies on Mark that also consider

Chapter 1: Introduction

latter and for that reason adopts Hays' guidelines. Likewise, Kelli S. O'Brien, in her study of Scripture in Mark's passion narrative, relies upon Hays for identifying allusions and assessing their impact on exegesis.[32]

According to Hays, the OT functions as a metaphor in Paul's intertextual reflections: "the great stories of Israel continue to serve for him as a fund of symbols and metaphors that condition his perception of the world, of God's promised deliverance of his people, and of his own identity and calling."[33] To understand how these symbols and metaphors manifest themselves in Pauline literature, Hays appeals to the trope of metalepsis and argues that allusive echoes of Scripture in Paul enable the reader to appreciate "a field of whispered or unstated correspondences" between the evoked and evoking texts.[34] This is a valuable approach for considering what appears to be Mark's extrapolation or development of the danielic SM. According to O'Brien, "the meaning of the New Testament passage is drawn out, clarified, or heightened, by the meaning of the Old Testament passage."[35] It will become evident that analyzing Mark's SM in light of its danielic background enables one to see not only how Mark develops the figure but also the significant contribution that his portrayal of the SM makes to his narrative. For instance, in Mark 2:1–12, Jesus as the SM manifests a divine authority "upon the earth" (v. 10) when he forgives the sins of a paralytic, which, as the on-looking scribes indicate, is Yahweh's prerogative. Although the SM is not an active figure in Dan 7, it is evident that Mark develops the figure who now executes a task associated with Yahweh himself. This appears to be a natural corollary of the investiture of the "one like a son of man" in Yahweh's presence, and the markan SM's ability to forgive sins introduces a function that is related to the purpose of his suffering and death revealed later in the story: "to be a ransom for many" (10:45b).

---

the importance of the OT context of a quotation or an allusion and the light it sheds on Mark's narrative: Watts, *New Exodus*; Marcus, *Way*; Hatina, *Search*.

32. O'Brien, *Use of Scripture*, 602–3.

33. Hays, *Echoes of Scripture*, 16. This approach is not unrelated to the work of C. H. Dodd on early Christian *testimonia* in the NT. These *testimonia* are related to one another because they arise out of a particular view of God's involvement with his people over the course of the history of Israel. Dodd comments that this history "coheres well with the entire Hebrew-Christian *Weltanschauung*: its conception of the nature of man, of the relations between man and the universe, and of the relation of both to their Creator" (*According to the Scriptures*, 128).

34. Hays, *Echoes of Scripture*, 20.

35. O'Brien, *Use of Scripture*, 49.

O'Brien observes that it is not just the NT authors who reuse Scripture in these ways, but rather they follow in a long tradition of biblical authors who appropriate earlier texts and reinterpret them in the service of new situations, usually crises which arise in the life of the nation.[36] She cites Michael Fishbane who claims that the Scriptures of Israel are the "imaginative matrix" for the nation's self-understanding generated in response to various events.[37] Applying this to the Gospel of Mark, we will see that his use of the OT, namely Dan 7, does not merely generate new meaning on a literary level to be contained within the text, but rather, these intertextual moments inform the self-understanding of the community for whom he writes who live somewhere in the Greco-Roman Empire in the latter half of the first century CE. Although it is difficult to determine the location of Mark's audience, this does not mean that nothing can be said about this group on the basis of Mark's text. I will argue that the destruction of the Jerusalem temple is a crucial concern for Mark and his use of the SM plays an important role in helping his audience, or at the very least the implied audience, see themselves as the new locus of Yahweh's dwelling in light of its destruction wherever they are located in the Empire.

As I indicated above, interpreters must employ a method by which they identify proposed allusions because, according to Hays, some allusions are clearer than others.[38] Further, if interpreters establish an allusion, whether faint or strong, they must also carefully consider how much of the context of the OT text contributes to the new meaning generated in the NT text itself. O'Brien asserts that those scholars who claim that allusions also evoke OT contexts do not argue that every allusion does so and those who are not as inclined to appreciate the relevance of context do not argue that context is never important. Rather, according to O'Brien, it is a question of degree: how often and how much of the context should interpreters consider?[39] Hays's comment "as we move farther away from overt citation, the source recedes into the discursive distance, the intertextual relations become less determinate, and the demand placed on the reader's listening powers grows greater" highlights the need for interpreters to establish,

---

36. On the reuse of the OT within the OT itself, see, for example, Williamson, "History," 25–38. For the "re-written Bible," see Alexander, "Retelling the Old Testament," 99–121 and also the seminal work of Vermes, *Scripture and Tradition*.

37. O'Brien, *Use of Scripture*, 51.

38. Hays, *Echoes of Scripture*, 29.

39. O'Brien, *Use of Scripture*, 56.

Chapter 1: Introduction

for example, clear terminological correspondences between the text of the referring passage and that of the referred.[40]

Since there is not a fixed definition for the term *allusion* for studies in biblical intertextuality, establishing one is a helpful starting point. Hays, for instance, does not make a formal distinction between *echo* and *allusion* because "allusion depends both on the notion of authorial intention and on the assumption that the reader will share with the author the requisite 'portable library' to recognize the source of the allusion."[41] As for *echo*, he argues that it is a metaphor of and for alluding that is unrelated to authorial intention.[42] Given the difficulty of classifying a passage as an allusion, something intended by Mark or Paul, or as an echo, something unintended, Hays uses the terms interchangeably focusing less on authorial intention. Interestingly, however, his seven criteria for testing the likelihood of OT echoes betray some level of concern for establishing what an author wants to communicate. It is a short step, I believe, from employing a set of criteria to validate the presence of an OT text in Paul and its exegetical worth to making the reasonable claim that Paul, then, intended his readers to come to a nuanced understanding of the text because of its interplay with an evoked text. The same can be said for Mark: if purported allusions satisfy Hays' criteria, then it is quite likely that they actually reflect Mark's intention. In this study, I use the term *allusion* to describe OT texts to which Mark intends to refer that have terminological and thematic correspondence with his text. Understanding allusion in this way involves, of course, actually making the case for an intended allusion through a careful study of the relevant parts of Dan 7, subsequent interpretation of the SM in other second-temple Jewish literature, i.e., the *Parables* and *4 Ezra*, the text of Mark where the proposed allusion occurs and, finally, how the proposed reading brings more coherence to Mark's Gospel. All of these things are covered by Hays' methodology. I understand *echo*, on the other hand, to be a category where the terminological correspondences, if any, and thematic parallels are not limited to just one OT text as with allusion but are rather a product of the scriptural imagery furnishing the mind of Mark. O'Brien refers to the latter as *influence* in which an OT passage(s) might have influenced the thinking of the author, but there is no explicit textual connection.[43]

40. Hays, *Echoes of Scripture*, 23.
41. Ibid., 29.
42. Ibid.
43. O'Brien, *Use of Scripture*, 24.

Daniel's Son of Man in Mark

Below, I list and briefly define Hays' seven criteria, but, like Hays, I will not explain how each of these criteria apply to every markan passage that I discuss. Rather, I will refer to specific ones at relevant points throughout the study, and when I do so, I will italicize his terms for the sake of clarity.

1. *Availability*: Is the text of a proposed allusion available to the NT author? In Mark, we have two very clear allusions to Dan 7 in 13:26 and 14:62 which establish that Mark has access to Daniel.[44]

2. *Volume*: How loud or noticeable is the allusion? This is determined by the number of lexical correspondences between the evoking and the evoked text. Hays also considers how much emphasis the allusion receives in the NT writing itself. Does it occur in a climactic moment in the epistle or narrative, for example? As I have already noted, Dan 7:13 is clearly evoked in some passages, such as 13:26 and 14:62, which occur at crucial points in the narrative. In other passages, the allusion can only be established on the basis of the SM phrase itself, such as in 10:45. For this reason, some argue that Dan 7 does not form the background of the "passion-resurrection predictions." In response, ὁ υἱὸς τοῦ ἀνθρώπου which does not exactly reflect ὡς υἱὸς ἀνθρώπου, is likely an instance of interpretative rendering, which, as we will see does not obviate an allusion to Dan 7.[45] Mark and other first-century Jewish authors have developed the "one like a son of man" for their own purposes and in the process have not retained the danielic phrase. The authors of the *Parables* and *4 Ezra* 13 do not use the phrase "one like a son of man" but rather evoke the figure in their respective texts through imagery from Dan 7. This means that in at least two first-century Jewish texts an allusion to the danielic SM is not established on the basis of the use of the "one like a son of man" phrase which interpreters of the markan SM need to bear in mind. This prompts N. T. Wright to conclude that "it ought to be out of the

---

44. For example, note the verbal correspondences between Mark 13:26 and the two Greek versions of Dan 7:13:
Mark 13:26: καὶ τότε ὄψονται τὸν υἱὸν τοῦ ἀνθρώπου ἐρχόμενον ἐν νεφέλαις μετὰ δυνάμεως πολλῆς καὶ δόξης.
Dan 7:13 LXX: ἰδοὺ ἐπὶ τῶν νεφελῶν τοῦ οὐρανοῦ ὡς υἱὸς ἀνθρώπου ἤρχετο
Dan 7:13 Theod.: ἰδοὺ μετὰ τῶν νεφελῶν τοῦ οὐρανοῦ ὡς υἱὸς ἀνθρώπου ἐρχόμενος ἦν

45. I borrow the phrase, interpretative rendering, from Christopher Stanley who comments that "within the Jewish sphere ... a long-standing tradition allowed for repeated reinterpretation and even rewriting of certain parts of the biblical record so as to draw out its significance for a later time" (*Paul and the Language*, 352).

question to discuss the 'son of man' problem on the basis of the occurrences of the phrase alone, or without consulting the root meaning of the imagery in Dan 7 itself." [46]

3. *Recurrence*: How many times does a NT author allude to the same OT passage? This criterion is particularly important for my investigation as I am building on Hooker's conclusion that Mark evokes nuanced aspects of the danielic figure and the context of Dan 7:13 in his portrayal of the SM at various points.

4. *Thematic coherence*: This criterion focuses on the exegetical impact that the allusion has on its narrative context and, more broadly, on the NT writing itself. This criterion and the preceding one need to be taken in tandem as Mark's recurring evocation of Dan 7 in his SM sayings make an important thematic contribution to his narrative. As I have mentioned earlier, Hooker argued that the themes associated with the markan SM, authority, suffering, and vindication, are all associated with the figure in Dan 7.[47] In order to ascertain the full impact of the thematic relationships amongst the sayings, it is crucial to examine them in their own narrative contexts, and even more broadly, to determine how these narratives contribute to the development of Mark's story vis-à-vis the SM.[48] As Jens Schröter puts it, the "designations applied to the main character Jesus have to be interpreted in connection with the narrated events."[49] It will become apparent that a careful narrative and intertextual analysis enables one to take Hooker's conclusions further providing a more nuanced and coherent interpretation of the function of Mark's SM.

5. *Historical probability*: This criterion, in distinction from the preceding ones, attempts to validate proposed allusions and, more importantly, their interpretative significance on an historical level. It seeks to determine if a proposed meaning could be understood by the audience. My argument that Mark's use of the SM prompts his implied audience

---

46. Wright, *New Testament*, 316.

47. Likewise, in his examination of Q, Tuckett observes that the SM sayings demonstrate a network of associated ideas which are in part inspired by Dan 7 and so it is "plausible to argue that the *term* 'SM' itself (at least in Greek) is also intended to be part of the way in which the Danielic scene is being alluded to in these sayings" ("Son of Man," 180).

48. Note that Gray, *Temple*, 5–6, takes an identical approach in his study of the temple in Mark. Below, I discuss the relevance of narrative criticism for this study in more detail.

49. Schröter, "Son of Man," 46.

to see themselves as a new covenant community in light of the second temple's destruction is bolstered by second-temple writings which depict groups of believers as a metaphorical temple over against the corrupt Jerusalem one. Further, a study of the status and function of the SM in the *Parables* and *4 Ezra* helps to determine what is "in the air" as far as first-century CE interpretations of the danielic SM are concerned. The Gospel of Mark, of course, is another first-century interpretation and so any conclusions I draw regarding the intertextual significance of the markan SM are strengthened when a similar portrayal is evident in contemporaneous texts. For instance, in the *Parables*, the SM executes the task of judgement which is a prerogative of Yahweh himself, e.g., *1 En.* 62:3–5, and I make the case that Mark portrays the SM in a similar fashion in 8:38, 13:26 and 14:62.

6. *History of interpretation*: This criterion covers a lot of territory from the early church fathers to modern scholars asking the question if others also have seen the same allusion. O'Brien rightly points out that the texts of Matthew and Luke reflect the earliest reading of Mark and that they, at times, make an allusion or proposed reading in Mark more explicit for the sake of their implied audience.[50] When I appeal to such comparative analysis to strengthen my argument, I will limit the use of this criterion to the first century.

7. *Satisfaction*: This criterion seeks to determine how logically compelling a proposed interpretation of an allusion might be; that is, "does it make sense"?[51] As Hays points out, this is a subjective criterion, but it should still be called upon as it forces interpreters to step back and consider the logical coherence, if any, a proposed reading creates in the writing itself.

Turning to a consideration of the narrative-critical approach of this study, there are an increasing number of publications on the literary creativity of Mark's text. Some studies consider its narrative features[52] while others investigate its function as a type of Greco-Roman drama.[53] One of the most influential studies on Mark's narrative, now in its second edition,

---

50. O'Brien, *Use of Scripture*, 60.
51. Hays, *Echoes of Scripture*, 31.
52. Malbon, "Narrative Criticism", 24–49; Malbon, *Mark's Jesus*; Carey, *Jesus' Cry*.
53. Dewey, "Aural Narrative," 45–56; Ibid., "Interwoven Tapestry," 221–36.

CHAPTER 1: INTRODUCTION

is *Mark as Story: An Introduction to the Narrative of a Gospel*.[54] The authors argue that discerning readers of the Gospel will discover that "the narrator's point of view is consistent. The plot is coherent: events that are anticipated come to pass; conflicts are resolved; prophecies are fulfilled. The characters are consistent from one scene to the next."[55] Such a reading involves an analysis of the following: 1. how the story is told; 2. various settings within the story; 3. conflict and resolution; and 4. the actors and their portrayal by the author.[56] Although the SM is not a character such as Peter or the high priest, the theological significance of this title must be considered in Mark's portrayal of Jesus. Narrative analyses of Jesus focus on him as God's son, and rightfully so, as he is introduced as such in Mark's opening statement. However, because Mark's Jesus refers to himself as ὁ υἱὸς τοῦ ἀνθρώπου in a way that reveals a coherent theme, literary critics must also consider the meaning of this title. Since Mark's Jesus does not use it in an arbitrary manner, this study examines the SM sayings in the order in which they occur in the Gospel. Hooker, in her monograph on Mark's SM to which I referred earlier, examines the sayings in the markan order for the same reason.

I do, however, take issue with the authors of *Mark as Story* who have an overstated assessment of the division between Mark's literary world and the cultural, religious, and political contexts of first-century Palestine. They conclude that "unless otherwise identified as helpful background information from the general culture of the first century, all subsequent references to people, places, and events refer *only* to the story world inside Mark's narrative [emphasis mine]."[57] Just because Mark is a story does not mean that its usefulness as a document for historical study is obviated. Conversely, the various contexts which make up life in the first century cannot be sidelined or overlooked when examining any aspect of Mark's narrative as his text is an ancient document, composed in an ancient language, and read (or heard) in an ancient culture. Therefore, I will attempt, whenever possible, to undergird my literary arguments about the SM in Mark with relevant data from the historical and literary worlds of second-temple Judaism.

---

54. Rhoads et al., *Mark as Story*.
55. Ibid., 3.
56. Ibid., 6–7.
57. Ibid., 5.

Chapter Outline

Since this work focuses on Mark's use of the danielic SM, I begin with an examination of Dan 7. In particular, I concentrate on the heavenly scene in vv. 9–10 and 13–14 and the historical context when the text was composed in the second century BCE. Regarding the former, I consider the parallels that this scene shares with the heavenly temple depicted in *1 En.* 14, canonical passages which depict Yahweh in a celestial context and other aspects of the scene which suggest a temple-centered vision. I conclude that Daniel sees Yahweh enthroned in his heavenly dwelling, not just a celestial courtroom as many scholars merely assume. My analysis of the historical world reveals that the priests during the time of Antiochus' rule actually colluded with the Syrian king to profane the temple which involved the abolishment of the *tamid* and the erection of a pagan shrine. These things have rendered the temple useless as a place to draw near to Yahweh and so its heavenly counterpart is revealed from which Antiochus' is judged. When the Ancient of Days comes, those who have been estranged from his presence because of corruption in the Jerusalem temple now draw near to the divine presence when the heavenly myriads present the SM, that is, faithful Israel, before Yahweh.

Chapter 3 examines the SM in *1 En.* 37–71 and *4 Ezra* 13:1–13a. While the intent is not to determine if these texts have a formative influence on Mark's understanding of the SM, this analysis is necessary as it reveals how other Jewish traditions interpreted the danielic figure providing a framework for my proposed readings which can bolster their historical probability. These are important texts because, along with the Gospel of Mark, they reflect in their own unique ways an updating of the danielic SM for their own theological interests, and they are two first-century CE texts contemporaneous with the composition of Mark. I argue that the author of the *Parables* locates the SM in the heavenly temple, which is where the vision in Daniel ends, and has him executing prerogatives of Yahweh, which is clearly a development. Similarly, in *4 Ezra* 13:1–13a, the SM is also associated with Yahweh's dwelling because he stands upon what might be termed an "otherworldly" temple mount from which he destroys his enemies, another instance of the SM carrying out a prerogative of Yahweh.

Chapter 4 examines the SM in Mark 2:10 and 2:28 and argues for a thoroughgoing evocation of the danielic SM in both cases which I establish through an application of Hays' criteria. The chapter begins with a study of relevant passages from Mark 1 which provide the context for the first appearance of the SM when he forgives the sins of a paralytic. I argue that the

Chapter 1: Introduction

markan SM has been endowed with Yahweh's authority and can therefore do that which only Yahweh can: forgive sins and exercise dominion over the sabbath. This presentation is similar to the one in the *Parables* and *4 Ezra* in which the SM judges sinners, saves the faithful, and destroys his adversaries, all of which in the biblical tradition are associated with Yahweh himself. However, unlike the SM in the *Parables* and possibly *4 Ezra*, he exercises this divine authority upon the earth in Mark 2.

Chapter 5 considers the passion-resurrection predictions, the ransom saying in 10:45 and the explication of Jesus' death in 14:24. This analysis demonstrates that the SM's rejection and redemptive death will result in the formation of a new people of God outside of the sacrifices offered in the second temple leading to the redundancy of its cult. Although scholars are wont to favor one OT or extra-biblical background over others for the passion-resurrection predictions, 10:45 and 14:24, I argue that interpreters must be attuned to a variety of intertexts. We will see that Dan 7, despite the fact that there is no evidence for the suffering of the "one like a son of man," is a formative intertext highlighting the corporate significance of the suffering, dying, and soon to be resurrected SM.

Chapter 6 focuses upon the future sayings of the SM in 8:38, 13:26–27, and 14:62. In this chapter, I argue that the SM comes in the heavenly temple to judge those who are opposed to him as well as the Jerusalem temple by analyzing Mark's evocation of Dan 7:13 and his description of the coming of the exalted SM in each of these three passages. This depiction parallels the enochic SM who is enthroned in heaven and judges those who have persecuted faithful Israel. These future sayings are a fitting denouement for Mark's SM who begins his ministry by executing divine prerogatives of Yahweh but then suffers at the hands of those who fail to recognize his authority. However, the future coming of the SM does not spell disaster for everyone. The picture of the SM sending his holy angels to gather the elect in 13:27 marks the full vindication of Jesus' faithful followers as a new covenant community founded upon the sacrificial death of Jesus and not the sacrifices of the temple cult. In the meantime, the rending of the temple veil at the moment Jesus dies and the command to go to Galilee at his resurrection anticipates the complete shift of the locus of Yahweh's dwelling from the earthly temple to Jesus' followers.

Chapter 2: Daniel's "One Like a Son of Man"

Introduction

THIS CHAPTER IS AN analysis of the "one like a son of man" (כְּבַר אֱנָשׁ) and the celestial scene in which he appears in Dan 7:1–14.[1] Since I argue that Mark evokes not only the danielic SM but also various aspects of the scene itself, it is important to provide a sustained examination of this material. Before looking at the text itself, this chapter begins with an investigation of the historical world of Dan 7. While many scholars rightly highlight that the vision comes as a response to the paganizing actions of Antiochus IV Epiphanes, few consider the complicity of a corrupt temple leadership and what interpretative light this sheds on the text. Another aspect of this vision which is often taken for granted is the setting in which the SM appears: is it merely a courtroom or is it actually a manifestation of Yahweh's heavenly temple from which judgement is meted out on Israel's pagan adversaries? If this is indeed the case, what significance does this celestial setting have for our understanding of the vision and the SM?

---

1. In this chapter, "one like a son of man" will be referred to as "the SM" for the sake of convenience. The comparative כְּ must not be ignored because it points to the human-like status of the figure. Goldingay comments that "the expression ['one like'] . . . parallels the varied, though more complex, כְּ phrases in 8:15; 10:16, 18. Like the figures who appear there, the one here entirely resembles a human being" (*Daniel*, 168). The human-like appearance of the SM coheres with the parallelism between his reception of "dominion" and "kingship" in 7:14 and those whom he symbolizes, "the people of the saints of the Most High" in v. 27, an argument I will take up later in the chapter. See also Lacocque, *Daniel*, 145–46, who also stresses the human status of the SM.

CHAPTER 2: DANIEL'S "ONE LIKE A SON OF MAN"

Historical Context

Many scholars agree that the book of Daniel, although containing earlier traditions from the Babylonian exile (Dan 1-6), was pseudonymously composed during the oppressive reign of the Syrian king Antiochus IV Epiphanes who desecrated the temple in 167 BCE.[2] C. F. D. Moule contends that these writings would not have appeared much later than 165 prior to the repossession of the temple by Judas Maccabeus.[3] After the exile, Jewish religion and politics centered around the re-built temple and its overseer, the high priest, due to the absence of a ruling Israelite king during the reigns of Persia and Greece.[4] As time passed, the temple was not only the locus of Israel's cult but also functioned as a royal palace so that the high priest executed both royal and priestly duties.[5] However, as shown below, Jewish writings of the second century criticize this royal high priesthood for its corruption. In examining the historical context of Dan 7, scholars do not often consider the complicity of the high priesthood in the desecration of the temple. According to a number of texts, the high priesthood after the return from exile does not exhibit covenantal faithfulness which continues into the time of Dan 7 and culminates in its collusion with Antiochus IV Epiphanes who transforms the temple into a pagan shrine.

Having become accustomed to foreign domination, many Jews, especially from the priesthood, did not resist Greek culture and religion. As early as the late third century BCE, the *Book of the Watchers* attests to the corruption of Israel's priests.[6] Fallen "watchers," or angels as in Gen 6:1-4,

2. Among the majority who posit a second-century BCE provenance for Dan 7-12 is Collins, "Son of Man," 54; Deissler, "Der Menschensohn," 82; Lacocque, "Socio-Spiritual," 335-37; Porteous, *Daniel*, 20; Montgomery, *Daniel*, 96-99. Hartman et al., *Daniel*, 16-18, propose a later date of 140 BCE which they believe accounts for Daniel's complex textual history. There are those, albeit a minority, who advocate a much earlier date for the book during the time of the Babylonian exile. These authors include Shea, "Neo-Babylonian," 31-36; Lucas, "Four Empires," 201-2; Baldwin, *Daniel*, 46. This thesis adopts a maccabean origin for the second half of Daniel realizing that chapters 1 to 6 likely reflect the exilic period which, nevertheless, have a unique literary relationship with chapters 7 to 12.

3. Moule, "Neglected," 416.

4. Davies, *Daniel*, 24.

5. Ibid.

6. Scholars who favour a third-century BCE date for this early portion of *1 Enoch* include Himmelfarb, "Prophecy to Apocalypse," 148; Suter, "Fallen," 131; Stone, "Enoch and Judaism," 482. Scholars can confidently date some parts of *1 Enoch*, i.e., *The Book of Watchers* and the *Astronomical Book*, to the end of the third century or the beginning of

come down from heaven, have sexual relations with women, and produce "giants" as offspring who ravage the earth (*1 En.* 6—11). The watchers represent corrupt priests who have married women from foreign nations and consequently have profaned the priestly bloodline.[7] George W. E. Nickelsburg comments that the author "has a grievance against the priesthood in his own time."[8] This is not unlike the concern of Ezra who, upon arriving in Jerusalem, realizes that many Israelites, including priests and Levites, have intermarried (Ezra 9:1–4).

David Suter also detects the theme of priestly corruption in the *Testament of Levi*, which is an early second-century BCE writing, and the *Damascus Document*, which is dated to the end of that century.[9] Martha J. Himmelfarb suggests that the *Testament of Levi* evolved in the same circles as that of the *Book of the Watchers* before the middle of the second century because of its focus on the corruption of the Jerusalem priests.[10] The *Testament of Levi* is clearly more relevant for the current argument because of its pre-maccabean origin. But the *Damascus Document* is valuable as well because, from the perspective of one group of Jews, it reveals a continued tradition of priestly corruption.[11] Specifically, these two texts are directed against the priesthood for being guilty of "whoredom, wealth, and the pollution of the temple."[12] The priests possess ill-gotten wealth from the tithes of the sanctuary (CD-A VI, 15–16; *T. Levi* 14:5), teach commandments that contradict God's ordinances (*T. Levi* 14:4; 16:2), and have an erroneous

---

the second century due to the appearance of fragments of these writings at Qumran. See, for example, 4QEna ar; 4QEnb ar; 4QEnc ar. For more on the dates of these writings and their relationship to Qumran, see the often criticized work of Milik, *Enoch*.

7. Suter, "Fallen," 130–31. For a discussion of the priestly character of the fallen angels, see Himmelfarb, "Prophecy," 152.

8. Nickelsburg, "Enoch, Levi, and Peter," 586. Nickelsburg proposes the northern area of Dan as the site for Enoch's revelatory activity, as opposed to Jerusalem, which may strengthen the text's anti-temple concern.

9. Milik, *Enoch*, 58.

10. See the discussion in Himmelfarb, *Ascent*, 30.

11. Note also the warnings given to Levi recorded in CTLevi ar Bd b, 14–23: "First, beware my son of all fornication and defilement and of all uncleanness. But you, marry a woman from my family and do not defile your seed with whores for you are a holy seed and holy is your seed like the sanctuary, for you are called a holy priest for all the seed of Abraham. You are close to God and close to all his holy ones. Therefore, keep yourself pure in your flesh from all the defilement of all men."

12. Suter, "Fallen," 125.

Chapter 2: Daniel's "One Like a Son of Man"

interpretation of the law to make that which is unrighteous righteous (CD-A I, 19–20; IV, 16–17; *T. Levi* 14:6–7).[13]

Another important text is *Jubilees*. This work is the product of those Jews who opted for violence and active rebellion in response to the hellenistic reform of 168 BCE.[14] The author of *Jubilees* condemns nakedness and uncircumcision (3:31), observance of the lunar calendar (6:17–22), consumption of blood (7:28–33), exogamy (30:7–23), and idolatry (20:7–9; 22:16–18).[15] According to Nickelsburg, these *halakhic* concerns reflect corrupt temple practices due to the influence of Hellenism.[16] It is likely that the author of *Jubilees* is a member of "a zealous, conservative, pious segment of Judaism which was bound together by its own set of traditions, expectations, and practices."[17] For this group, failure to observe Jewish days and festivals, for example, is to rebel against Yahweh's ordering of the cosmos.[18] The author attempts to reinforce the absolute necessity of observing sabbath and traditional festivals because they have their roots not in the Mosaic legislation but in the patriarchal age and even in creation itself.[19] This is paralleled in Dan 7:25 where Antiochus' desire to change the "sacred seasons and the law" reflects an undoing of the created order in keeping with the savage and chaotic character of the fourth beast from which this "little horn" emerges. Not surprisingly, the author of *Jubilees* calls for an active and violent stance against the corruption of the priesthood. The author endorses Levi's slaughter of unfaithful Jews at Shechem by stating that Levi was upholding the law prohibiting exogamy (*Jub.* 30; Lev 20:2; 21:9), even though Jacob himself condemns the incident in the biblical text (Gen 34; 49:5–7). Because of his zeal for the law, the author exalts Levi and his descendants to the priesthood (*Jub.* 30:18–20), and, despite the unabated

---

13. Ibid., 130.

14. Nickelsburg, "Rewritten," 100. Davenport suggests that the document was composed in three stages beginning in 200 BCE and was concluded somewhere between 140 to 104 BCE in the Qumran community (*Eschatology*, 10–18).

15. Nickelsburg, "Rewritten," 98, 103.

16. Ibid., 100.

17. Wintermute, "Jubilees," 45.

18. Note, for example, *Jub.* 6:17: "Therefore, it is ordained and written *in the heavenly tablets* that they should observe the feast of *Shebuot* in this month, once per year, in order to renew the covenant in all [respects], year by year."

19. VanderKam, "Interpretation," 121.

corruption of the current priesthood, it will be purified and reinstated through a violent priestly figure.[20]

The *Animal Apocalypse* is another writing which parallels *Jubilees'* concern to purify Jerusalem violently by ridding it of hellenizing priests (*1 En.* 85—91).[21] The author schematizes history into four periods, the fourth of which is composed of four subperiods ruled by seventy shepherds. The fourth period is followed by the establishment of God's kingdom (90:14-39). In the second subperiod (of the fourth period), the temple is rebuilt, but the cultic food is still considered "polluted and impure" (89:73).[22] The author describes the sheep, those who re-built the temple and reinstituted its cult, as being "so dim-sighted that they could not see" along with the seventy shepherds (89:74; 90:7). This most likely reflects not a rejection of the second temple itself *per se* but rather of its leadership, a rejection which continues into the author's own time.[23] In the third subperiod, various birds ravage the sheep "until the sheep became few" (90:4) which refers to an oppressive period under the Ptolemies.[24] Then, in the fourth subperiod of the shepherds' reign, white sheep give birth to lambs who, representing faithful Israel, "began to open their eyes and see" (90:6). Despite the cry of these lambs, the blind sheep refuse to listen but instead persecute them. In the opinion of Patrick A. Tiller, the oppressive sheep signify the hellenizing efforts of the high priests Jason and Menelaus (90:7).[25] In the next verse, ravens seize the lambs and crush the sheep which points to the oppressive rule of the Seleucid kingdom (90:8).[26]

Importantly, Tiller argues that the lambs reflect the author's own social group who experienced persecution both from within Israel, i.e., from

20. Ibid., 123.

21. Ibid., 113.

22. Collins, *Apocalyptic*, 68–69; Fröhlich, "Symbolical Language," 630–31.

23. Tiller, *Animal*, 337; Collins, *Apocalyptic*, 69.

24. Tiller, *Animal*, 345–48.

25. Tiller, *Animal*, 352. There are variant readings of v. 7. Based on internal grounds, Tiller selects MS "m": "and they afflicted" in which the subject is the blind sheep and the object is the seeing lambs. See also Charles, *Ethiopic*, 352. More recently, Nickelsburg and VanderKam translate v. 7 as follows: "But they [the white sheep] did not listen to them nor attend to their words, but were extremely deaf, and their eyes were extremely and excessively blinded" (*1 Enoch*, 133). Although this differs from Tiller's translation, it does not alter the central point that the priestly aristocracy, because of their corruption, pays no heed to those who wish to purify the temple and remain faithful to Yahweh.

26. For more on Jewish life under the Ptolemaic and Seleucid kingdoms, see Hengel, *Judaism*, 267–309.

Chapter 2: Daniel's "One Like a Son of Man"

the blind sheep who represent the priestly aristocracy, and from without, i.e., from the ravens who symbolize the Seleucids who crush them in their attempt at an armed rebellion (90:9–10).[27] Many scholars agree that the seized lamb of v. 8 could be Onias III who in light of his nefarious successors, Jason and Menelaus, could be viewed in a positive light by the author of the *Animal Apocalypse*.[28] Daniel refers to him as "the prince of the covenant" (נְגִיד בְּרִית) (Dan 11:22b).[29] The persecuted plight of the sheep changes when "a big horn sprouted" on one of them (90:9). This horn represents the military agenda of Judas Maccabeus, against whom the ravens or the shepherds cannot prevail (90:12–13; see 1 Macc 3:10–26; 3:38–4:27), who fights against the Seleucids and hellenized Jews. After this victory, God's kingdom is then established and the temple is restored (90:20–37).[30]

These extracanonical texts demonstrate that at least three groups before and around the time of Daniel viewed the temple and/or its leadership as corrupt and defiled largely due to the priests's capitulation to Hellenism. The author of Daniel has a similar view of the Jerusalem priesthood. According to Daniel, "he [Antiochus] shall make a strong covenant *with many* for one week" (9:27a). The term רַבִּים certainly refers not only to priests but also to all those Hellenized Jews who forsook the law (see 1 Macc 1:11–15). One of the "many" would include Menelaus and the close relationship that he and his priestly compatriots had with the Seleucid king from the end of 172 until 165 BCE after having deposed Jason.[31] According to Dan 11, Antiochus will "pay heed to those who forsake the holy covenant" (v. 30;

---

27. Tiller, *Animal*, 355.

28. Tiller notes that August Dillmann assumes that Onias III was a full-fledged Hellenizer (*Animal*, 354). However, Tiller comments that "once he [Onias III] has been disassociated from the temple leadership, it is possible that his views on the temple and its purity could approximate those expressed in the *An. Apoc.*" (*Animal*, 354). Although Onias III was not overly zealous for the law, he is certainly outdone by the high priest Jason who, along with the priestly aristocracy, wished to transform Jerusalem into a *polis*, Antioch in Jerusalem, which results in favor and benefits from the ruling Seleucid king; see 1 Macc 1:11; Dan 11:23. Succeeding Jason was Menelaus who purchased the priesthood from Antiochus IV and was from a non-Zadokite priestly line. See Hengel, *Judaism*, 1:277–80.

29. Lacocque, "Socio-Spiritual," 196.

30. Fröhlich, "Symbolical," 631.

31. Hengel, *Judaism*, 1:288. Lacocque incorrectly implies that Jason was the last high priest before Antiochus desecrated the temple (*Daniel*, 125). While Onias III is likely the referent of the cut off "anointed one" in 9:26, the high priest Menelaus was in control prior to Antiochus's attack on Jerusalem.

see v. 28b) and will "seduce with intrigue those who violate the covenant" (v. 32a). After analyzing the phrase "holy covenant" (בְּרִית קֹדֶשׁ) in 11:28 and 30, Arie van der Kooij concludes that it refers to the "central cultic institution of the Jews" so that those who forsake and violate the covenant at least includes those priests who fail to carry out their responsibilities in the temple (2 Macc 4:14).[32] Nested between references to Antiochus "paying heed" in v. 30b and "seducing with intrigue" in v. 32a those who abdicate covenant responsibilities is the mention of the cultic practice which Antiochus abolishes: the "regular burnt offering" in v. 31 (see 8:11). As I will discuss below, this daily sacrifice preserves the continued presence of Yahweh in the temple and now it is no more.

The complicity of the priestly aristocracy is quite evident in Josephus: "it was this man [Menelaus] . . . who had been the cause of the mischief by persuading the king's father [Antiochus IV Epiphanes] to compel the Jews to abandon their fathers' religion" (Josephus, *Ant.* 12.384 [Marcus, LCL]).[33] The author of 2 Maccabees characterizes Menelaus as a "traitor both to the laws and to his country" because he guides Antiochus IV in his desecration of the temple (5:15).[34] In light of this evidence, Emil Schürer comments that even at the start of the second century, Hellenism would have been considerably pervasive in Palestine because "the aristocratic and educated classes in particular [of Israel], willingly consented to the Hellenizing programme of Antiochus Epiphanes, and indeed promoted it."[35]

The pervasive corruption of the priesthood in the middle of the second century reveals that Antiochus IV Epiphanes is not solely responsible for the desecration of the temple and the cessation of its cult. Daniel, in chapters 9 and 11, implies that the priestly aristocracy is quite corrupt and unfaithful to the Mosaic covenant not resisting Antiochus's profanation. The author of the *Animal Apocalypse*, which is a writing contemporaneous with Daniel, makes this involvement explicit through the imagery of the blind and deafened sheep, symbolizing the priests, who fail to heed the

---

32. van der Kooij, "Covenant," 500. See also Lebram, who refers to these priests as "Abtrünnigen" priests" ("Apocalyptik," 513).

33. Earlier, Josephus indicates that "Menelaus and the Tobiads withdrew, and going to Antiochus informed him that they wished to abandon their country's laws and the way of life prescribed by these and to follow the king's laws and adopt the Greek way of life" (Josephus, *Ant.* 12.240 [Marcus, LCL]).

34. Josephus also records that the "sons of Tobias" request that Antiochus use them in his attack on Judea (Josephus, *J. W.* 1.32).

35. Schürer, *History*, 145.

Chapter 2: Daniel's "One Like a Son of Man"

cries of the faithful ones. Despite what is commonly thought, Antiochus does not merely plunder the temple so that the Jews will turn from their God to worship his gods. The ruling high priest consorts with the Syrian king resulting in unfaithfulness to Israel's laws and, specifically, a failure to execute temple responsibilities which enable Israel to maintain her status as a kingdom of priests and a holy nation (Exod 19:6).[36]

Despite the capitulation of Israel's leadership, there are those who remain faithful to the law of Moses, refusing to bow down to pagan idols.[37] These faithful or *hasidim*[38] realize that Antiochus' domination is "more subtle, more insidious than that of Babylon. It was not concerned, in the first place, with the removal of the people of the land, but with their removal from the law of Yahweh."[39] This type of persecution serves to undermine Jewish self-identity. Israel's traditions and laws define the nation as a people of the Presence, for this is what makes them distinct from all the nations (Exod 33:14-16). The laws which safeguard the holiness of the temple and guide its cultic practices are now abolished. The text of Daniel indicates, in chapter 8, that a little horn removed the regular burnt offering as part of its desecrating sacrilege (Dan 8:11). A passage in Exodus describes this offering (29:38-42), known as the *tamid* in rabbinic literature (see the adverb תָּמִיד in v. 38). The priests are instructed to offer a lamb in the morning and evening as well as a drink and cereal offering to accompany it (vv. 39-41). This type of burnt offering needs to be offered regularly because it ensures the continued presence of Yahweh in the tabernacle and, later, in the temple: "it shall be a regular burnt offering throughout your generations at the entrance of the tent of meeting before the Lord, *where I will meet with you, to speak to you there*" (v. 42).[40] With the cessation of the *tamid*, faithful Israel is now estranged from the divine presence, and the temple no longer serves as a place in which to worship Yahweh.[41]

---

36. Noteworthy is that Antiochus's intolerance of Judaism went as far as the Jerusalem city limits. Hengel indicates that Jews in Syria, Antioch and Babylon were not oppressed by Antiochus, which may suggest that it is the temple leaders who initiate the king's oppressive rule in Jerusalem (*Judaism*, 1:280, 287 fn. 200).

37. 1 Macc 1:57-64.

38. For a helpful discussion on the background of the *hasidim*, see Lacocque, "Socio-Spiritual," 317-43.

39. Caragounis, "Greek Culture," 302. See also Lacocque who acknowledges the "life-threatening danger" of this persecution on a religio-cultural level ("Socio-Spiritual," 323).

40. Klauck, "Sacrifice," 878; Durham, *Exodus*, 396.

41. Goldingay, *Daniel*, 211.

Literary Context

Before turning to an examination of the SM in Dan 7, it is important to consider briefly the function of chapter 7 in the book.[42] A number of scholars argue that it has a unique literary relationship with the first half of the book and, for some, the second half as well. Chapters 2 and 7 have a number of significant parallels and together form the outer element of a chiastic structure.[43] The four parts of the idol in Dan 2 parallel the four kingdoms which arise from the sea in Dan 7. Daniel elaborates on the fourth kingdom in each chapter, highlighting its divisive nature. In Dan 2, the idol's feet, representing the fourth kingdom, are an admixture of iron and clay (vv. 40–43), while the fourth beast in chapter 7, far more grotesque and destructive than the preceding beasts, has ten horns out of which an eleventh one springs up and destroys three of the original horns (vv. 7–8). The four kingdoms are different in their appearances—in chapter 2 they are dazzling, impressive, and humanlike—while in chapter 7 they are beastly and animalistic culminating in the "terrifying and dreadful" fourth beast (v. 7).[44] In each chapter, the kingdom of God replaces the fourth kingdom which in Dan 2:34 is represented by a "stone" (אֶבֶן) and in Dan 7:13 "one like a son of man" (כְּבַר אֱנָשׁ). According to Chrys Caragounis, the visionary character of chapter 7 indicates that Daniel no longer interprets these kingdoms on merely an historical level.[45] The vision reveals their true nature as inherently evil, failing to recognize their place in Yahweh's kingdom. As a whole, the court tales in Dan 1–6 are crucial for a proper understanding of chapter 7. P. R. Davies indicates that the heroes, settings, and themes of the tales are presupposed in the visions.[46] For example, the theme of vindication after some type of persecution is almost consistent throughout chapters 1 to 6 and is evident again in chapter 7.[47] The faithfulness of the human figures, Daniel and his three friends, in the face of suffering (1:6–8, 12–13; 3:16–18;

---

42. Collins, "Saints," 54; Raabe, "Daniel 7," 267–75; Patterson, "Daniel 7," 245–61; Goldingay, *Daniel*, 157–58; Lenglet, "Structure," 169–90.

43. The entire structure expresses the literary coherence of Dan 2–7. For a diagram, see Lenglet, "Structure," 171.

44. Goldingay, *Daniel*, 158. Davies points out that the four kingdoms of Dan 2 signal a gradual "decline" in power and glory while the ones of Dan 7 indicate an "increase" in power and might ("Eschatology," 45).

45. Caragounis, "Greek Culture," 304–5.

46. Davies, "Eschatology," 34. See also, Lacocque, "Socio-Spiritual," 9.

47. Wright, *People*, 293–94; Davies, "Eschatology," 35.

Chapter 2: Daniel's "One Like a Son of Man"

6:11–12) foreshadows the faithfulness of the "holy ones" (7:21) symbolized by the SM.

Unlike many scholars, John J. Collins argues that chapters 7 to 12 represent a literary unity exclusive of 2 to 6.[48] The fact that Dan 7 completes the Aramaic section beginning in Dan 2:4 does not detract from his case because, according to Collins, "no fully satisfactory solution to the problem of the two languages in the Book of Daniel can be found."[49] However, this does not constitute decisive evidence for the literary unity of 7–12 but places the burden of proof on Collins, who argues that 7–12 is a unit, despite the fact that 2–7 are written in the same language, possibly suggesting a common author or redactor, and, more importantly, have an obvious literary relationship.[50] Collins's emphasis on the unity of Dan 7–12 has a direct bearing on his methodology by which he examines the danielic SM, which will be summarized and evaluated below. Responding to Collins, Davies claims that he does not take seriously a maccabean "re-reading" of the tales which underscores the importance of these stories for the readers of Daniel in the mid-second century BCE.[51] This is not to deny that chapter 7 has a relationship with 8 to 12. It clearly does as 7–12 are apocalyptic visions communicated in the first-person, while the tales are recorded in narrative form in the third-person. An author(s) most likely composed the visions during the maccabean revolt at which point the tales were "re-read" to serve as an historical counterpart to the visions, as Davies rightfully claims.[52]

Turning to Dan 7 itself, the first half contains the dream and visions of Daniel (vv. 2–14) while the second half records their interpretation (vv. 15–27). The author describes the beasts and their undesirable fate in mere

---

48. Collins, "Saints," 54–55.

49. Ibid., 54.

50. However, in a monograph published a few years later, Collins modifies his view: "they [the court tales] are integrated in the book by a careful editorial process of interlocking, which is attained by the symmetry of ch. 7 with chs. 2–6," (*Apocalyptic*, 19) but he does not seem to allow this observation to guide his interpretation of the "one like a son of man."

51. Davies, "Eschatology," 34.

52. Ibid., 36. However, Lindenberger dates the Aramaic material to maccabean times and the Hebrew sections (1:1—2:4a; 8:1—12:13) to a later period ("Daniel 7:13–14," 186). However, the material of chapter 8, for example, about the little horn and his eventual demise in chapter 11 is pertinent to the Antiochene crisis. The suggestion of Moule is instructive: "the Aramaic bits in both books [i.e., Dan and Ezra] are fortuitous, and probably due to the copyist's having a defective exemplar, and, *faute de mieux*, filling in the lacunae from an Aramaic Targum" (cited in Wright, *People*, 293 fn. 33).

prose in vv. 2–8 and 11–12, but for the exalted, celestial scene he uses poetry in vv. 9–10 and 13–14. This difference contrasts the stately and exalted "one like a son of man" being presented before Yahweh and the kingdom he subsequently receives with the oppressive and violent fourth beast and the kingdom he symbolizes that Yahweh destroys. Daniel's dream begins with "the four winds of heaven stirring up 'the great sea'" (לְיַמָּא רַבָּא) out of which four beasts arise (vv. 2–3). The sea in aNE thought connotes chaos and destruction which is commensurate with the character of these beasts.[53] In a brief essay, A. E. Gardner discusses three passages which highlight the mythological nature of the sea: Isa 51:9–10; Ps 74:13–14; 104:25–26.[54] In these passages, it is the abode of the fierce and vicious sea monsters Rahab and Leviathan over whom Yahweh has dominion and control. Especially significant is Ps 104:25–26 in which הַיָּם גָּדוֹל, which is the Hebrew equivalent of יַמָּא רַבָּא, contains "both small and great beasts."[55] Similarly in Dan 7:3, four "great beasts" (אַרְבַּע חֵיוָן) arise from the sea. This is an insightful Psalm for understanding the nature of the Mediterranean, or any ancient sea (see Isa 51:9–10), because the "distinction between an actual and a mythological sea" is blurred, which seems to be the case in Dan 7.[56] The Mediterranean as "the great sea" is the abode of savage monsters and beasts.

These four beasts, in the opinion of most scholars, represent the great world empires of Babylon, Media, Persia, and Greece.[57] In his description of the four beasts, Daniel claims that they were "different from one another" (v. 3b) which, according to Hartman and Di Lella, points to the

53. Gardner indicates that the majority of scholars allude to the chaotic nature of the sea ("Daniel 7:2–14," 244). However, she does mention that Casey and Goldingay both claim that "the sea" in vv. 2–3 refers only to the Mediterranean, having no mythological associations (see Casey, *Son of Man*, 18 and Goldingay, *Daniel*, 160). Given the mythological tone of the whole scene, it seems odd that Daniel would intend that the sea exclusively represent a body of water.

54. Gardner, "Great," 412–15.

55. According to Gardner, the Aramaic Targumim translate the Hebrew הַיָּם גָּדוֹל as ימא רבא in the following instances: Num 34:7; Josh 1:4; 9:1; 15:12, 47; 23:4; and Ezek 47:10, 15, 19, 20; 48:28 ("Great," 412).

56. Gardner, "Great," 414. Mosca draws attention to Gen 41:1–8 in which creatures rise out of the Nile ("Ugarit and Daniel 7," 500 fn. 20).

57. See Colpe, "ὁ υἱὸς τοῦ ἀνθρώπου," 421 fn. 164; Gurney, "Kingdoms," 39; Lindenberger, "Daniel," 177; Porteous, *Daniel*, 104–6; Lacocque, "Socio-Spiritual," 139–40; Collins, *Daniel*, 297–99; Montgomery, *Daniel*, 286–94; Heaton, *Daniel*, 176–77; Lucas, "Four Empires," 194. However, some deviate from this scheme. For example, Kellner argues that the first three beasts represent neo-Babylon, Persia, and Greece while the fourth beast signifies the Greek armies and their "Maschinen" of war (*Traum*, 32–43).

Chapter 2: Daniel's "One Like a Son of Man"

successiveness of each of these kingdoms (v. 17).[58] The first beast "was like a lion and had eagles' wings" (v. 4a) while the second "looked like a bear. It was raised up on one side, [and] had three tusks in its mouth among its teeth" (v.5). The third one appeared to be "like a leopard . . . [and] had four wings of a bird on its back and four heads" (v. 6). Since each of these beasts are mutations, the phrase "different from one another" contrasts with the oft-repeated expression "after their kind" in Gen 1:11, 21 meaning that God's creation is not supposed to mutate through reproduction.[59] These monsters from the abyss appear to be aberrations of God's creation. Daniel describes the fourth beast as still a mutation of the preceding three: "it was different from all the beasts that preceded it, and it had ten horns" (v. 7b; see 23–24).[60] Like the second beast, the fourth one is predatory: "it had great iron teeth and was devouring, breaking in pieces, and stamping what was left with its feet" (v. 7). The iron teeth of this beast that devour and "crush" (v. 7: וּמְדֲקָה) recall the iron of the fourth kingdom in Dan 2 that also "crushes" (v. 40: מְהַדֵּק) everything. The dominant characteristic of this beast is its ten horns (7:7b) from which a "little horn" appears, and three horns are uprooted to make room for it (v. 8a). This vicious depiction of the fourth beast is fitting given that its little horn desecrates the temple which is described in 8:11. As to which kings these eleven horns refer is a near insolvable matter of debate,[61] but most scholars agree that the eleventh horn having anthropomorphic characteristics of eyes and a mouth is Antiochus IV Epiphanes (v. 8b).[62]

---

58. Hartman and Di Lella, *Daniel*, 212; Porteous, *Daniel*, 104.

59. Wilson, "Creation," 201; Dumbrell, "Daniel 7," 26–31.

60. On the basis of a form-critical approach, Hampel indicates that the original vision ended with 7:7a and that the description of the ten horns and the little horn that comes up among them (7:7b–8) would have been added later along with the interpretation in the second part of the chapter (*Menschensohn*, 9). Most likely, Jews would have been responsible for this accretion during the maccabean revolt, according to Hampel.

61. For one of the most comprehensive proposals, see Caragounis, "Interpretation," 106–13.

62. Van Henten argues that the author of Daniel interprets the oppression of Antiochus partly on the basis of Egyptian and Greek myths about Seth and Typhon respectively ("Antiochus IV," 223–43). There are some striking similarities between these figures and the description of the little horn. Especially interesting is Typhon's rejection of the laws which parallels Antiochus's changing of the times and seasons (Dan 7:25). However, Henten discusses a wide variety of Egyptian and Greek texts which the author of Daniel may or may not have known. One also wonders how many second-century BCE Palestinian readers would have been acquainted with these pagan sources.

In both biblical and non-biblical sources, horns represent power, strength and authority (Zech 1:18–21; *1 En.* 90:9; 1QSb V, 26).[63] In Zechariah, four horns symbolize nations that have scattered the people of Judah which is similar to the fourth beast that devours, crushes and tramples its prey, which in the interpretation turns out to be faithful Israel (v. 21). In keeping with its power and authority, the little horn has "arrogant eyes" (Isa 2:11; 5:15; Ps 101:5) and a "boastful mouth" (Isa 37:23; Ps 12:3).[64] Its arrogance is evident when he "makes war" against the holy ones and "prevails over" them (v. 21). He also speaks against the Most High, "harasses" the holy ones, and finally attempts to manipulate the "appointed times and laws" (v. 25). In Dan 8:11b, the little horn takes "the regular burnt offering away from him [the prince of the host] and overthrows the place of the sanctuary" clearly manipulating Yahweh's laws. As mentioned above, this "offering" (הַתָּמִיד) is the one offered up each morning and evening in the temple to preserve Yahweh's presence.[65] The cessation of these burnt offerings and the temple's desecration leads to the estrangement of faithful Israel from the divine presence. Such profanation befits the chaotic and savage nature of the fourth beast from whence the little horn comes, whose activities were aided and abetted by a colluding priesthood. Consequently, the end of this oppressive kingdom is imminent, just as the pagan kingdoms in Dan 2 met their end. Divine judgement will come.

Judgement from the Heavenly Temple

After Daniel describes the savagery and arrogance of the fourth beast, the scene shifts to what many designate a celestial courtroom. There are a number of features that indicate a great assize is about to transpire. In the first movement, "thrones are set in place and an Ancient of Days took his throne" (v. 9a) that parallels the last line of the scene: "the court sat in judgement, and the books were opened" (v. 10c). In the biblical tradition, Yahweh is envisaged as a judge who sits enthroned in the council of various

---

63. Collins incorrectly cites Zech 2:1–4 which mentions nothing about horns (*Daniel*, 299). Collins suggests that the horn imagery partly derives from its use on coins by Antiochus's predecessors symbolizing the power of the king.

64. Ibid., 299. Kellner cites pagan sources which likewise associate arrogance with the eyes and mouth (*Traum*, 46).

65. Goldingay, *Daniel*, 211.

Chapter 2: Daniel's "One Like a Son of Man"

heavenly beings (Ps 82:1; 1 Kgs 22:19).[66] Next, Daniel describes the appearance of Yahweh's clothing and hair and the throne upon which he sits (v. 9b–c). A few commentators suggest that the white clothing, in the context of a description of Yahweh's throne, communicates that he has an unsullied royalty and nobility befitting his role as judge.[67] The image of the throne as "fiery flames" (v. 9c) recalls various OT theophanies such as the burning bush and God's descent on Mount Sinai (Ex 3:2; 19:18). While fire has a number of associations in the OT, here it is a symbol of judgement in which case the fire flowing from the presence of the Ancient of Days is likely the "blazing fire" into which the body of the forth beast is cast (v. 11; Deut 4:24; Ps 18:9–14; 21:10; 50:3; 97:3).[68]

Some scholars argue that the scene Daniel depicts in vv. 9–14 occurs in the Jerusalem temple.[69] John Goldingay, although recognizing the celestial features of the scene, claims that God judges on earth more often than not, e.g., Jer 49:38; Zech 14:1–5; Ps 96:10–13, and so this courtroom has a terrestrial temple context.[70] Further, he assumes that the phrase "until the Ancient of Days came," found in the interpretation of Daniel's vision in v. 22a, depicts the coming of Yahweh to earth.[71] However, there is no indication in the chapter from whence Yahweh comes; he just comes to judge, much like the "one like a son of man" who "comes" with the clouds for vindication (v. 13). Goldingay is correct that the plural "thrones" is only evident here and in Ps 122:5 where the setting is the Jerusalem temple. He does not use Ps 122:5 to argue against a heavenly setting but to suggest that the thrones are merely for emphasis and part of the architecture of the scene. There are, however, several examples of Yahweh judging from a heavenly context in which he is surrounded by a myriad of angelic/divine beings, not unlike Dan 7, in biblical

---

66. Hartman and DiLella, *Daniel*, 217; Ferch, *Son of Man*, 146.

67. Goldingay, *Daniel*, 165; Hartman and DiLella, *Daniel*, 218; Ferch, *Son of Man*, 150.

68. Goldingay, *Daniel*, 165–66. See, for example, Ps 97:3: "Fire goes before him [Yahweh] and consumes his foes on every side" (see Ps 50:3).

69. Ibid., 164–65; Fletcher-Louis, "High Priest," 176. Beasley-Murray argues that the scene is a theophany and so the judgement transpires on earth but not necessarily in the temple ("Interpretation," 48–49). In his commentary on Daniel, Collins curiously suggests that the vision occurs in "mythic space" since Daniel does not indicate where the vision occurs (*Daniel*, 303). It seems to me that with many of these apocalyptic visions, the location is never spelled out but is implied through the imagery used.

70. Goldingay, *Daniel*, 164.

71. Ibid., 165.

Daniel's Son of Man in Mark

and extra-biblical texts, which Goldingay cites but does not discuss.[72] In 1 Kgs 22, the prophet Micaiah, much to the chagrin of King Ahab, does not relay a favorable message from Yahweh but rather predicts disaster will come upon the King. The message of judgement begins with the following: "Therefore hear the word of the Lord: I saw the Lord sitting upon his throne, with all the host of heaven standing beside him to the right and to the left of him" (1 Kgs 22:19). Similarly, in Ps 82, God takes "his place in the divine council" (v. 1a) and then the Psalmist declares "in the midst of the gods he holds judgement" (v. 1b). The setting for this is a celestial one from which God is called to judge to the earth (v. 8).[73] Finally, in Isa 6, the prophet witnesses "the Lord sitting on a throne, high and lofty; and the hem of his robe filled the temple. Seraphs were in attendance above him" (v. 1b–2a). Because of the presence of celestial beings attending Yahweh and that only the hem of his robe fills the earthly temple, Isa 6 is a vision of Yahweh in his heavenly dwelling who is about to pronounce judgement (see vv. 8–13). Hans Wildberger argues that "it is by no means clear, as is presumed by the majority of exegetes, that Isaiah is speaking of the temple in Jerusalem. Based on the form-historical parallels in 1 Kgs 22:19 and Ezek 1:1 ("the heavens were opened, and I saw visions of God"), but also Gen 28 and Ps 29, it would seem much more likely that the heavenly dwelling place is meant."[74] This brief survey indicates that there is indeed a precedent for conceiving of Yahweh judging from a heavenly context when surrounded by heavenly beings which should inform interpretations of the courtroom scene in Dan 7 where a heavenly entourage is also present.

An especially important text that does not often receive the attention that it should in studies of the celestial scene in Dan 7 is Enoch's description of the heavenly temple in *1 En.* 14:8–24 which dates from the early second century, if not the late third century BCE.[75] Some rightfully argue that this text inspired Daniel's vision of the Ancient of Days due to a number of terminological correspondences.[76] Heldge S. Kvanvig concludes his analyzes with

---

72. According to Himmelfarb, the Israelite heavenly council is likely drawn from their aNE counterparts (*Ascent*, 13). For instance, in Ugaritic literature, the gods who surround El do not council him but rather ratify his decisions which is paralleled in the biblical instances of Yahweh reigning in the context of angelic beings.

73. Kraus, *Psalms 60—150*, 154; Weiser, *Psalms*, 558.

74. Wildberger, *Isaiah 1—12*, 263. For a similar assessment, see Watts, *Isaiah 1–33*, 72-74 and Lioy, *Axis*, 40–44.

75. Nickelsburg, "Apocalyptic," 389–91.

76. Kvanvig, "Henoch," 101–33 [esp. 119–30]; Black, "'Parables'" 7; Glasson, "Son of Man," 82. In a recent article, Stokes argues that Dan 7 is the primitive form of the vision

CHAPTER 2: DANIEL'S "ONE LIKE A SON OF MAN"

the following: "Andererseits aber ist die Verwandtschaft zwischen den Texten so eng, besonders im Wortschatz, dass Dan 7 in seiner jetzigen Form von Hen 14 beeinflusst worden sein muss".[77] This does not mean that the literary correspondences between these texts translate into sociological correspondences, but it should be noted that the group who composed Daniel found some usefulness for this enochic literature.[78] The text of 1 En. 14 is a part of *The Book of Watchers* (1–36), which is a protracted development of the short narrative in Gen 6:1–4 about the "sons of God" who have sexual relations with the "daughters of man".[79] Specifically, these "sons of God" are interpreted as fallen priests from Yahweh's heavenly temple who have lain with women and taught wickedness to humanity. Now, they petition Enoch to intercede on their behalf for forgiveness as they have been condemned (13:1–3). The patriarch ascends to the heavenly temple in which he receives a word of confirmation from "the Great Glory" that their giant sons will face destruction and the watchers themselves "will have no peace" (16:4b). Of particular

---

versus 1 En. 14 ("Throne Visions," 340–58). Stokes highlights the differences between the two and claims that "if certain divergences in one text may be easily explained based on the agenda of its author, especially if this agenda is observable elsewhere in the work, then this text is more likely to be the one making use of the other" ("Throne Visions," 346). In other words, Stokes makes his case on the basis of alleged changes that the author of 1 En. 14 makes to his source text, Dan 7, in light of other parts of chapter 14. However, this does not constitute a compelling case for the priority of 1 En. 14 especially when many scholars agree that the text of *The Book of Watchers* found at Qumran predates that of Dan 7. Further, Stokes only discusses two differences between the texts on which he builds his case, and, in my opinion, they are not significant ones.

Collins indicates that Dan 7:9–10 is considered by many to be an ancient hymn which would predate the Antiochene crisis (*Daniel*, 299). If this could be historically verified, then Stokes's argument would be more convincing. If anything, however, the evidence tips in favour of its composition in the maccabean period. For instance, the only other references to "thrones" in a heavenly context is the first-century BCE Qumran document the *Songs of the Sabbath Sacrifice* (11QShirShabb X, 5–6). It seems to me that the one who composed Dan 7, especially in light of his fanciful description the four beasts and the coming of the SM, is clearly an imaginative author who drew some of his inspiration for vv. 9–10 from 1 En. 14.

77. Kvanvig, "Henoch," 130.

78. Boccaccini argues that "yet, in spite of many similarities [between 1 *Enoch* and Daniel], a fundamental difference makes Daniel representative of yet a different party ("Covenantal Theology," 41). Daniel opposes the enochic doctrine of the superhuman origin of evil, and strenuously defends the tenets of Zadokite covenantal theology." See also Boccaccini, *Beyond*, 68–79. For criticisms of articulating specific groups as having composed these texts, see Collins, "Response," 59–66.

79. Black notes that, despite the traditional understanding, Milik argues the reverse is true: Gen 6:1–4 has borrowed from Enoch (*Enoch*, 14).

Daniel's Son of Man in Mark

interest for the purposes of this study is Enoch's description of the heavenly temple. After flying to heaven (v. 8), Enoch comes to a wall constructed of fiery hailstones through which he passes (v. 9). He then comes to a great house also built of hailstones "and the walls of this house were like stone slabs, and they were all of snow, and the floor was of snow" (v. 10b). The ceiling of this house "was like shooting stars and lightning flashes and among them were fiery cherubim, and their heaven was water, and a flaming fire encircled all their walls, and the doors blazed with fire" (vv. 11–12). He enters this surreal house, "hot as fire and cold as snow" (v. 13), and, being overcome with fear, he falls prostrate until he sees a yet greater house with an open door, which is composed of "tongues of fire" (v. 15). It is at the door of this house that he witnesses the presence of Yahweh in his heavenly temple, which "so excelled in glory and splendor and majesty that I am unable to describe for you its glory and majesty" (v. 16). Himmelfarb argues that this vision of Yahweh's celestial dwelling reflects the layout of the first and second temples: the first wall that Enoch passes through represents the vestibule or outer chamber (1 Kgs 6:3; Josephus, *JW* 5:207–19), the second wall is part of the "great house" (v. 10a) which is the sanctuary or *hekhal* and finally, the third "even greater house" in which Enoch sees the Great glory seated upon the throne is the holy of holies or *devir*.[80]

While there are many differences between Enoch's description of the heavenly temple and the vision of the celestial courtroom in Dan 7:9–10 and 13–14, not the least of which is the brevity of the danielic vision, there are some distinct similarities which point to an indebtedness on the part of Daniel. Matthew Black contends that "comparison of the shorter Daniel apocalypse with the fuller Enoch vision does suggest that Daniel is abridging or adapting phrases or excerpting a whole line (Dan 7.9 = En. 14.22) from Enoch."[81] On historical grounds, this seems to make the most sense as *The Book of Watchers*, due to its discovery at Qumran is at the very least an early second-century document while Daniel is traditionally dated to the period of the Antiochene crisis.[82] Below is a reproduction of Dan 7:9–10 and *1 En.* 14:18–23 in tabular form.

---

80. Himmelfarb, *Ascent*, 14. Nickelsburg also claims that this third dwelling is the holy of holies (*1 Enoch*, 50).

81. Black, *Enoch*, 151.

82. Ibid., 151. Regarding the date of *The Book of Watchers*, Nickelsburg concludes that one is "justified in treating these chapters as a product of the period before 175 BCE" (*Jewish Literature*, 46).

Chapter 2: Daniel's "One Like a Son of Man"

Dan 7:9–10	1 *En.* 14:18–23

And as I watched,
 thrones were set in place,
  and the Ancient of Days took his throne,
 his clothing was white as snow,
  and the hair of his head like pure wool;
 his throne was fiery flames,
  and its wheels were burning fire.
A stream of fire issued
 and flowed out from his presence.
A thousand thousands served him,
 and ten thousand times ten thousand stood attending him.
The court sat in judgment
 and the books were opened.
	And I was looking and I saw a lofty throne;
	 and its appearance was like ice,
	 and its wheels were like the shining sun,
	 and the voice (or sound) of the cherubim,
	 and from beneath the throne issued rivers of flaming fire.
	And I was unable to see.
	The Great Glory sat upon it;
	 his apparel was like the appearance of the sun and whiter than much snow.
	No angel could enter into this house and look at his face because of the splendor and glory,
	 and no human could look at him.
	Flaming fire encircled him and a great fire stood by him,
	 and none of those about him approached him.
	Ten thousand times ten thousand stood before him,
	 but he needed no counselor; his every word was deed.
	And the holy ones of the watchers who approached him did not depart by night,
	 nor <by day> did they leave him.

There are three clear parallels between these two texts.[83] First, the wheeled throne is described similarly in both visions. In Daniel, it is composed of "fiery flames" and its wheels are "burning fire" (v. 9c) while in 1 *Enoch*, its wheels are "like the shining sun" (v. 18) and from beneath it flow "rivers of flaming fire" (v. 19)[84]. Likewise, in Daniel, "a stream of fire issued and flowed out from his presence" (v. 10a) which likely comes from the throne on which Yahweh is seated (v. 9a). Black notes that both Dan 7:10 LXX and the extant Greek text of Enoch (G) contain the words "river of fire" (ποταμὸς πυρός).[85] Second, the apparel of Yahweh is "white as snow" (v. 9b) in Daniel and similarly in Enoch it is "whiter than much snow" (v. 20). Third, the "thousand thousands" who "serve" (יְשַׁמְּשׁוּנֵּהּ) the Ancient of Days (Dan 7:10bα) and the "ten thousand times ten thousand" who "stand attending him" (יְקוּמוּן) (Dan 7:10bβ) recalls the "ten thousand times ten thousand" who "stood before him" (1 *En.* 14:22b) and "the holy ones of the watchers who approached him" (1 *En.* 14:23) in Enoch's vision. Again, the Greek of Daniel, this time in both the LXX and Theodotion as they have identical readings, is very similar to Enoch G: μύριαι μυριάδες παρειστήκεισαν αὐτῷ (v. 10b) parallels μύριαι μυριάδες ἑστήκασιν ἐνώπιον αὐτοῦ.[86] The activity of standing before the throne is a priestly one as is evident in Enoch's vision where the angels *stand* before the throne (14:22–23) and have the mandate to intercede on behalf of humanity (15:2).[87] Since the earthly temple is thought to mirror its celestial counterpart, which seems to be the case with the one depicted in 1 *En.* 14,[88] it is not surprising that the posture of standing is specifically a role of the priests in the earthly temple. In 2 Chron 20:19 and Neh 9:3, two post-exilic texts, the subjects of the verb קום are priests who "stand up" to praise and worship God (see also 2 Chron 30:27; Neh 9:4).[89] Although Daniel's heavenly beings do not appear to intercede for humanity, they still seem to have a priestly status because

---

83. Stuckenbruck highlights a number of parallels between Dan 7:9–10 and 4QEnb ar II, 15b–20 ("Daniel," 380). See also, Stuckenbruck, "Throne," 216–20.

84. Black points out that the wheeled throne that is surrounded by fire ultimately has its source in Ezekiel's vision of the divine chariot throne (Ezek 1:15–21, 27) (*Enoch*, 149). For a fuller treatment of Enoch's dependence on Ezekiel, see Himmelfarb, *Ascent*, 9–13.

85. Ibid., 149.

86. Ibid., 150.

87. Himmelfarb, "Ascent," 211.

88. Ibid., 14–15. For more on this topic, see Levenson, *Sinai and Zion*, 137–42.

89. After the dedication of the second temple, Ezra records that "then they set (וַהֲקִימוּ) the priests in their divisions and the Levites in their courses for the service of God at Jerusalem, as it is written in the book of Moses" (6:18).

Chapter 2: Daniel's "One Like a Son of Man"

of their posture of standing before the throne in the presence of Yahweh (v 10b). Daniel's use of the verb שמשׁ translated as "serving" or "ministering" (7:10ba: a thousand thousands *served* him) likewise recalls the Aaronic priests who drew near to the altar in order "to minister" (שָׁרֵת) in the holy place (Exod 28:35, 43; 30:20).[90] Similarly, the Zadokite priests "approach the Lord to 'minister' (מְשָׁרְתִי) to him" in Ezekiel's vision of an eschatological temple (Ezek 45:4-5; 46:24; see also 42:14).[91] *Targum Neofiti*, despite the vexed question of the text's date of composition, employs the Aramaic verb שמשׁ in Exod 28:43 and 30:20 to describe the activity of the priests "serving" where the MT uses שרת.[92] This at least demonstrates a trajectory of the cultic usage of שמשׁ in Daniel where we have heavenly beings in a priestly posture of "standing" in Yahweh's presence.

In Dan 7:13cβ, the heavenly myriads are likely the subjects of the verb "present" (הַקְרְבוּהִי). Most English translations render this verb in the passive voice, but this *haphel* verb, which is in the active voice, has a third person plural subject, the antecedent of which is the heavenly multitude, and a third person singular object, the SM.[93] The *hiphel* of קרב in biblical Hebrew expresses the act "of presenting, dedicating, or offering to."[94] In the Pentateuch, this verb describes the presentation of Israel's first priests before the Lord's presence in the tabernacle. In Exod 29:4, Moses is commanded to "bring (*hiphel*: תַּקְרִיב) Aaron and his sons to the entrance of the tent of meeting, and wash them with water" (see 29:8). This act is also recorded in Lev 7:35; 8:6, 13, 24 and Num 8:9, 10; 16:5.[95] It is unwarranted, however, to argue that the danielic SM is, therefore, a priest as Crispin Fletcher-Louis has recently attempted.[96] What is important to realize is that the language used to describe the presentation of the SM in this celestial setting is used to designate priestly activity in the earthly tabernacle. Likewise, as I discussed earlier, the verbs that describe the activity of the heavenly myriads who *serve* Yahweh and *stand* attending him also apply to the priests in

---

90. BDB, "שָׁרַת, 1058".

91. Ibid.

92. Kaufman et al., *Key-Word-In-Context*, 1310. Kaufman et al. also list Exod 28:1, 4; 29:44; Deut 17:12.

93. NRSV: "and was presented before him;" NIV: "and was led into his presence."

94. BDB, "קָרַב," 898.

95. Ibid. In the Qal form, it is the priests themselves who "draw near" (Ezek 44:15; 16; 45:4).

96. Fletcher-Louis, "High Priest," 167.

the tabernacle and temple. Finally, the SM's mode of transportation, "the clouds of heaven" (עִם־עֲנָנֵי שְׁמַיָּא) are often associated with manifestations of Yahweh's presence both in the tabernacle (Exod 40:34–35) and in the temple (1 Kgs 8:10–11; 2 Chron 5:13–14). Although these examples are not the only use of clouds in the OT by any means, e.g., Gen 9:13, this imagery is, however, associated with cultic contexts.[97] This data, along with aspects of Enoch's description of Yahweh in his heavenly temple that appear in the throne vision of Daniel and the parallels the latter shares with canonical instances of Yahweh exercising judicial rule in his celestial dwelling (see 1 Kgs 22:19; Ps 82:1; Isa 6), support my claim that Daniel describes more than a celestial courtroom, but actually Yahweh reigning and, particularly, judging from his heavenly temple.

Another point of contact between in *1 En.* 14 and Dan 7 is that the heavenly temple depicted in both texts appears in response to the defilement of the earthly temple and its priesthood. The author of *The Book of Watchers* is communicating a message of priestly corruption, of fallen watchers who no longer intercede in heaven, which is likely directed at some segment of the Jerusalem priests.[98] Nickelsburg indicates that the polemic against the Jerusalem priests is evident in *1 En.* 15:3–4 where Yahweh chastises the fallen priests for abdicating their eternal and priestly role in the eternal sanctuary by defiling themselves with the daughters of men.[99] But not all priests are evil as there are those heavenly watchers still before Yahweh's throne (14:23). Although the danielic vision centers on the oppressive and destructive nature of the "little horn," I have argued above, in light of a variety of Jewish texts, that the priests were not above reproach and, in light of Dan 11, were in collusion with the Seleucid king. In both *1 En.* 14 and Dan 7, the heavenly temple is revealed due to the corruption and profanation of the terrestrial temple so that God may continue his saving purposes for faithful Israel which involves, in these visions, executing judgement on the perpetrators of covenantal disloyalty and temple profanation. This pattern, that Yahweh's heavenly dwelling is revealed in response to terrestrial temple corruption, is also related to the first-century BCE text, the *Songs of the Sabbath Sacrifice*. For the Qumran community, the denunciation of the earthly

---

97. Reynolds, *Apocalyptic Son of Man*, 30.

98. Himmelfarb, *Ascent*, 22.

99. Nickelsburg, "Enoch," 584–85. See also the helpful discussion and secondary literature cited in Wardle, *Jerusalem Temple*, 52–56 on the priestly polemic of *The Book of Watchers*.

temple is uncompromising because of its corruption and, therefore, this document depicts the worship of Yahweh at Qumran as being that which mirrors the worship of Yahweh in the heavenly temple.[100] Timothy Wardle comments that "the idea that humans may, alongside the angels, partake in the divine worship appears to have been an important tenet for those living at Qumran, for in this shared praise they were able to participate in the worship of the God of Israel even though they were separated from the [Jerusalem] temple."[101]

The Danielic Son of Man and Faithful Israel

This section focuses on current interpretations of the danielic SM and concludes with my contention, as well as that of others, that he is a symbol for faithful Israel, "the people of the holy ones of the Most High" (v. 27a) and as such his vindicated status restores those to Yahweh's presence who did not capitulate to the ways of the Seleucid king and corrupt priests. Contemporary interpretations of the figure include the Messiah, an angelic or divine being, or faithful Israel.[102] All three approaches recognize that the SM either represents or symbolizes the "holy ones" (קַדִּישִׁין: vv. 18, 21, 22, 25, 27), but the referent of this group is also the subject of much debate. Advocates of the angelic or divine interpretation claim that קַדִּישִׁין refer to heavenly beings.[103] Collins is widely known for his contention that the SM

---

100. Nickelsburg, *Jewish Literature*, 151–54.
101. Wardle, *Jerusalem Temple*, 155.

102. Regarding the messianic interpretation, Beasley-Murray claims that the figure represents both the "rule of God" and the people under that rule analogous to the function of the Messiah in the OT ("Interpretation," 55–57). Support for the messianic approach has greatly waned in recent years in light of an emphasis on variegated messianic expectations in pre-Christian times. Wright indicates that "modern scholarship has made one thing quite clear: there was no single, monolithic and uniform 'messianic expectation' among first-century Jews" (*People*, 307). See also Sanders, *Judaism*, 295–98. Additionally, Collins correctly notes, "the traditional view, which identifies the 'Son of Man' with the Messiah, has scarcely any scholarly support now, as it is widely recognized as the product of a Christian interpretation, in the light of the NT" (*Vision*, 124). For defenses of the messianic interpretation, see Horbury, "Messianic," 34–55; Rowe, "Daniel's 'Son of Man,'" 71–96; Shepherd, "New Testament Son of Man," 100–6. For further criticisms of this approach, see Collins, *Vision*, 308–9.

103. Collins, *Vision*, 313; Noth, "Holy Ones," 228; Colpe, "ὁ υἱὸς τοῦ ἀνθρώπου," 442; Dequeker, "Daniel 7," 353–92.

is the archangel Michael who leads the angelic קַדִּישִׁין.[104] However, not every occurrence of קַדִּישִׁין in both the Hebrew Bible and the DSS favors an angelic referent.[105] For example, in Ps 34:10 the קְדֹשָׁיו are humans, along with the ἁγίους in 1 Macc 1:46, although the latter postdates Daniel.[106] Since Collins's interpretation is either endorsed or disputed in the major commentaries and, more significantly, is at odds with my own reading of the danielic SM, I offer the following evaluation of his work. Collins arrives at his conclusion via a circuitous path of exegesis which begins in Dan 10–12 and concludes in chapter 7.[107] To begin, Collins attempts to demonstrate that Antiochus speaks against Yahweh's "angelic host"(אֵל אֵלִים) in 11:36.[108] There is nothing in the text of Dan 11 itself to support this reading; rather, Daniel is contrasting the pagan gods of Antiochus, along with the one on which he relies, the "god of fortresses" in v. 38 with the "God of gods" (אֵל אֵלִים) against whom Antiochus speaks "horrendous things" (v. 36a). The phrase "God of gods" also contrasts with the preceding phrase "greater than any god" (v. 36a), a designation which Antiochus ascribes to himself.[109] At this point, the battle is not between Antiochus and the heavenly hosts but between the paganism of Antiochus and the one true God, the "God of gods" of the Jews, not unlike the theme of Dan 3.

Victory comes when Michael, "the great prince, the protector of your people, shall arise" (12:1a) and "the wise shall shine like the brightness of

---

104. Likewise, see Chilton, "Son of (the) Man," 276 and Nickelsburg, *Jewish Literature*, 78. Meanwhile, Zevit claims that the SM is Gabriel ("Structure," 394–96). Black advocates that the SM is a divine being: "Dan 7 zwei Manifestationen der Gottheit kennt: den Alten der Tage und den Menschensohn" ("Die Apotheose Israels," 98). For a similar interpretation, see Bittner, "Gott—Menschensohn," 351 and Caragounis, *Vision*, 74–80.

105. Collins, *Vision*, 313.

106. Di Lella, "Human Likeness," 7.

107. Collins, *Vision*, 144.

108. Ibid., 135. He supports this interpretation of אֵל אֵלִים with the DSS where אלימ is often a synonym for "angels" and in one instance in the War Scroll. Y. Yadin translates אל אלימ "god of angels" (*Scroll*, 230). Collins also cites the phrase "lord of spirits" in the *Parables* as supporting evidence (*1 En.* 37:4; 38:2, 6). However, the *Parables* are largely irrelevant in determining the meaning of terminology in Daniel as it post-dates the book by at least 100 years. Hartman and DiLella indicate that "God of gods" is a superlative expression, i.e., God is the highest God (*Daniel*, 301). This same phrase appears in Dan 2:47 contrasting the true monotheistic God with the pagan gods: "Truly, your God is a God of gods (אֱלָהּ אֱלָהִין) and Lord of kings." Note also that it appears in Deut 10:17a: "For the Lord your God is God of gods (אֱלֹהֵי הָאֱלֹהִים) and Lord of lords."

109. Porteous, *Daniel*, 169; Hartman and Di Lella, *Daniel*, 301; Montgomery, *Daniel*, 462.

Chapter 2: Daniel's "One Like a Son of Man"

the sky, and those who lead many to righteousness, like the stars forever and ever" (12:3). Collins argues that the wise, a symbol for righteous Israel, become "stars" to join the angelic host because in biblical and extra-biblical traditions stars refer to heavenly beings (see Judg 5:20; Job 38:7; *T. Mos.* 10:9; *1 En.* 104:2-6).[110] But this is figurative exaltation language describing the "wise" *as* the "brightness of the sky" and "those who lead many to righteousness" *as* "stars."[111] Furthermore, assuming that the wise did join the angelic ranks, this status applies exclusively to this group, that is, "those who are wise/those who lead many" (v. 3) and not to all of those delivered (v.1c: "your people").[112] In Dan 7, קַדִּישִׁין denotes all of faithful Israel (v. 27), not a particular group such as the הַמַּשְׂכִּלִים in 12:3.

Collins then turns to Dan 8. According to him, the parallelism between the "host" (צָבָא) and the "stars" in 8:10 indicates that the former are heavenly beings because, as mentioned above, "stars" refer to angels in the biblical tradition.[113] He claims that "here, as in Dan 11, Epiphanes passes over from the purely human domain and launches an attack on the heavenly host."[114] Collins then cites 8:24b-25a: "He will destroy mighty ones and a people of holy ones and against his plotting, and deceit will prosper in his hand." Recognizing the corruption of the MT text, Collins reconstructs the Hebrew based on the LXX which reads: "He will destroy powerful ones and a people of holy ones and his plotting shall be against the holy ones." Collins appeals to dittography to dismiss the authenticity of עַם־קְדֹשִׁים because of the similarity between this expression and אֶל קדושן. Many commentators fail to see the need to excise עַם־קְדֹשִׁים from 8:24c, hence rendering this expression hardly "superfluous."[115] Further, according to Goldingay, the "many" of 8:25b is a phrase Daniel often uses to refer to faithful Jews and in

---

110. Collins, *Vision*, 136-37; Davies, "Eschatology," 43.

111. Porteous, *Daniel*, 170-71; Goldingay cautions against a literal reading of 12:1-3 when he claims that the phrase "'Like the stars' ... *compares* the discerning with these [the stars], but does not necessarily thereby suggest that they will be located among them, still less will *become* stars/angels" (*Daniel*, 308).

112. Lacocque, *Daniel*, 245; Hartman and Di Lella, *Daniel*, 310.

113. Collins, *Vision*, 138.

114. Ibid., 138. Collins supports this with reference to Dan 11:36 in which Antiochus lifts himself up above עַל־כָּל־אֵל where אֵל refers to "heavenly being." But, as I have argued above, Daniel is concerned with Antiochus's own arrogation to the divine realm in which he sees himself "above every *god*."

115. Collins, *Vision*, 139. See Lacocque, *Daniel*, 170; Hartman and Di Lella, *Daniel*, 229; Montgomery, *Daniel*, 350.

8:24–25 the "people of the holy ones" (v. 24c) parallels the "many" (v. 25b) because both are objects of the verb "destroy" (v. 24c/v.25b).[116] Antiochus's destructive hostility is directed at the "people"/"many" of Israel (see 7:25); they are the קַדִּישִׁין as Dan 7:27 explicitly states.

Some scholars have criticized both Collins's methodology and conclusions.[117] He, however, does recognize the weakness inherent in using Dan 10–12 to interpret Dan 7–8.[118] According to Wright, "the later visions in Daniel 8–12, in my opinion, are to be read as developments from this basic position [reading Dan 7 in light of 1–6], rather than as themselves determining the meaning of the earlier portions of the book."[119] Further, there are no indications within chapter 7 itself that קַדִּישִׁין and by implication כְּבַר אֱנָשׁ are angelic figures. Rather, Wright argues that Dan 7 evinces "literary representation" in which the four beasts who represent pagan empires parallel the SM who represents the earthly holy ones, that is, faithful Israel who has been recently estranged from God's earthly dwelling.[120] Wright accuses Collins of mixing categories of representation. The SM cannot be both a heavenly figure existing in some other realm as in metaphysical representation and at the same time representing the plight of the "saints of the Most High" as in literary representation. However, given the parallels between the holy ones and the SM, which I discuss below, I contend that the SM is a symbol for the saints and is not an independent figure separate from faithful Israel which Wright's comment seems to suggest. Despite this, his criticism still stands.

There are clear parallels between the SM and the saints in the text; for example, both the SM and the "*people* of the saints of the Most High" are given "kingship" (v. 14a: מַלְכוּ; v. 27a: מַלְכוּתָה) and "dominion" (v. 14a: שָׁלְטָן; v. 27a: שָׁלְטָנָא). The court ruling in favor of the SM at the appearance of the Ancient of Days (vv. 9–14) is likewise ruling in favor of the suffering saints at which point the kingdom is taken from the beast and given to the SM/saints (vv. 14, 22).[121] Hooker argues that this reception of dominion "means that the dominion of Adam is restored to the rightful owner,

---

116. Goldingay, *Daniel*, 218.

117. For example, see Beasley-Murray, "Interpretation," 52–55 and Di Lella, "Likeness," 7–13.

118. Collins, "Saints," 58.

119. Wright, *People*, 296.

120. Ibid., 291, 295–96. See also Delcor, *Le Livre de Daniel*, 61 fn. 52.

121. Moule, "Neglected," 418–19.

Chapter 2: Daniel's "One Like a Son of Man"

and the saints are seen to be what they have always been—the inheritors of God's promises, the elect and true 'Man', in contrast to those whose sin and rebellion has reduced them to the level of the beasts."[122] It is clear in Gen 1:26 that אָדָם has a divine mandate "to rule" (רָדָה) over all the animals whether in the sky, sea or upon the earth. This injunction is repeated again in v. 28 using the verb כָּבַשׁ as well as רָדָה in which humanity is to "subdue" the earth. According to J. E. Hartley, the verb כָּבַשׁ is more intense than רָדָה as it means to conquer or subjugate pagan nations (see 2 Sam 8:11).[123] The danielic SM, then, is first and foremost a symbol for faithful Israel who embodies the vindication of the nation over beastly, oppressive empires.[124] Some scholars argue that before the SM's vindication, he suffered at the hands of the little horn just like the saints (vv. 21, 25).[125] If the SM does suffer, it is of a secondary concern to Daniel as it is not clearly evident.

A crucial element, as many scholars have recognized, is that despite faithful Israel's current plight of suffering and persecution, God will vindicate them and restore to them his kingdom. However, a consideration of the heavenly temple features of the vision as well as a nuanced study of the historical context in which it was composed, enables interpreters to see that not only is Israel receiving Yahweh's royal authority when he judges in their favor, but also that she is being reconnected with his presence despite Antiochus's successful mission to paganize the Jerusalem temple by, among other things, prohibiting the *tamid*. Although the vision itself makes no mention of the priests's complicity in the temple's profanation, there are references to it later in Daniel and in other Jewish literature from the period. Essentially, they have forsaken their divinely sanctioned cultic duties and have instead supported the Syrian king in his attempts to paganize Jerusalem. When we consider this background, the associations that Daniel's vision has with earthly tabernacle and temple, as well as the celestial one depicted in *1 En.* 14, serve an important purpose. The use of temple imagery in this celestial context indicates that, despite the desecration of the Jerusalem temple and the malfeasance of its leaders, faithful Israel is

---

122. Hooker, *Son of Man*, 29.

123. Hartley, *Genesis*, 49.

124. France, *Old Testament*, 146; Goldingay, *Daniel*, 171. Reynolds argues that because of the royal investiture of the SM in 7:14, he is a "kingly representative of the holy ones of the Most High" (*Apocalyptic Son of Man*, 33).

125. Moule, "Neglected," 418–19; Wright, *People*, 524; Caragounis, *Vision*, 76; Goldingay highlights that "the picture is one of conflict and victory, rather than suffering and affliction" (*Daniel*, 171).

now restored to Yahweh's presence. When the angelic beings present the SM before Yahweh, they are echoing Moses' presentation of Aaron and his sons before Yahweh's terrestrial presence in the tabernacle. Eric W. Heaton is quite accurate in his assessment that the people of the holy ones of the Most High, "symbolized by the figure [the SM] were no ordinary members of Israel but a special group nearer to the ideal of 'a kingdom of priests, a holy nation' (Exod 19:6), than the rank and file of Judaism."[126] It is these ones who have remained faithful and so are now once again in the divine presence because of the vindication of the symbolic SM. The enemies of Israel, in particular, the little horn of the fourth beast and those who colluded with him, will no longer hinder them. A. Fuellet rightly concludes:

> Qu'est-ce à dire, sinon que les trios oracles de 7:13–14; 8:14; et 9:24 se complètent mutuellement et contribuent à exprimer la même réalité? Le sanctuaire tout spirituel que Dieu oint (9:24) est assuré de la présence divine grâce à la venue avec les nuées du Fils de l'homme (7:13–14), et c'est de cette manière que Dieu venge (8:14) le temple matériel profané par Antiochus.[127]

Conclusion

I have argued in this chapter that faithful Israel or "the holy ones of the Most High" have been estranged from Yahweh's dwelling because the aggressive, tyrannical Syrian king, Antiochus IV Epiphanes, desecrated the Jerusalem temple along with a colluding high priesthood. Antiochus's desire to turn the temple into a pagan shrine in addition to the abdication of cultic duties by the priests means that it can no longer serve its redemptive purposes. The priests in Daniel's day who have colluded with Antiochus are yet another example of priestly corruption in the third and second centuries BCE, which likely includes their involvement in the cessation of the daily burnt offering. This underscores my assertion about the desecration's effects on faithful Israel: they are now estranged from Yahweh's presence. It is impossible for them to draw near to Yahweh when the temple is in such a deplorable state. The vision in Dan 7 reveals the solution, however. Yahweh, enthroned in his heavenly temple, will reverse the oppressed and

---

126. Heaton, *Daniel*, 187. Lacocque claims that the קַדִּישִׁין form a "spiritual Temple" (*Daniel*, 126). Likewise, Fuellet, "Le Fils," 197–98.

127. Ibid., 197–98.

Chapter 2: Daniel's "One Like a Son of Man"

persecuted plight of Israel through not only the destruction of their adversary but also through the symbol of the SM who is presented before Yahweh. This marks the reinstatement of their God-given dominion and the reestablishment of the divine presence for the persecuted holy ones.

This chapter's reevaluation of the scene of Dan 7:9-10 and 13-14, which as I have argued, describes not merely a celestial courtroom but the heavenly temple and brings to light the full significance of the vindication of faithful Israel beyond the reinstatement of their royal investiture. Despite the different opinions held by scholars as to Yahweh's location in Daniel's vision, the scene shares a number of similarities with Enoch's vision of the heavenly temple in *The Book of Watchers* and other canonical texts which describe the same setting. Not only are there parallels between *1 En.* 14 and Dan 7, which suggests that the latter is more than a celestial courtroom, but also their similar historical contexts of a corrupt priesthood and temple appears to elicit the manifestation of Yahweh's celestial dwelling from which judgment is meted out. In Daniel, this judgement results in the destruction of the impure, chaotic four beasts, especially the little horn of the fourth one, leading to Israel's presentation before Yahweh's presence.

Chapter 3: The Son of Man in 1 Enoch 37–71 and 4 Ezra 13

Introduction

THE PURPOSE OF THIS chapter is to examine subsequent interpretations of the danielic SM in two Jewish texts that are close to the time of the composition of Mark's Gospel. The examination of these "interpretative renderings," as they appear in the *Parables* and *4 Ezra*, enables one to appreciate the range of interpretations of the danielic SM current in first-century Judaism which will then provide a framework for my study of the markan figure.[1] The authors of these texts have exploited the SM in such a way that he is now an active, messianic agent engaging in tasks specifically associated with Yahweh. In the *Parables,* he executes judgement from the heavenly temple against corrupt kings and sinners which in Daniel is implicitly carried out by Yahweh himself in his celestial dwelling. The enochic SM is also the agent of eschatological salvation for those who have been victimized and oppressed by these earthly despots. In *4 Ezra*, the SM acts as a warrior situated on a cosmic temple mount from which he destroys those who wish to make war against him, similar to the portrayal of Yahweh as divine warrior in a number of biblical texts. It is not insignificant that the SM in both the *Parables* and *4 Ezra* is still associated with Yahweh's heavenly dwelling.

---

1. Chialà comments that "the book [Daniel] contains the basic *imagistic repertoire* that was taken up and elaborated in the centuries that followed [in a number of Jewish and Christian texts], and the expression 'son of man', which Daniel uses in a totally neutral way, is part of this repertoire" ("Son of Man," 158).

CHAPTER 3: THE SON OF MAN IN 1 ENOCH 37–71 AND 4 EZRA 13

The Son of Man in the Parables

Date of Composition

Since the time of R. H. Charles, until the discovery of the Aramaic and Greek fragments of the Enoch corpus at Qumran, it was widely believed that the *Parables* or the "Second Vision of Enoch" (*1 En.* 37:1) constituted pre-Christian evidence of a heavenly messianic SM who is both savior and judge.[2] However, this was seriously called into question with the publication of J. T. Milik's work, *The Books of Enoch: Aramaic Fragments of Qumrân Cave 4*. Milik argues that the *Parables* are a third-century Christian work because this writing is not found in any Qumran fragments. As for their usefulness for NT studies, Milik declares that "it will be necessary henceforth to dismiss definitively all the alleged references to the Book of Parables, since the latter is a Christian work of the third century, if not later."[3] This assessment has not gone unchallenged. Probably the most glaring deficiency is Milik's argument from silence that the *Parables* are not pre-Christian because they did not turn up in the Qumran Aramaic fragments.[4] Further, the writings themselves do not evince any distinctly Christian aspects or themes as a number of scholars have noted.[5] The close similarities between Matthew's SM and the enochic one does not necessarily mean that the author of the *Parables* was inspired by Matthew but rather the opposite is likely true.[6]

Scholars often use the passage about the Parthians and Medes to determine a date for the *Parables*, as Milik himself does:[7]

---

2. Charles published his translation of the enochic writings using 29 ethiopic MSS in 1912 in *The Book of Enoch or 1 Enoch*.

3. Milik, *Enoch*, 74.

4. Fitzmyer claims that the argument from silence is precarious not least because only twenty fragments for the other sections of *1 Enoch* have been found ("Implications," 342 fn. 16). Greenfield notes that the authenticity of Esther has not been called into question despite the fact that it did not appear in the Qumran fragments ("Enochic Pentateuch," 55). Hooker comments that this "negative evidence . . . cannot be regarded as in any sense decisive" (*Son of Man*, 48). See also the discussion in Suter, "Enoch in Sheol," 415–43.

5. Fuller, *Foundations*, 37–38; Fitzmyer, "Implications," 343; Black, "Throne-Theophany," 66; Hooker, *Son of Man*, 48.

6. According to Theisohn, the Gospel *Menschensohntradition* is influenced by "Typ des partiellen Einflusses" which includes material from the *Parables* (*auserwählte Richter*, 153).

7. Milik, *Enoch*, 91–96.

> In those days, the angels will assemble themselves, and hurl themselves toward the East against the Parthians and Medes. They will stir up kings, and a spirit of agitation will come upon them, and it will rouse them from their thrones. They will break out like lions from their lairs, and like hungry wolves in the midst of their flocks. They will go up and trample the land of his chosen ones, and the land of his chosen ones will be before them as a threshing floor and a (beaten path); but the city of my righteous ones will be a hindrance to their horses (1 En. 56:5–7).

Matthew Black argues that the reference to the Parthians in this text is indicative of "an *earlier* rather than a *later* date in that period."[8] This early date is between 40 and 38 BCE when the Parthians occupied Palestine prior to the reign of Herod the Great.[9] It is difficult to determine a precise date for the *Parables* on the basis of this passage, however, because the reference concerns the *future* and the Parthians were in fact successful in securing Jerusalem.[10] Nonetheless, it may have been composed in response to that particular invasion as a way of seeking revenge because in the text the Parthians are predicted not to make any advance on Jerusalem (56:7a) but instead will be thrown into confusion (56:7b) and, finally, swallowed up by Sheol (56:8). The Parthian invasion appears to be fresh in the author's mind and, therefore, lends at least tacit support for a pre-Christian time frame for the text's composition.

Another text indicating a possible historical reference is *1 En.* 67:8–13 which likely refers to the warm healing waters of Callirrhoe. According to Josephus, Herod bathed in these waters to soothe the pain of his physical ailments (Josephus, *Ant.* 17.171) which have come as the result of God's judgement for his "lawless deeds" (Josephus, *Ant.* 17.168 [Marcus and Wikgren]). Enoch refers to those who use these waters as "kings, mighty, exalted, and those who dwell on earth" (67:8a). For Enoch, these healing waters serve a beneficial purpose, but for those kings, such as Herod, who fail to believe in the Lord of Spirits, the waters will become "a fire

---

8. Black, "Composition," 27.

9. Mearns, "Dating," 362; Black, "Composition," 27; Caragounis, *Vision*, 89–91; and, most recently, Nickelsburg and VanderKam, *1 Enoch*, 6.

10. Josephus indicates that the foreign army plundered all of Jerusalem including the royal palace (Josephus, *Ant.* 14.363). Both Suter and Mearns caution scholars who appeal to this one historical reference to determine a date (Suter, *Tradition and Composition*, 24; Mearns, "Dating," 362). Suter argues that "we are dealing with updated apocalyptic myth or a vague memory of the invasion of the Parthians in 40–39 BCE" ("Sheol," 6). See also Knibb, "Parables of Enoch," 349.

CHAPTER 3: THE SON OF MAN IN 1 ENOCH 37–71 AND 4 EZRA 13

that burns forever" (67:13). Interestingly, the passage about these waters is one of the so-called "Noahic fragments" which are clear allusions to the *Book of Watchers* where fallen angels, referring to temple priests as I have mentioned earlier, lead humanity astray. Enoch recalls their judgement in 67:4–5 which he later deems a "testimony for the kings and mighty who possess the earth" (67:12). This could indicate that the kings in the Parables are not generic figures but rather are ones who rule over the Jews vis-à-vis King Herod.[11] There are also some noticeable parallels between Enoch's record of the deplorable behavior of the "kings" and "sinners" with Josephus's account of the reign of King Herod. These include:

1. the persecution of the righteous (46:8; 47:1, 4; 53:7) with Herod's persecution of the Jewish people (Josephus, *Ant.* 16.158–59), the Pharisees who refused to support Herod (Josephus, *Ant.* 17.41–45), and the revolutionaries who pulled down the eagle from the Temple (Josephus, *Ant.* 17.149–67);

2. kings and mighty who build idols (46:7b) with Herod's erection of idols (Josephus, *Ant.* 15.276, 278) and the construction of pagan temples outside of Jewish territory (Josephus, *Ant.* 15.328–330; 16.147);

3. the impiety of the kings and mighty (46:5; 48:10b; 63:7) with Herod's impiety (Josephus, *Ant.* 15.182, 375; 17.171);

4. ill-gotten wealth of the kings (63:10) with, for example, Herod stealing valuables from David and Solomon's tomb (Josephus, *Ant.* 16.179–182).

All of these correspondences make a compelling case for the composition of the *Parables* in the late stages of Herod's reign and the writing itself could very well be a response to it.

Although scholars do not attempt to date the book with a high degree of precision, a *terminus ad quem* is before destruction of the Jerusalem temple and, in light of *1 En.* 56:5–7 and 67:8–13, a *terminus a quo* is 40 BCE.[12] In the preface to a collection of essays from the 2005 Enoch Seminar

---

11. See also 64:1–2 which *prima facie* seems out of place but, when analyzed in its literary context, fits well. These two verses refer to the fallen angels which immediately follows an extended discussion in *1 En.* 63 on the judgement of the kings and mighty. This again suggests a close association between the figures of the fallen angels and the kings for the author of *Parables*.

12. Suter argues for a date before the last third of the first century CE (*Tradition*, 24) and Collins advocates pre-70 ("First-Century," 452); meanwhile, Knibb claims that

held at Camaldoli, Italy, Gabriele Boccaccini comments that "most of the participants passionately argued for a composition of the Parables at the turn of the era; no one suggested a date before the Roman period or after the first-century CE."[13] In light of this scholarly consensus as well as the discussion above, it is unwarranted to diminish the importance of the *Parables* for the study of the NT, particularly in relation to the SM not because of any literary dependence on them but, as I have mentioned above, to understand how other traditions interpreted the danielic SM which are contemporaneous with the NT writings.

Literary Structure

The first line of the prologue characterizes the rest of the work: "The vision of *wisdom* that Enoch saw" (37:1a). This wisdom is given to the patriarch by "the Lord of Spirits" for "those who dwell on the earth" (37:4–5), which is divided into three "parables" (38–44, 45–57, and 58–69). At various points in the last two, some Noahic material has been inserted after the original composition (54:7—55:2; 60; 65:1—69:25).[14] The writing concludes with a so-called "double epilogue" constituting chapters 70 and 71. Because of Enoch's identification with the SM in 71:14 and possibly in 70:1, depending upon which MS is viewed to be authentic, these final chapters continue to be the object of much scholarly debate.[15] Some argue that both of these chapters are from the same hand as the rest of the work.[16] James C.

---

the writing dates from the end of the first century because he is unconvinced that the lack of a reference to the destruction of the temple means that the *Parables* predate this event ("Date," 358–59). However, the burden of proof rests on him because to counter this negative evidence is the positive data that Jerusalem has not been attacked (*1 En.* 56:6). His other argument discussing the parallels between *2 Baruch* and *4 Ezra* with the *Parables* does not constitute a late first-century date, but rather could mean that certain groups of Jews had parallel interpretations of the SM which does not imply that each writing was composed contemporaneously. Knibb himself realizes the weakness of his argument when he concedes that "I am fully aware of how tentative this must be" ("Date," 359).

13. Boccaccini, "Enoch Seminar," 16.

14. See Collins, "Heavenly Representative," 112 fn. 8 and Hooker, *Son of Man*, 33 fn. 5. Hooker also includes 39:1–2a.

15. See Olson, "Enoch," 27–38 and Schreiber, "Henoch als Menschensohn," 1–17. For criticisms of Olson's argument, see Hannah, "Elect Son of Man," 153–54.

16. Black, "Messianism," 165; Hooker, *Son of Man*, 42–43. Schreiber, for example, sees 70:1—71:13 as original in which Enoch ascends to the SM, but 71:14-6 reflects the work of

CHAPTER 3: THE SON OF MAN IN 1 ENOCH 37–71 AND 4 EZRA 13

VanderKam suggests that the idea of Enoch as the SM would be presumed throughout the text.[17] For VanderKam, the preceding parables chronicle the visions revealed to Enoch while on earth and the final two chapters indicate his ultimate removal echoing Gen 5:24.[18] The name revealed to the Lord of Spirits and the elect in 48:2 and 69:26 respectively is finally expressed to the reader in 71:14.[19] In support, Daniel C. Olson marshals new textual evidence in support of the minority MS *u* for 70:1 which implicitly identifies Enoch with the SM.[20] Following is Olson's translation of this MS: "And it happened afterwards that the immortal name of that Son of Man was exalted in the presence of the Lord of Spirits beyond all those who live on earth. He was raised aloft on a chariot of wind, and his name was often spoken among them."[21] All of this lends support to the literary coherence of these two chapters with the preceding visions so that the final moment of the *Parables*, in which Enoch is identified as "that SM" (71:14), functions as a conclusion. André Caquot, in support of *1 En.* 70–71, states that "puisqu'ils racontent les moments successifs d'une seule aventure, et qu'ils presentent un aspect original de la légende d'Hénoch."[22] Others, however, argue that the epilogue or portions thereof are inauthentic because, for example, nowhere within the *Parables* does the author indicate that Enoch is the SM.[23] But one must bear in mind that this is apocalyptic literature

---

a Jewish redactor ("Menschensohn," 8). Many years ago, Black advocated that the last two chapters are prior to the *Parables* because of their links with *1 En.* 14 ("Eschatology," 8).

17. VanderKam, "Righteous One," 177–85. Casey finds that "the term 'son of man' is used in the Similitudes in exactly the same way as we know the Aramaic and Hebrew expressions 'son of man' were used elsewhere, namely, as an ordinary expression for 'man,'" which is in coherence with VanderKam's point above ("Use of the Term," 11).

18. VanderKam, "Righteous One," 179. However, 37:1–2, as I will demonstrate below, read as though they are narrated from heaven.

19. For criticisms of the view that Enoch's name is presupposed throughout the vision, see Collins, "Heavenly," 121–22.

20. Olson, "Enoch," 30–31.

21. Compare this with the traditional reading in Nickelsburg and VanderKam: "And after this, while he was living, his name was raised into the presence of that son of man and into the presence of the Lord of Spirits from among those who dwell on the earth. He was raised on the chariots of the wind, and his name departed from among them" (*1 Enoch*, 92).

22. Caquot, "Remarques," 115.

23. Alexander argues that Enoch is presented as quite distinct from the SM in the *Parables* ("Son of Adam," 103). Hannah mounts several convincing criticisms against the authenticity of these last two chapters as well ("Elect Son of Man," 152–58).

in which revelations progressively unfold. The various epithets which describe the eschatological figure are even gradually introduced: Righteous One (38:2), Elect One (39:6) and Messiah (48:10) culminating with the revelation of Enoch as the SM in 71:14. Darrell D. Hannah contends that the last revelation is a little too unexpected and surprising to be authentic likely because it functions as anti-Christian polemic in the late first century correcting the emergent Christian view that Jesus is not the SM but rather Enoch.[24] Even if the final two chapters are a later addition, they still provide us with another picture of Jewish interpretation of the danielic figure in the first century and so I will not attempt to argue for either their authenticity or inauthenticity. The Parables, including the final chapters, are important for determining the *historical probability* of readings of the markan SM which I will propose in the following chapters.

The Reign of "that" Son of Man in the Heavenly Temple

There are two passages in the second parable (*1 En.* 45–57) where the author clearly evokes the celestial scene of Dan 7 and we will examine each of these in turn. The first is found in *1 En.* 46:1–5:

> There I saw one who had a head of days, and his head was like white wool. And with him was another, whose face was like the appearance of a man; and his face was full of graciousness like one of the holy angels. And I asked the angel of peace, who went with me and showed me all the hidden things, about that son of man—who he was and whence he was (and) why he went with the Head of Days. And he answered me and said to me, "This is the son of man who has righteousness, and righteousness dwells with him. And all the treasuries of what is hidden he will reveal; for the Lord of Spirits has chosen him, and his lot has prevailed through truth in the presence of the Lord of Spirits forever. And this son of man whom you have seen—he will raise the kings and the mighty from their couches, and the strong from their thrones. He will loosen the reigns of the strong, and he will crush the teeth of the sinners. He will overturn the kings from their thrones and their kingdoms, because they do not exalt him or praise him or humbly acknowledge whence the kingdom was given to them.

---

24. Hannah, "Elect Son of Man," 157–58.

Chapter 3: The Son of Man in 1 Enoch 37–71 and 4 Ezra 13

As in the heavenly scene in Dan 7, the first character described is Yahweh. He is "one who had a head of days" and a head "like white wool" both of which recall the Ancient of Days whose hair is "like pure wool" (Dan 7:9). Accompanying him is another individual whose countenance is similar to "the appearance of a man" and "full of graciousness like one of the holy angels" recalling, of course, the danielic "one like a son of man" who is presented before Yahweh. Unlike Daniel's vision in which the SM comes into Yahweh's presence, in the enochic scene the SM is already there. It seems as though this vision begins where the one in Daniel leaves off.[25] Further, both Enoch's question, "about that SM", and the seer's response (vv. 2–6) indicates that the danielic SM is no longer a symbol but some type of divine being who is clearly an individual.[26] Chialà suggests that the phrase "whose face was like the appearance of a man" recalls not Dan 7 but rather Dan 10 in which two phrases are used to describe an angelic being: "one in the likeness of sons of men" (v. 16a: כִּדְמוּת בְּנֵי אָדָם) and "one like the appearance of a man" (v. 18: כְּמַרְאֵה אָדָם). He argues that although the face of the enochic SM looks *like* a man, he is not merely human but is rather an angelic figure like the one in Dan 10.[27] However, the SM is introduced in the presence of the Head of Days and so the scene in *1 En.* 46:1–5 evokes Dan 7, not Dan 10. Nonetheless, his divine-like status is confirmed in the Third Parable (58–69), as we will see, in which he is seated upon a throne and is the object of worship. Unlike Daniel's vision in which judgement is meted out before the SM appears, here the figure judges arrogant kings, mighty and sinners who fail to recognize his authority (46:4–8) reminiscent of the danielic fourth beast who failed to recognize the kingdom of the SM/saints. It is the enochic SM, not Yahweh, who topples haughty kings and rulers.

---

25. Wright, *People*, 317.

26. Enoch's identification of the figure as "*that* son of man" in 46:2 occurs with the demonstrative "this" or "that" another 13 times (46:3, 4; 48:2; 62:5, 7, 14; 63:11; 69:26, 27, 29; 70:1; 71:14, 17). SM in the ethiopic text is rendered from three different expressions that do not differ in meaning and hence can be considered translational variants. See Casey, *Interpretation*, 102 and, recently, Hannah, "Elect Son of Man," 141. For a discussion of each of the ethiopic phrases, see VanderKam who notes that "the reason for the changes is not always clear" ("Righteous One," 174).

Some suggest that the articular form of SM points to the danielic figure: Moule, *Origin*, 14–15; Fitzmyer, "New Testament Title," 143–60; Manson, "Son of Man," 123–45.

27. Chialà, "Evolution," 160.

Daniel's Son of Man in Mark

The second text is *1 En.* 47:3—48:6:

> In those days I saw the Head of Days as he took his seat on the throne of his glory, and the books of the living were opened in his presence, and all his host, which was in the heights of heaven, and his court, were standing in his presence.... And in that hour that son of man was named in the presence of the Lord of Spirits, and his name, before the Head of Days. Even before the sun and the constellations were created, before the stars of heaven were made, his name was named before the Lord of Spirits. He will be a staff for the righteous, that they may lean on him and not fall; and he will be the light of the nations, and he will be a hope for those who grieve in their hearts. All who dwell on the earth will fall down and worship before him, and they will glorify and bless and sing hymns to the name of the Lord of Spirits. For this (reason) he was chosen and hidden in his presence before the world was created and forever.

This second evocation of Dan 7 begins with the Head of Days sitting upon his glorious throne, the books being opened, and all of his host and court are standing before him which essentially summarizes the scene in Dan 7:9–10. A great judgement is about to transpire in response to the prayers of the righteous whose earthly counterparts have been martyred (47:4b). The SM then reappears and Enoch learns that he was "named in the presence of the Lord of Spirits" (48:2) and was in fact named before creation itself (48:3), which for some suggests his pre-existence much like that of wisdom existing before creation (see Prov 8).[28] As in the preceding text, the SM is an individual but note that now the emphasis falls on his deliverance of righteous Israel and his restoration of her vocation: a "staff for the righteous," "a light for the Gentiles," and "the hope of those who are sick in their hearts" (48:4). Toward the end of this chapter, the judgement of the earthly rulers is once again described. In this instance, they will perish before the once persecuted holy and righteous ones (v. 9) because not only have these earthly rulers denied the Lord of Spirits but also his royal vice-regent, the Anointed SM (v. 10b). The designation "anointed" in v. 10 makes explicit the messianic status of the enochic SM, which is anticipated by the terminology used in v. 4 that depicts the deliverance he will effect for faithful Israel and, later in the vision, is confirmed when he is seated upon a glorious throne by the Lord of Spirits (61:8; 62:2). According to Ps 89 and

---

28. VanderKam, "Righteous One," 179–82; Venter, "Spatiality," 410.

Chapter 3: The Son of Man in 1 Enoch 37–71 and 4 Ezra 13

110, a throne is the place for Yahweh's anointed.[29] When this exalted messiah delivers his people, "all who dwell on the earth will fall down and worship before him [the SM], and they will glorify and bless and sing hymns to the name of the Lord of Spirits" (v. 5). The SM is not the object of worship, yet, but he does have an elevated position in the context of the worship the Lord of Spirits.

The SM's role in the great judgement of Israel's adversaries and in the salvation of the righteous is depicted again in *1 En.* 62. When the adversaries of the faithful ones see the SM, they shall at that point be judged: "And one group of them will look at the other; and they will be terrified and will cast down their faces, and pain will seize them when they see that son of man sitting on the throne of glory" (62:5), but also at that time "the congregation of the chosen and the holy will be sown; and all the chosen will stand in his presence on that day" (62:8). Echoing the implied posture of the Ancient of Days in Dan 7, the SM is seated upon "the throne of glory" from which he executes this judgement (v. 5). The connection between the SM and Yahweh also intensifies in this chapter as he is worshipped by the kings and mighty "who will fall on their faces in his presence; and they will *worship* and set their hope on that son of man, and they will supplicate and petition for mercy from him" (*1 En.* 62:9). In the next chapter, this same group attempts to worship the Lord of Spirits, all of which is in vain (vv. 1–12). It appears as though that this SM, who was described as an angelic figure having a face "like the appearance of a man" and "being full of graciousness like one of the holy angels" when he was first introduced to Enoch is in some respects on par with Yahweh himself as one who is an agent of eschatological salvation and judgement and because of this earthly kings worship him in a hopeless attempt to garner his favor (see 62:10–12).

As I demonstrated in the preceding chapter, a careful study of the setting of the celestial scene in Dan 7 enables a fuller appreciation of what is described in the scene itself. I contend that the *Parables* are no different and, as is the case with Dan 7, scholars give scant attention to the setting of the visions. Not unlike Dan 7:9–10 and 13–14, the heavenly temple setting of the *Parables* is evident. In the introduction before the First Parable (37:1–5), the wisdom that Enoch receives is from the Holy One (v. 2b)

---

29. There is some debate regarding the ethiopic behind the verb "sat" in 62:2. Knibb and Ullendorff translate it as "the Lord sat down" in keeping with the majority of MSS (*Ethiopic*, 150), but Charles suggests an emendation to the passive voice in keeping with 61:8 (*Enoch*, 123). See also the note in Nickelsburg and VanderKam, *1 Enoch*, 79, for further support for the latter reading.

which he will take to those who "dwell on the earth" (v. 2a, 5) implying that his journey takes him to a supra-terrestrial realm. After a summary about the judgement to befall the kings of the earth in the First Parable and a reference to the descent of angels (38:1—39:2), Enoch's ascent to heaven is recorded: "And in those days, a whirlwind snatched me up from the face of the earth and set me down within the confines of heaven" (39:3). The description of his ascent appears to draw upon the one recorded in the *Book of Watchers*: "Look, clouds in the vision were summoning me, and mists were crying out to me; . . . and winds in my vision made me fly up and lifted me upward and brought me to heaven" (14:8). Helge Kvanvig convincingly argues that the reference to Enoch's ascent in 39:3 is but one theme in a succession of themes in the First Parable which are modelled on the structure of the *Book of Watchers*.[30] Regarding this particular theme, he observes that "all that happens next in the Parables is based on this ascent to the heavenly realm (i.e., Enoch does not return to earth again). This is one way to read the Book of Watchers as well, because when we follow the story line, there is no report of Enoch returning to the earth."[31] This is a crucial piece of information for any study of the *Parables*. While it is true that the emphases of the visions concentrate less on setting and more on the characters, their actions, postures, and words, it still needs to be considered in tandem with the latter.

Following his ascent, Enoch states, "And there I saw another vision" which is the dwelling and resting place of the holy and righteous ones who once lived on earth (39:4) who now, together with the righteous angels and heavenly holy ones, intercede for the sons of men (v. 5).[32] This recalls the intercessory work of the angelic beings in the heavenly temple described in the *Book of Watchers*, some of whom abdicated their celestial duties. Turning again to *1 En.* 39, in the presence of the Lord of Spirits, the holy and righteous ones continually offer praise: "their mouths were full of blessing, and their lips praised the name of the Lord of Spirits" (v. 7). Enoch also witnesses those who do not sleep but continually "bless and praise and exalt, saying, 'Holy, holy, holy is the Lord of Spirits, he fills the earth with spirits . . . blessed are you, blessed is the name of the Lord forever and ever'" (v. 12). This is not unlike Isa 6 which depicts Yahweh enthroned in his heavenly dwelling and Seraphs attending him and calling out "Holy, holy, holy

30. Kvanvig, "Son of Man," 184–85.
31. Ibid.
32. VanderKam, "Righteous One," 184.

Chapter 3: The Son of Man in 1 Enoch 37–71 and 4 Ezra 13

is the Lord of Hosts; the whole earth is full of his glory" (v. 3). This angelic praise may even be the source text for *1 En.* 39:12. In short, the intercessory work of these angelic beings coupled with the continual praise of Yahweh in such a celestial context in this early part of the *Parables* suggests that Enoch ascends to the heavenly temple.

The same scenario is evident in 47:1–2, in the Second Parable. These two verses describe the "holy ones" who are offering praise to Yahweh and are interceding in his presence on behalf of the suffering righteous (47:1–2bd).[33] This scene segues to Enoch's vision of the Head of Days and the SM whose judgement will put to right the injustices experienced by the terrestrial righteous, and Enoch himself indicates that this vision occurs in heaven: "the Head of Days ... took his seat on the throne of his glory, and the books of the living were opened in his presence, and all his host, which was *in the heights of heaven*, and his court, were standing in his presence (47:3)." The phrase "heights of heaven" is used in the last chapter of the *Parables* to describe the location of a fiery house which is the heavenly dwelling of holy angels and, importantly, the Head of Days (71:9–10). Enoch reports that "Michael and Raphael and Gabriel and Phanuel, and the holy angels who (are in) *the heights of heaven*, were going in and out of that house (v. 8b)." This constitutes a clear indication that when Enoch sees the Head of Days earlier in the *Parables*, in whose presence is the SM, the setting is the heavenly temple "in the heights of heaven" which is not made explicit until the end, much like the SM who is not identified until the final scene as well. If chapters 70–71 are a later addition, it would appear that this author understands the celestial setting of the *Parables* to be the heavenly temple as he reuses this phrase in an explicit description of Yahweh's heavenly dwelling. Finally, as I have stated in my argument for the heavenly temple setting of Dan 7, it is difficult to conceive of Yahweh's throne being located anywhere but in the celestial temple, just as it is here and in the *Book of Watchers* (*1 En.* 14:18–20). Thrones are also part of the architecture of the celestial temple in the *Songs of the Sabbath Sacrifice* (11QShirShabb X, 5–6) and the prophet Micaiah sees Yahweh seated upon his throne flanked by the heavenly hosts (1 Kgs 22:19; see also Isa 6:1).

In the final two chapters, Enoch has a vision in which the description of the heavenly temple figures prominently (70—71). Some argue that this

---

33. Later in the Parables, priestly themes may also be evident in the righteous and chosen who put on "the garment of glory" (62:15b), which is "the garment of life from the Lord of Spirits" (62:16a). Unlike Moses' countenance after being in the presence of Yahweh, their "glory will not fade in the presence of the Lord" (62:16).

section evinces a coherent literary structure modelled on Enoch's journey through the three edifices of the celestial dwelling in *The Book of Watchers*: wall (14:9), outer house (14:10-14), and inner house (14:15-17) which itself reflects the earthly temple's vestibule (*'ulam*), sanctuary (*hekhal*), and holy of holies (*dvir*).[34] Enoch is first elevated to paradise (70:2-4), the vestibule, then his spirit enters the lower heavens (71:1-4), the sanctuary, and finally the heaven of heavens, (71:5-16), which is likely the counterpart to the earthly holy of holies, where Enoch sees a fiery structure out of which comes the Head of Days (vv. 9-10). It seems to me that the most convincing correspondence is between "the heaven of heavens" and the earthly holy of holies which in both instances are associated with Yahweh's presence. At any rate, VanderKam rightly argues that "[these] three major units are not parallel accounts about the same event but are rather a series of reports regarding the stages of Enoch's ultimate ascent."[35] Regarding the first stage, Enoch ascends to the heavenly temple "on the chariots of the wind" (70:2) which recalls not only 39:3 in which he ascends to the heavenly temple by means of the clouds and a whirlwind (v. 3) but also his ascent in 14:2, and for that matter, the coming of the SM to the Ancient of Days in Dan 7, although there is no indication that the SM ascends to Yahweh in Daniel.[36] Jumping to the third stage, Enoch describes the heavenly temple as "a house built of hailstones" (71:5; see 14:9-10) surrounded by heavenly beings, some of whom are the Cherubim (71:7), which recalls the "fiery cherubim" of 14:11. This house occupies a prominent role in this third section (71:5-16) as a myriad (thousands of thousands and ten thousand times ten thousand) of angels surround it (71:8a) whereas in 14:22, the myriad of angels stood before the throne. Further, unlike *1 En.* 14 and Dan 7, the Head of Days comes out of the house with his angelic entourage to greet Enoch (71:9-10).[37] Recalling the description of the Ancient of Days from

---

34. VanderKam, "Righteous One, 177-78; Hengel, *Studies*, 105. Himmelfarb argues for correspondence between the three areas of the celestial temple in *1 En.* 14 with those of the Jerusalem temple ("Ascent," 210).

35. VanderKam, "Righteous One," 187.

36. Nickelsburg and VanderKam indicate that only some MSS have "clouds and" in 39:3 (*1 Enoch*, 52 n. g). They have not included this reading in their text; however, Knibb and Ullendorff do (*Ethiopic*, 126). The addition of "clouds" in some MSS could reflect a harmonization with 14:8.

37. See, however, Dan 7:21-22: "As I looked, this horn made war with the holy ones and was prevailing over them, until the Ancient of Days *came*; then judgment was given for the holy ones of the Most High, and the time arrived when the holy ones gained possession of the kingdom."

CHAPTER 3: THE SON OF MAN IN 1 ENOCH 37–71 AND 4 EZRA 13

both *1 En.* 46:1a and Dan 7:9b, the Head of Days has a head "white and pure as wool and his apparel was indescribable" (71:10). At the sight of him, Enoch falls prostrate and blesses the Lord (71:11–12). In 71:14, the author repeats that the Head of Days and his myriad of angels came to Enoch at which point an angel, likely speaking on behalf of Yahweh, declares, "You are that son of man who was born for righteousness, and righteousness dwells on you, and the righteousness of the Head of Days will not forsake you" (71:14). Whether one views these last two chapters as either original or a later addition, one thing is made clear, which the text has hinted at all along: the abode of the Head of Days is the heavenly temple.

The Son of Man in 4 Ezra

Date and Provenance

Many scholars agree that the text of *4 Ezra* 3–14 was composed at the turn of the first century CE in response to the destruction of the second temple.[38] In support of this, the three heads of the eagle in Ezra's fifth vision, for example, likely correspond to the Flavian dynasty which spans most of the second half of the first century (11:1—12:51).[39] On a literary level, the book is set thirty years after the destruction of Solomon's temple which connects the second temple's destruction with that of the first (*4 Ezra* 3:1a). While there may be a substantial amount of consensus on the date and occasion of the text, there is much less on its provenance. Broadly speaking, *4 Ezra* could have originated within apocalyptic circles or, alternatively, within a particular strain of emergent rabbinic Judaism.[40] Because the text reflects apocalyptic themes and has an emphasis on the law, Lester Grabbe suggests there may have been some

---

38. Longenecker, "Locating 4 Ezra," 278; Collins, *Apocalyptic*, 196; Lichtenberger, "Zion," 238; Harrington, "Holy Land," 665; Stone, *Fourth Ezra*, 41. However, there are some exceptions, such as Zimmerman, who argues for 150 CE ("Language," 203–18).

39. Grabbe, "Chronology," 51. DiTommaso resurrects an older theory that the three heads reflect Severus (193–211 CE) and his sons, Geta (211–212 CE) and Caracalla (211–217 CE) ("Dating," 6). DiTommaso still recognizes, however, that *4 Ezra* dates from the end of the first century, and the eagle vision, in its extant form, "is a drastic Severan-era reworking of a Flavian-era original" ("Dating," 6).

40. Grabbe, "Chronology," 58. Those who argue for a sectarian background include Knibb, "Apocalyptic," 64 and Kee, "Fourth Ezra," 199. Longenecker even goes so far as to claim that Ezra's audience would include the rabbinic leadership ("Locating," 284–85). Those who propose a more exoteric provenance include Esler, "Social," 113–14; Rowland, "Apocalyptic Literature," 184–85; Stone, *Fourth Ezra*, 38–39; Collins, *Apocalyptic*, 212.

"apocalyptic speculation" in rabbinic circles in light of the temple's destruction.[41] According to Bruce W. Longenecker, "the polarisation of apocalyptic and rabbinic interests has received support from an unjustified assumption that a literary text or corpus presupposes a distinct community . . . so that rabbinic literature is thought to emerge from a different social matrix than apocalyptic literature."[42] Possibly, then, a rabbinic segment with apocalyptic interests composed *4 Ezra* which would explain the dual features of the text.[43] Whatever the case, it is still important to realize and accept, despite the demurrals of some, that a particular historical group produced this writing and was grappling with the devastating effects of the temple's destruction rendering Israel devoid of her place of worship.

Literary Structure

The textual history of *4 Ezra* is very complicated not least because extant versions are two steps removed from the original Hebrew.[44] The Jewish section of the work, chapters 3 to 14, is bracketed by what many consider to be later Christian addenda, *4 Ezra* 1-2 and 15-16.[45] The original Jewish composition contains seven visions, the first three of which are more precisely termed "dialogic visions" between Ezra and Uriel (3:1—5:20; 5:21—6:34; 6:35—9:25).[46] Following the three dialogues are four visions which are more apocalyptic in character (9:26—10:59; 11:1—12:51; 13:1-58; 14:1-48). Michael E. Stone comments that the fourth vision of the lamenting woman who is transformed into Zion is a pivotal section which "shares structural

---

41. Grabbe, "Chronology," 59. Grabbe correctly points out that the Pharisees's messianic hope reflects apocalyptic concern.

42. Longenecker, "Locating," 282.

43. The Talmud records two rabbis, Johanan b. Zakkai and R. Akiba who have messianic interests. The former awaited the messiah (*b. Ber.* 28b) while the latter supported Simeon b. Koshiba (*y. Ta'an.* 68d).

44. For a lucid discussion of *4 Ezra's* complex textual history and how extant versions relate to one another, see Stone, 1-9.

45. O'Neill refutes this because "2 Esdras 1-2 contains at least one passage that no Christian or Gentile Christian, could have written; and that 2 Esdras 1-2 contains no passage that a Jew could not have written" ("Desolate," 227). Conveniently, passages which evince the influence of Jewish Christian scribes are mere corruptions, according to O'Neill. Although it is possible that the first two chapters are authentically Jewish, the theme of God's rejection of Israel and salvation of the Gentiles (*4 Ezra* 1:24-37) is the opposite of the message of chapters 3 to 14.

46. Stone, "Reactions," 202.

Chapter 3: The Son of Man in 1 Enoch 37–71 and 4 Ezra 13

elements with those visions which precede it and with those which follow it."[47] In it, Ezra encounters a woman weeping over the death of her only son who immediately died upon entering the wedding chamber (9:26—10:59). Ezra responds by rebuking the woman for lamenting over one child when all of Israel laments for her mother, Zion, now destroyed by the Romans (10:19–24). While Ezra consoles her, the woman is transformed into a glorious and majestic city (10:25–28) which Uriel interprets as a restored Zion (10:44) which is far more superior to the Jerusalem temple. Ezra is commanded to see it for himself: "Therefore do not be afraid, and do not let your heart be terrified; but go in and see the splendor or the vastness of the building, as far as it is possible for your eyes to see it" (10:55).

Five sections constitute the sixth vision in which a figure recalling the danielic SM appears: dream (13:1–13a); response (vv. 13b–24); interpretation (vv. 25–50); rationale for the revelation (vv. 51–56); and an epilogue (vv. 57–58). Much of the imagery and symbolism of the vision, along with the fifth one, is heavily indebted to Dan 7.[48] Based on *4 Ezra* 12:11 and the danielic allusions in these visions, it appears that the author "consciously intended to update and rewrite Dan 7"[49] or, in the words of Gregory Beale, the text "is a result of direct creative reflection only on Dan 7."[50] Symbolism from Dan 2 and 7 is particularly prominent in the "dream" segment (13:1–13a) of the sixth vision, which is the most relevant part of *4 Ezra* for this study.

Danielic Imagery in 4 Ezra 13:1–13a

As in Dan 7:1, Ezra "dreamed a dream in the night" (v. 1), and the vision begins with ominous imagery of primeval chaos in which the winds churn the sea (v. 2; Dan 7:2). But unlike Dan 7 where four beasts arise out it (Dan 7:3), "something like the figure of a man" unexpectedly comes up at which point he begins his journey "with the clouds of heaven" (v.

---

47. Stone, *Fourth Ezra*, 29; Ibid., "Reactions," 202–4. See also Harnisch, "Die Ironie," 79–104.

48. Wright, *People*, 314–17; Knibb, "Wisdom," 70; Stone, "Concept," 301, 304, 308; Beale, "Problem of the Man," 184; Collins, *Apocalyptic*, 207, 384; Hayman, "'Man from the Sea,'" 9.

49. Hayman, "'Man from the Sea,'" 6.

50. Beale, "Problem," 184. Knibb highlights that the formulaic expression "And I looked, and behold" (13:3, 5, 6, 8) is reflected in Dan 7:2, 6, 7, 13 ("Wisdom," 71).

3b).⁵¹ This man-like figure recalls the "one like a son of man" who also comes "with the clouds of heaven" (Dan 7:13).⁵² Finally, "the stream of fire and the flaming breath and the great storm [of sparks] (v. 11a)" from the mouth, lips, and tongue of the SM, that destroy his enemies, recall the stream of fire flowing from the presence of the Ancient of Days leading to the destruction of the fourth beast (vv. 10–11; Dan 7:10–11). Knibb claims that only the burning of the multitude in v. 11 echoes the burning of the fourth beast in Dan 7:11.⁵³ However, Ezra's description of the "stream of fire" from the SM's mouth (v. 10) evokes more clearly the "stream of fire" emitted from Yahweh's presence in Dan 7:10.

Scholars are divided as to why SM rises from the sea. According to Peter Hayman, "the wind," that enables the SM to rise up from the depths of the sea, parallels Ba'al who needs the assistance of Kothar and Hasis to defeat Yam, the personification of the chaotic sea, before he ascends to his heavenly palace.⁵⁴ Hayman also admits that the biblical tradition can serve as a background because it attests to Yahweh's defeat of the sea monsters (Ps 74:12–17; 89:9–11) and the SM coming up from the sea could imply Yahweh's dominion.⁵⁵ But possibly the answer lies within the text of *4 Ezra* itself. In *4 Ezra* 6, we learn that at creation Leviathan is spared and has possession of the waters; however, Yahweh has "kept them [one of whom is Leviathan] to be eaten by whom you wish, and when you wish" (6:52b) and has placed Adam "over all the works that you had made" (6:54a).⁵⁶ For Ezra, then, the sea is not the place where chaotic monsters reign, but, rather,

---

51. Stone claims that the "sea" is not the same "sea" of Dan 7:3 from whence the beasts arise because the "heart" or "midst" of the sea in *4 Ezra* 13:3 is El's dwelling (*Fourth Ezra*, 384). However, given the danielic symbolism evident in this passage, the use of the "sea" here, from which the SM arises, could reflect an ironic twist, but more on this below.

52. Since *4 Ezra* is clearly depicting the SM from Dan 7, I will refer to this individual as the SM even though Ezra does not use this title in his description of the dream.

53. Knibb, "Wisdom," 71.

54. Hayman, "Sea," 11–12. For those who question how a late first-century author would have been acquainted with the ancient Canaanite Ba'al cycle, Hayman points out the reuse of this material in *1QHa* XIV, 22–35 (Hayman erred on this reference, it is actually column 14, not 6) and a late second-century CE text, *Odes Sol.* 22. Nonetheless, the parallels which Hayman draws between the latter texts and the Ba'al cycle are still tenuous.

55. Hayman, "Sea," 12. See also Beale for moments in which Yahweh judges his enemies via the sea in the later Jewish works *Sib. Or.* 3:72–74 and *2 Bar.* 53:1–12 ("Problem," 183 fn. 10).

56. For a helpful discussion of *4 Ezra* 6, see Cook, "Creation," 131–35.

Chapter 3: The Son of Man in 1 Enoch 37–71 and 4 Ezra 13

it is under Yahweh's authority. Similarly, Beale claims that Ezra employs a "polemical irony" in portraying the SM as rising from sea because in Dan 7 it is the dwelling of chaotic monsters: "the same way in which the enemy will try and subdue God will be used by God himself to subdue this enemy in the end."[57]

The Temple-Mountain and the Son of Man

As with the enochic SM, the figure here is clearly an individual and now functions as a warrior much like Yahweh: "wherever he turned his face to look, everything under his gaze trembled, and whenever his voice issued from his mouth, all who heard his voice melted as wax melts when it feels the fire" (vv. 3b–4). In a depiction of Yahweh coming in judgement, the author of Ps 104 describes him as "one who looks upon the earth and it trembles" (v. 32a). The imagery of melting wax is also used to describe the effect of Yahweh's judgement: "the mountains will melt under him and the valleys will burst open, like wax near the fire" (Mic 1:4a; Isa 66:15–16; Jdt 16:15).[58] In this opening scene of the vision, Stone comments that "the man [SM] is described using symbolic language that is drawn largely from biblical descriptions of God, particularly, his epiphanies as warrior."[59]

In the next scene, Ezra sees that "an innumerable multitude of people were gathered together from the four winds of heaven to make war against the man who came up out of the sea" (13:5). The SM responds by carving for himself a "great mountain," interpreted as Mount Zion in 13:35–36, and then flies upon it from which he burns up his adversaries: "I saw only how he sent forth from his mouth something like a stream of fire and from his lips a flaming breath, and from his tongue he shot forth a storm of sparks . . . all of these were mingled together . . . and fell on the onrushing multitude . . . and burned up all of them" (vv. 10–11a). As I have indicated above, the SM's destruction of his enemies is similar to the portrayal of Yahweh in Dan 7 from whose presence a stream of fire issues burning up the body of the fourth beast.

In his account of the dream, Ezra is unable to identify the "great mountain" which the SM carves out for himself (13:7). According to Jacob M. Myers, he might not have been able to determine this because it is a

57. Beale, "Problem," 186.
58. Burkett, *Debate*, 105.
59. Stone, *Fourth Ezra*, 212.

part of the heavenly Jerusalem which is not of this world.[60] It also may be related to the heavenly city/temple of the fourth vision revealed only to Ezra but is now revealed to all of Israel as well as her adversaries (see 13:36).[61] This great "carved out" (v. 6) mountain recalls the "cut out stone" of Dan 2 which in that vision eventually becomes a "great mountain and fills the whole earth" (2:35b).[62] In the interpretation of Nebuchadnezzar's vision, Daniel likens the stone to the kingdom of God (2:44-45), but stone and mountain imagery is also associated with the dwelling of God in the OT (Gen 28:22; Isa 28:16; Zech. 4:7-10; Jer 26:18; Mic 4:1; Isa 66:20). In keeping with this, the angel who interprets Ezra's vision identifies the "great mountain" as Mount Zion which will "come and be made manifest to all people, prepared and built, as you saw the mountain carved out without hands" (13:36).

After coming down from the mountain, the SM calls and gathers to himself a "multitude that was peaceable" (13:12) which is possible now that he has destroyed his enemies. This group is composed of those who are joyful, sorrowful, bound, and of those who bring others as "offerings" (13:13a). All of these are likely victims of the oppressors destroyed by the SM and now their deliverance has come.[63] The manifestation of the great mountain, which is associated with Yahweh's dwelling, might explain why some of the multitude appears to execute a priestly role in bringing others as offerings. This act of offering people parallels Isa 66:20: "they [the Gentiles] shall bring all your kindred [Israelites] from all the nations as an offering to the Lord . . . to my holy mountain Jerusalem, says the Lord, just as the Israelites bring a grain offering in a clean vessel to the house of the Lord."[64] The next verse indicates that some of these Gentiles will also serve as priests and Levites in a restored Jerusalem Temple (66:21).[65] Likewise,

---

60. Myers, *1 and 11 Esdras*, 308. See also, Bryan, *Jesus and Israel's Traditions*, 194-95.

61. Lichtenberger argues that the vision of Zion does not disappear at the conclusion of the fourth vision ("Zion," 246-47), which, in my opinion, is an argument from silence as it does not play a role in the following visions. In fact, at the conclusion of the fifth vision, Ezra is at prayer seeking mercy from God because of the destruction of the Jerusalem temple (12:48).

62. Stone, "Concept," 308.

63. Myers, *1 and 11 Esdras*, 314. Stone argues that the "sorrowful" are the Gentiles but there is nothing in the vision or in the interpretation (13:39-50) that suggests this (*Fourth Ezra*, 387).

64. Knibb, "Wisdom," 71.

65. Watts, *New Exodus*, 104-5.

Chapter 3: The Son of Man in 1 Enoch 37-71 and 4 Ezra 13

Psalms of Solomon records that "nations [will] . . . come from the ends of the earth to see his glory, to bring *as gifts* her children who had been driven out" (17:31a). Although the mountain in Ezra's dream is not a heavenly temple by any means, it is certainly associated with Yahweh's dwelling and is revealed in response to the devastating effects caused by the destruction of the Jerusalem temple and, once again, the SM is at the center of executing Yahweh's justice. The carved out temple mount in *4 Ezra* seems to be functioning as a surrogate for the once-standing Jerusalem temple, and it is to this mountain of an other-worldly origin that the multitude comes, not unlike what was once prophesied for Mt. Zion itself, e.g., Mic 4:1-5. This finds support when we realize that this scene is a response to Ezra's prayer regarding the "desolation of Zion" and the "humiliation of our sanctuary" (12:48) at the conclusion of the preceding vision. As in the *Parables*, the SM puts to right what is wrong in the world by destroying adversaries, albeit not from Yahweh's celestial dwelling, but from a surrogate temple mount of a heavenly origin which he has carved out for this purpose.

4 Ezra 13:1-13a: An Older Tradition

Ezra's vision in 13:1-13a is likely older than its interpretation (13:25-50) and the fifth vision and its interpretation (11:1—12:51). According to Stone, this later material lacks the cosmological themes of the sixth vision (13:1-13a).[66] Stone attributes this difference to "the legalizing of the eschatological battle leading to the description of the activities of the Messiah in legal terms."[67] He contends that the author of *4 Ezra* imports many of the judicial characteristics and roles of the Messiah from chapters 11 and 12 into the interpretation of the sixth vision: "Thus, not only does the man, central to the vision, play little role in the interpretation, but there are features of the Messiah presented by the interpretation which are not hinted at in the vision."[68] For example, the legal activities of the messianic figure in 13:37-38 are not mentioned in the vision, and the fiery breath of 13:10 is

---

66. Stone, "Concept," 308-9.
67. Ibid., 302.
68. Ibid., 309. Further, Stone argues that the interpretation is quite confusing and repetitive compared to the orderly and coherent interpretations found in the fourth and fifth visions ("Concept," 395-96). According to Stone, this is likely a reflection of the author's own struggle to interpret and apply the earlier SM vision (13:1-13a) to his own historical situation. Myers notes the apparent difficulty in the interpretation which evinces a rabbinic bent (*1 and 11 Esdras*, 316).

interpreted as the law in 13:38. Stone concludes that the judicial features of the interpretation parallel the rest of *4 Ezra*.[69] It does seem quite probable that the dream recorded in 13:1–13a is an older tradition in which judicial and legal concerns did not figure as prominently as in the rabbinic Judaism of post-70 CE.[70] Since *4 Ezra* is a response to the second temple's destruction, one can see why the author would find this dream material about a figure punishing his enemies, possibly representing the Romans, from an other-worldly temple mount relevant for his historical situation.

If the dream reflects a tradition which predates the temple's destruction, *4 Ezra* 13:1–13a becomes another example of how the danielic SM was interpreted before the composition of Mark's Gospel. Although the SM is not enthroned in a heavenly temple as in the *Parables* from which he judges his enemies, the earthly kings and mighty, the SM in *4 Ezra* does destroy those who oppose him from a location associated with Yahweh's earthly dwelling, although not of this world. The SM in both texts is no longer a symbol for faithful Israel but is an individual who executes prerogatives of Yahweh from either the heavenly temple or an extra-terrestrial mountain. This provides an important interpretative framework for my analysis of the markan SM, particularly for the so-called "earthly" and "future" SM sayings.

Conclusion

It is likely that the *Parables* are a Jewish work written at some point before the destruction of the temple. The historical references to the Parthian threat, the healing waters of Callirrhoe, and hints throughout the text that the "kings of the earth" are not necessarily generic figures, make a date sometime during the reign of Herod, which spanned from 37 to 4 BCE, possible. Even if the final two chapters are indeed later additions, they make explicit what is implied throughout the *Parables* that the heavenly temple is the dwelling of the Head of Days in whose presence "that" SM appears. Although not much has been made of the setting of the visions in the *Parables*, a careful reading suggests that Enoch has a vision of the SM and Yahweh in the heavenly temple. Early on in the First Parable, Enoch is swept up into "the confines of heaven" (37:3) and never is it mentioned that he returns to earth again. A little later, Enoch witnesses the intercessory work of the righteous and holy ones which, as we have seen in the *Book of*

69. Stone, "Concept," 309.
70. See also, Müller, *Messias*, 108–9.

Chapter 3: The Son of Man in 1 Enoch 37–71 and 4 Ezra 13

Watchers, occurs in the heavenly temple. It is difficult to conceive of that type of activity occurring anywhere else but in the celestial temple where these heavenly beings also continually praise the Lord of Spirits. In *1 En.* 47:3, Enoch himself declares that he witnessed the Head of Days upon his throne of glory in the presence of his hosts in "the heights of heaven." This phrase is used again in *1 En.* 71 to describe the location of the fiery house, which is the temple of Yahweh, which supports my claim that its first occurrence in 47:3 likewise designates the heavenly temple. Further, the presence of Yahweh's throne in 47:3 is a key piece of heavenly temple architecture in other descriptions of his celestial abode.

In contrast with the SM in Daniel, the enochic figure is now a messianic savior and judge reigning in the heavenly temple of the Lord of Spirits and is, toward the end of the *Parables*, seated upon his throne. From here the SM will one day execute judgement on behalf of the persecuted terrestrial holy, righteous, and chosen, which is a prerogative of Yahweh in Dan 7. These judicial actions will not only mark the end of "the kings and the mighty" who have persecuted faithful Israel and disrupted their congregations (46:4–8; 48:9–10; 62:11) but also will result in salvation for those who have persevered through suffering on earth (48:4; 62:8).

Although *4 Ezra* 3–14 most likely dates from the end of the first century CE, Ezra's dream in the sixth vision contributes to our understanding of how the danielic SM was interpreted before the destruction of the temple as the dream appears to reflect a tradition which predates the material in chapter 12 and its interpretation in 13:25–50. As an older piece of tradition, this text provides us with another view of pre-70 Jewish interpretations of the danielic SM which becomes important for our study of the markan figure. At the same time, this older material in which the SM lands upon a mountain, which he carves out for himself, fits with preceding material in the book. The turning point of *4 Ezra*, for instance, comes in the fourth vision in which a lamenting woman is transformed into the heavenly Jerusalem before Ezra's eyes. This is connected with the appearance of the other-worldly temple mount in the sixth vision from which the SM destroys those who make war against him and to which the faithful come. The dream fittingly comes in response to Ezra's prayer about the destruction of Zion at the conclusion of the preceding interpretation (12:48). In light of Dan 7, the SM in the dream is associated with Yahweh himself and his dwelling when he executes destruction through a "stream of fire" and does so from a mountain, which is imagery traditionally associated with

Yahweh's abode. It appears that the SM in both the *Parables* and the dream account in *4 Ezra 13*, which pre-date the temple's destruction, is associated with Yahweh himself and his dwelling, whether it be the continued presence of the SM in the heavenly temple from which he executes Yahweh's justice for the oppressed or from a temple mount from which he annihilates his enemies making space for those who are peaceable to come to him.

Chapter 4: The Son of Man's Divine Authority on Earth

Introduction

UNLIKE THE SM IN Daniel and the *Parables* who is in heaven, namely the heavenly temple, the markan SM first appears "on earth" exercising Yahweh's divine authority. In Daniel, the "one like a son of man" is presented before Yahweh in his celestial dwelling and receives ἐξουσία while "that SM" in the *Parables* exercises authority seated upon a throne in the heavenly temple from which he judges the earthly "kings" and "mighty." Although the heavenly temple is not part of the setting in *4 Ezra* 13, the SM is still associated with Yahweh's dwelling as he flies upon an other-worldly temple mount from which he, as a warrior like Yahweh, annihilates his adversaries. Both the *Parables* and *4 Ezra* develop the passive figure of Dan 7 so that he now engages in activities associated with Yahweh himself. These first-century CE Jewish interpretations of the danielic SM provide an interpretative framework for the following analysis of the markan SM who likewise executes divine prerogatives but on earth.

This chapter begins with a brief analysis of specific passages that precede the so-called "conflict cycle" of Mark 2:1—3:6, in which the SM makes his first two appearances. Particular passages in Mark 1 contain programmatic material for a markan understanding of Jesus as the SM. The chapter then examines Mark 2:1–12 and 2:23–28 in light of Dan 7 and other relevant OT passages to determine the meaning of Mark's interpretative rendering of the danielic figure. Essentially, I argue that the SM manifests Yahweh's divine authority which is demonstrated in his ability to forgive sins and to exercise dominion over the sabbath, not from heaven, but "upon the earth." However, not all are willing to recognize it.

Daniel's Son of Man in Mark

Literary Context of Mark 2:1–12 and 2:23–28

Mark 1 contains at least three accounts that express a high Christology and so complement and support my proposed interpretations of the SM in Mark 2. The baptism of Jesus (vv. 9–11), the exorcism of an unclean spirit by the Holy One of God (vv. 21–28), and the cleansing of a leper (vv. 40–45) are particularly relevant. Starting with Mark's baptism scene, the heavens "are torn apart" (σχιζομένους) and the Spirit of God descends upon Jesus when he is coming up from the water. A crucial background text is Isa 64:1 (LXX: Isa 63:19): "O that you would 'tear open' (ἀνοίξῃς) the heavens and come down, so that the mountains would quake at your presence."[1] This text describes the desire of Isaiah that Yahweh would come down from his heavenly dwelling and manifest his judgement on Israel's enemies (64:2). The descent of the Spirit in Mark also recalls Isa 63:10 LXX. Here the prophet speaks of Yahweh who had put his "holy spirit" (v.10: τὸ πνεῦμα τὸ ἅγιον; MT: רוּחַ קָדְשׁוֹ) in the midst of Israel at the time of the Exodus event. According to Watts, "if the memory of Yahweh's great redemptive act, from Isa 63's point of view, is characterized by his 'placing' of his רוּחַ-presence in the midst of his people then it is hardly surprising if the long-awaited repetition of the saving event should also be so characterized."[2] In other words, not only does Isaiah desire that Yahweh rend the heavens and come down to judge Israel's enemies, but also that he would once again dwell in the midst of his people (see 65:17–25). For Mark, the heavenly dwelling is torn open and Yahweh's Spirit descends upon Jesus so that he is now filled with the divine presence in order to deliver those who believe in the good news (v. 15). As the narrative unfolds, especially in regard to the SM, we will see that Jesus, in some way, is Yahweh in the flesh with his people and is the one who will one day judge those opposed to God's kingdom.[3]

The next passage relevant for this study is the exorcism of the unclean spirit (vv. 21–28), for a few reasons. First, it foreshadows conflict between Jesus and the scribes. People in the synagogue are "astounded" at his teaching "for he taught them as one having authority, and not as the scribes" (v. 22b). Framing this scene with an *inclusio*, Mark at the end of

---

1. Gundry, *Mark*, 51. For a helpful proposal as to why Mark uses σχίζω instead of the LXX's ἀνοίγω, see Watts, *New Exodus*, 103.

2. Ibid., 106.

3. Watts argues that the theme of Yahweh's coming for judgement is not discontinued in Mark because Jesus does battle with Satan, e.g., 1:24 and 3:27, and will judge the resistant temple leadership, e.g., 11:12–24 (*New Exodus*, 107).

Chapter 4: The Son of Man's Divine Authority on Earth

the pericopé again highlights the authoritative teaching of Jesus: "a new teaching with authority" (v. 27). Not surprisingly, the first encounter that Jesus has with the scribes develops into conflict when they, albeit in their minds, label Jesus' action of forgiving the sins of a paralytic as blasphemy in 2:7.[4] Later, in the passion-resurrection predictions, Jesus predicts that the scribes, as well as the elders and chief priests, e.g., 8:31, will reject the SM. Although these scribes are associated with Jerusalem, it is noteworthy that almost all of the scribes in the story resist him. The Gospel's audience, after hearing the narrative only once, will subsequently "hear" this passage as a foreshadow of future conflict between them and Jesus.[5] Second, this narrative, like the account of the baptism, reveals a unique aspect of Jesus' authority. While it seems clear that conflict revolves around authority early in Mark (1:22; 2:10; 2:28), scholars have overlooked exactly what type of authority Jesus exhibits in this passage other than that it characterizes his teaching, as the synagogue crowds acknowledge. However, this does not seem to be the point for Mark because he does not disclose the content of Jesus' instruction.[6] It is important to realize that the *inclusio*, which underscores Jesus' authoritative teaching, surrounds the first miracle that Mark's Jesus performs—exorcizing a man with an "unclean spirit" (v. 26: τὸ πνεῦμα τὸ ἀκάθαρτον). Mark employs the phrase τὸ πνεῦμα τὸ ἀκάθαρτον three times in this passage (vv. 23, 26, 27) and between the first and second occurrence, the unclean spirit addresses Jesus as "the holy one of God" (v. 24: ὁ ἅγιος τοῦ θεοῦ). Consequently, Mark's emphasis on the authority of Jesus and the "uncleanness" of the spirit, who is threatened by "the holy one of God," expresses that his authority is over that which is unclean and is not demonstrated primarily by his teaching.[7] This authority is evident again when Jesus touches the unclean leper and heals him in vv. 40-45. Third, this passage reveals the unique relationship that Jesus, as "the holy one of God," shares with Yahweh. For some, the connection between the authority of Jesus over the unclean spirit and the designation, "the holy one of God," becomes clearer if one views Jesus from a priestly framework. The phrase "the holy one of God" may recall passages such as Ps 106:16 in which Aaron

---

4. Kingsbury, *Conflict*, 66.

5. It is likely that Mark was dramatically re-told as either oral or aural narrative. See Dewey, "Aural Narrative," 45-65.

6. Kingsbury, *Conflict*, 66 fn. 11; Dewey, *Public*, 124; France merely indicates that Jesus' teaching contradicts "accepted halakhic teaching" (*Mark*, 102).

7. In Mark 3, this authority extends to the disciples (v. 15; 6:7).

is τὸν ἅγιον κυρίου (LXX: 105:16; see Num 16:7). This echo suggests a priestly connotation for the person of Jesus that corresponds with Mark's emphasis on the "uncleanness" of the spirit.[8] However, other than one or two references to the phrase "the holy one of the Lord" in the LXX that refer to priests, there is nothing else to support the claim. Further, Elisha (2 Kgs 4:9 LXX) and Samson (Judg 16:17 LXX) also receive the designation.[9] Nonetheless, these echoes do point to a unique status that Jesus shares with Yahweh. In Mark, the title, "the Holy One of God," is related to his divine sonship which is attributed to him not only by Yahweh himself at the baptism in v. 11 but also by unclean spirits in 3:11: "Whenever the unclean spirits saw him, they fell down before him and shouted, 'You are the son of God!'"[10] As the "Holy One of God," the authoritative teaching of Jesus, which is manifested in his exorcism of the "unclean spirit," derives from Yahweh himself with whose Spirit Jesus has been endowed and with whom he has a unique familial relationship. Through his Son, Yahweh is at work purifying his people from that which is unclean.[11]

Finally, in the third passage, which immediately precedes 2:1–12, the theme of purity emerges again when Jesus acts as a healer granting the request of a leper that he be made "clean" (vv. 40–45), complementing the portrayal of Jesus as "the Holy One of God" who has authority over an "unclean" spirit. After he touches the leper, Mark comments that "immediately the leprosy left him, and he was made clean" (1:42). As long as one still has the disease, according to Lev 13:46, that person is still "unclean" (LXX: ἀκάθαρτος), hence Mark's statement that the leprosy left him before the declaration of being made clean. The utterance of Jesus, "be made clean," introduces a priestly dimension to his ministry because this is a pronouncement made only by priests, which is amply evident in Leviticus (Lev 13:6, 13, 17, etc.).[12] However, it is unwarranted to go so far as Fletcher-Louis and argue that Jesus acts as a full-scale priest here mainly because there is no evidence that priests actually heal in the way that Jesus does.[13] That Jesus

---

8. Fletcher-Louis, "High Priest," 30–31; Lührmann, *Das Markusevangelium*, 51. See also Gnilka who lists scholars holding this view (*Das Evangelium*, 1:81 fn. 28). He also draws attention to *T. Levi* 18:12 in which a messianic high priest "shall bind Beliar" (*Das Evangelium*, 1:81).

9. Guelich, *Mark 1—8:26*, 57.

10. See the discussion in Brower, *Holiness*, 86–88 and Hurtado, *Lord*, 287.

11. Brower, "Able," 184.

12. Chilton, *Baptism*, 60.

13. See his discussion in "High Priest," 30–36.

Chapter 4: The Son of Man's Divine Authority on Earth

can heal a leper by merely touching him indicates that he has a power that transcends the earthly priests who merely declare that someone is clean subsequent to natural healing. Although impurity is contracted through contact (Lev 13:46; Num 5:1–4; Hag 2:11–13), the opposite occurs here.[14] According to Fletcher-Louis, "instead of the contagion of impurity flowing from impure to pure, it [the contagion of purity] flows from pure to impure."[15] Not only does "the Holy One of God" have authority over the "unclean" spirits, he also can heal and by implication make clean that which is unclean by means of a contagious purity. This is yet another manifestation of the power of Yahweh at work in Jesus.

After healing the leper and declaring that he is clean, Jesus commands him to tell no one but rather to offer those sacrifices "for your cleansing what Moses commanded, as a testimony to them" (v. 44b). According to Lev 14, specific sacrifices had to be offered before the candidate's cleansing is complete. Matthew and Luke (see Luke 5:15) say nothing more about the leper at this point leading one to believe that he obediently followed Jesus' instruction. However, Mark indicates that the leper did not obey: "*but he went out and began to proclaim it freely, and to spread the word*" (v. 45a). From Mark's perspective, it appears that sacrifices and offerings are no longer needed for cleansing but rather just the purifying touch and authoritative words of Jesus. According to N. T. Wright, "when Jesus healed a leper and told him to go to the priest and make the required offering, the point was of course that an ex-leper needed the official bill of health in order to be readmitted to his community."[16] In other words, the rituals of temple priests and offering of sacrifices are not needed to complete this cleansing. In my opinion, the command that the leper show himself to the priests as a "testimony" or "witness" has more to do with sending a message to the temple establishment. The phrase εἰς μαρτύριον αὐτοῖς can also be translated as "a testimony *against* them" (v. 44) which is how the phrase is often translated in Mark 6:11 in which the disciples are to shake the dust off their feet as εἰς μαρτύριον αὐτοῖς, that is, against those who reject the gospel message.[17]

14. Chilton defines the disease of leprosy more generally as "outbreak" so that whoever comes in contact with that which has gone beyond its boundaries, such as blood, becomes impure (*Baptism*, 58–59).

15. Fletcher-Louis, "High Priest," 33. For a list of those who support the contagion of purity reading of 1:40–45, as opposed to the idea that Jesus dispenses with purity laws altogether, see Ibid., "High Priest," 33 fn. 101.

16. Wright, *Challenge*, 45.

17. France argues that the phrase in 13:9 should be interpreted in a confrontational

The fact that Jesus has not only declared the leper to be clean but also has healed the cause of impurity could mean that his testimony will reveal to the priests the redundancy of the temple's purification system. It is no longer necessary for accomplishing that which it was originally intended to do. This is strengthened when we consider that by the time of the composition of Mark's Gospel the temple establishment is either over-run with Jewish rebels in the Jewish-Roman war, or has already been destroyed, and when we consider Mark's portrayal of the acrimony between Jesus and the temple leaders later in the narrative and the way in which, as I will argue later, the SM's sacrificial death renders the temple cult unnecessary.

The Son of Man's Authority to Forgive Sins

In this scene, Jesus returns to his house in Capernaum, and the crowds gather *en masse* since his popularity is increasing rapidly due to the healings and exorcisms he has been performing (1:28, 32–34, 37, 45). Four men attempt to bring a paralyzed man to him, but since they cannot do so because of the crowd, they remove the roof above Jesus and lower the mat on which the paralytic is lying (v. 4). Seeing this act of faith, Jesus announces to the paralytic, "Son, your sins are forgiven" (v. 5). For the first time, the scribes play a role Mark's narrative, other than just being mentioned as in 1:21–27, and they do not respond favorably to this declaration. Instead, they "reason" (διαλογιζόμενοι) in their hearts that Jesus has abused or insulted God by assuming his prerogative of forgiving sins (v. 6). A number of OT passages indicate that Yahweh is the source of forgiveness (Exod 34:6–7; Isa 43:25; 44:22). They, therefore, conclude that Jesus is guilty of blasphemy (v. 7). Assuming his own authority to forgive sins and that the scribes should have recognized it, Jesus then asks them, "Why do you raise such questions in your hearts?" (v. 8). He appears to perceive some level of opposition from them and proceeds to heal the paralytic which he claims demonstrates that ὁ υἱὸς τοῦ ἀνθρώπου has authority "on earth" to forgive sins (v. 10). At seeing the paralytic walk out of the house, everyone is amazed and gives glory to God saying, "We have never seen anything like this" (v. 12b).

---

sense as well (*Mark*, 120).

Chapter 4: The Son of Man's Divine Authority on Earth

Establishing an Allusion to Dan 7:13 in Mark 2:10

As I have indicated in the chapter 1, there has been quite a bit of debate over the significance of the phrase ὁ υἱὸς τοῦ ἀνθρώπου found in the Gospel tradition and its background. What will become apparent throughout this study is that, in light of Dan 7, it functions as a title in Mark communicating specific ideas about Jesus which make an important contribution to Mark's theology.[18] A. Y. Collins, however, is quite right that "the critical reader of Mark today cannot assume that everyone in the audience of Mark understood this epithet as a title."[19] Initially, this would likely be the case if the phrase is not a common Greek idiom, but through repeatedly hearing this Gospel, the audience would soon realize that Mark is doing something more than employing an unidiomatic circumlocution by which Jesus refers to himself as "man."

When we consider the intertextual significance of ὁ υἱὸς τοῦ ἀνθρώπου, the terms υἱὸς and ἀνθρώπου lay the foundation for establishing an allusion to an OT text where υἱὸς ἀνθρώπου likewise occurs, which is not, by any means, limited to Dan 7.[20] An application of the relevant criteria for establishing an allusion, which I described earlier, will provide convincing support for my claim that Mark alludes to the danielic SM in 2:10. A good place to start is with *volume*: how loud or noticeable is the allusion? Dan 7:13–14 seems quite audible when Mark's Jesus proclaims that ἐξουσίαν ἔχει ὁ υἱὸς τοῦ ἀνθρώπου (v. 10).[21] The markan SM's possession of ἐξουσία clearly alludes to the danielic figure and his investiture of the same following the angelic multitude's presentation of him before the Ancient of Days. Both Theodotion and the LXX contain the attribution ἐξουσία in Dan 7:14: "his authority (ἐξουσία) is an everlasting authority (ἐξουσία) which will not pass away" (NETS) and the beginning of v. 14 in the LXX reads: "and royal authority (ἐξουσία) was given to him" (NETS).[22]

---

18. Responding to those argue that the Greek phrase makes little sense, Moule remarks that it is no more "ponderous" than the title ὁ υἱὸς τοῦ θεοῦ ("Son of Man," 277).

19. Collins, *Mark*, 186. See also Hurtado, "Summary," 160.

20. According to Hurtado, the LXX contains 112 uses of the singular and anarthrous construction "(a) son of man" ("Summary," 161). The majority of these are found in the vocative case in Ezekiel (υἱὲ ἀνθρώπου). Other examples include: Ps 8:5: υἱὸς ἀνθρώπου; 79:16: υἱὸν ἀνθρώπου; and Num 23:19: υἱὸς ἀνθρώπου.

21. Many scholars agree that Mark alludes to the SM of Dan 7:13 in 2:10: Hooker, *Son of Man*, 93; France, *Mark*, 127; Gundry, *Mark*, 119; Pesch, *Das Markusevangelium*, 160; Gathercole, "Son of Man," 369; Ibid., *Pre-existent*, 258.

22. English translations of the LXX/Theod. are taken from Pietersma and Wright,

Also, but much less audibly, the phrase "upon the earth" (ἐπὶ τῆς γῆς, v. 10) may recall the earthly realm in which the terrestrial "holy ones," that is, faithful Israel, share in the authority of their heavenly counterpart, the SM (Dan 7:14, 27).[23]

However, there is a significant point of discontinuity between Dan 7 and the scene in Mark 2. Nowhere in Daniel or in any surviving Jewish literature either preceding or contemporaneous with Mark does the SM forgive sins.[24] This has led Casey, for instance, to dismiss the background of Dan 7 altogether because forgiving sins is not a part of that scene.[25] When we apply the criterion of *thematic coherence*, which considers the exegetical insight the allusion sheds on the evoking passage, *prima facie*, there seems little to glean. Even in the text of Mark itself, it seems odd that Jesus forgives the paralytic's sins when one expects that he would heal him of his disability as this was likely the intention of the man's friends (vv. 3–4). The last time in Mark in which people were gathered around "the door," they wished to have the sick healed and the demon possessed exorcised (1:32–34). Further, form critics argue that vv. 5b-10 are a later accretion because the line "he said to the paralytic" (λέγει τῷ παραλυτικω) at the end of v. 10 artificially resumes Jesus' original address to the paralytic in v. 5a: λέγει τῷ παραλυτικω and so without this interpolation, the focus remains on healing.[26] Before addressing the connection between the SM and for-

---

Septuagint.

23. Marcus, "Forgive," 203–4.

24. Marcus attempts to argue that 2:10 is midrash combining Dan 9:9, which speaks about God's mercy and forgiveness, with Dan 7:13–14 ("Forgive," 205). Midrash does not seem as evident here as it is, for example, in 14:62 in which Mark clearly combines Dan 7:13 and Ps 110:1. Further, Marcus argues that the *Apoc. Abr.*, which includes SM terminology from Dan 7 and refers to the angel who can forgive sins from Exod 23:20–22, provides a parallel for the connection between the SM and this action (Ibid., "Forgive," 205–8). The most glaring deficiency with this is that the angel, Iaoel, in the *Apoc. Abr.* 10–11 does not forgive sins but merely prescribes for Abraham the sacrifices that he needs to offer (*Apoc. Abr.* 12:3–10).

25. Casey, "Method," 29. Casey holds this view in his most recent publication, *Solution*, as well. He argues that such interpretative problems "arise from studying this verse in Greek, in the light of Christian tradition. From these habits comes the whole idea that 'Son of man' is a messianic title in this verse, and refers to Jesus alone. All the other problems flow from these assumptions" (*Solution*, 163). As I hope is obvious from the argument above, my claim that Mark is evoking Dan 7 in this passage is not an assumption.

26. For example, Gnilka, *Das Evangelium*, 1:96 and Higgins, *Son of Man*, 26–28. For arguments against the inauthenticity of vv. 5b-10, see Gundry, *Mark*, 121–23; Guelich, *Mark*, 88; Dewey, *Public*, 74–76.

Chapter 4: The Son of Man's Divine Authority on Earth

giveness, we can say that Jesus likely forgives the man's sins first because in the OT as well as Jewish tradition physical illness was thought to occur because of personal sin in which case vv. 5b–10 is a reasonable interpolation if indeed this passage is inauthentic.[27] In other words, Jesus first deals with the cause of the paralysis. The healing, in v. 10 as Jesus himself proclaims, demonstrates his authority as the SM to forgive sins "upon the earth" and, at the same time, introduces an important aspect of the SM's role in Mark.

The Son of Man and the Forgiveness of Sins

There are a variety of proposals that connect Jesus with his assertion that the paralytic's sins are forgiven in v. 5, which incidentally tend to ignore the function of v. 10, the climax of the passage. A number of scholars argue that he functions as a priest when he makes the declaration of forgiveness which recalls the oft-repeated phrase from Leviticus "they shall be forgiven" (Lev 4:20b) occurring after the prescriptions for various offerings.[28] Jesus, then, does not commit blasphemy, despite the accusation of the scribes, because "mann im antiken Judentum dem Priester bzw. dem Hohenpriester die Vollmacht der Sündenvergebung zugeschrieben habe."[29] Ernst Haenchen claims that in addition to God forgiving sins, "auch der Priester kann nach jüdischer Überzeugung von Sünden lossprechen!"[30] According to Ernst Lohmeyer, priests have the earthly authority to forgive sins "durch Opfer und Weihe."[31] The major difficulty with the claims of Haenchen and Lohmeyer is that the scribes's accusation of blasphemy is founded on the idea that *only* Israel's God can forgive sins, not a priest or

---

27. Hooker, *Son of Man*, 89; Ibid., *Mark*, 85; Casey, *Solution*, 151–52. A number of OT texts express that physical sickness and ailments are related to sin or God's judgement. One example is found in Ps 32 in which the supplicant acknowledges his body is wasting away due to sin that he has not confessed, but after his confession, the Psalm implies that the individual's body is restored. See also Lev 26:14–16; Jer 16:3–4; Isa 33:24; 2 Chron 21:18–19.

28. Hofius discusses a number of these arguments ("Vergebungszuspruch," 115–20). Collins notes that the LXX uses ἀφίημι, the same verb Mark uses in vv. 5 and 7, to describe the result of atonement for sin in Lev 4:20, 26, 31, 35; 5:6, 10, 13, 16, 18, 26; 19:22 (*Mark*, 185 n. 27).

29. Hofius, "Vergebungszuspruch," 115. See also Haenchen, *Der Weg Jesu*, 102 and Lohmeyer, *Das Evangelium*, 52.

30. Haenchen, *Der Weg Jesu*, 102.

31. Lohmeyer, *Das Evangelium*, 53.

the high priest.³² Jesus is performing a prerogative of Yahweh. Validated throughout Israel's Scripture is the notion that Yahweh is the one who forgives sins: Exod 34:7; Num 14:18-20; Neh 9:17; Ps 130:4; Mic 7:18; Dan 9:9.³³ Further, in Lev. 4:20b, the Niphal verb in the statement וְנִסְלַח לָהֶם, which is translated "they shall be forgiven," is in the passive voice and the unstated agent is God himself, and there is also no indication that this was an audible formula pronounced by the priests.³⁴ Rather, the focus in the cult is on the duties of the priest and the consequent atonement and forgiveness.³⁵

Others suggest that the notion of a "salvation oracle" uttered by the priests in the temple could include a reference to the forgiveness of sins which provides a background for the declaration of Jesus. In Ps 130, the supplicant seeks forgiveness from the Lord and hopes upon "his word" (v. 5c) that forgiveness will come, a "word" from the priest as the "Zuspruch der Sündenvergebung."³⁶ A possible parallel to this might be 2 Sam 12:13 in which Nathan declares to David, "Now the Lord has put away your sin." However, Nathan is a prophet and not a priest. One striking example of the oracle of salvation is evident in the words of one of the Seraphim, priestly figures who attend to the Lord: "Now that this [the live coal] has touched your lips, your guilt has departed and your sin is blotted out (תְּכֻפָּר)" (Isa 6:7). In 1QS II, 1-10, the priests bless new initiates into the community, but they also curse those associated with Belial (II, 4b-5a). Included in the curse is the opposite of the priestly oracle, employing the same verbs from Lev 4:20: "May God not be merciful when you entreat him. May he not forgive (יסלח) by purifying (לכפר) your iniquities" (II, 8b).³⁷ Finally, some suggest Simon's blessing in Sir 50:20-21 includes the pronouncement that

---

32. Lohmeyer suggests the following reconstruction of 2:7: "Wer has die Vollmacht, außer dem Priester, die Vergebung der Sünden durch Gott auszusprechen?" (*Das Evangelium*, 53).

33. Ellingworth lists the following excerpts from prayers which depict God as the forgiver of sins: 1 Kgs 8:30-50; 2 Kgs 5:18; Ps 25:11; 79:92; 2 Chron 6:21-39 ("Forgiveness," 241).

34. Casey, *Solution*, 155; Milgrom, *Leviticus 1-16*, 1:56.

35. Milgrom, *Leviticus 1-16*, 1:260.

36. Hofius, "Vergebungszuspruck," 118-19. See also Broyles for the secondary literature he cites (*Psalms*, 469). Kraus cites the following passages as evidence of an oracle of salvation: Ps 107:20; 114; 119:81-82; 138:4; 147 (*Psalms 60-150*, 467).

37. This English translation is taken from Martínez and Tigchelaar, *Dead Sea Scrolls*, 73.

Chapter 4: The Son of Man's Divine Authority on Earth

the nation's sins are forgiven subsequent to the sacrifice that he offers in the sanctuary (vv. 13–19) which follows the pattern of Leviticus.[38] The major weakness with the "salvation oracle" alternative, much like the "declaration of forgiveness," is that there is no evidence that in fact the priests pronounce that one's sins are forgiven after executing priestly duties on behalf of a supplicant or the nation. Accordingly, Otfried Hofius rejects these proposals as lacking any "Quellengrundlage."[39]

Fletcher-Louis argues that Jesus acts as a priest in 2:1–12 by appealing to Exod 28:36–38 in which "Aaron shall bear/remove/forgive (MT: נָשָׂא; LXX: ἐξαρεῖ) any guilt incurred in the holy offerings that the Israelites consecrate as their sacred donations" (v. 38) and Lev 10:17 where Eleazar and Ithamar are to eat the sin offering "for it is most holy, and God has given it to you that you may remove/forgive/bear (MT: לָשֵׂאת; LXX: ἀφέλητε) the guilt of the congregation, to make atonement on their behalf before the Lord."[40] However, Aaron and the priests do not forgive sins themselves but rather mediate God's forgiveness by, in the case of Exod 28:36–38, being set apart or "holy to Yahweh" (28:36) or, as in Lev 10:17, having been charged with the duty by God to eat the sin offering. Jacob Milgrom comments that the priest "removes iniquity" (לָשֵׂאת אֶת־עֲוֹן) because he "serves as the divine surrogate on earth and exclusively so in the sanctuary", but forgiveness ultimately derives from Yahweh himself, e.g., Exod 34:6–7; Isa 43:25; 44:22.[41] Although Mark has ἀφίενταί and not ἐξαίρω or ἀφαιρέω found in the two passages from the LXX, נָשָׂא is translated as ἀφίημι in Ps 25:18b [LXX 24:18b] and 32:1b, 5c [LXX 31:1b, 5c]. The subject, however, is not the high priest but God himself in each case (25:18b; 32:5c). Finally, Fletcher-Louis's contention that Jesus is acting as a priest, or the eschatological high priest, does not account for the response of the scribes in v. 7 who attribute forgiveness, as previously noted, not to the priesthood or an expected eschatological high priest, but rather to Yahweh himself.[42]

---

38. See Hofius for the literature he cites ("Vergebungszuspruch," 119 fn. 25).

39. Ibid., 125.

40. Fletcher-Louis, "High Priest," 41.

41. Milgrom, *Leviticus 1–16*, 1:623–24.

42. Marcus comes to a much more tentative conclusion regarding the priestly status of the SM in 2:10. Concentrating on the Adamic background of the Greek phrase ὁ υἱὸς τοῦ ἀνθρώπου and noting the instances in which Adam is portrayed as a priest, Marcus concludes that "since a major part of a priest's job is to *make atonement for sins* by performing sacrifices, these passages [about Adam's priestly status/function] provide a partial parallel to the Markan description of the Son of Man having the authority to

On the one hand, Jesus himself is the one offering forgiveness in Mark 2 and not Yahweh; his authority appears to be something he himself as the SM possesses, but, on the other hand, the narrative context of 2:1–12 reveals that Jesus is clearly associated with Yahweh. His baptism reveals that he is now endowed with the divine presence through Yahweh's Spirit, a presence that manifests itself authoritatively through the Holy One of God who casts out an unclean spirit in 1:21–28 and through his ability to purify a leper by healing him of his disease in 1:40–45. In 2:1–12, Jesus demonstrates this authority again. In response to the scribes's question, "Who is able to forgive sins?" (v. 7b), it is, for Mark and his implied audience in light of the preceding narrative, the authoritative Son of Man. Robert Guelich comments that Jesus answers the scribes's question head on: "He leaves his inquisitors to resolve how this might be or whether indeed it is blasphemy."[43] Now that his adversaries know, as well as the audience, the question remains: who is this Son of Man and why should he possess authority to do that which is manifestly a prerogative of Yahweh? What we can say at the outset is that for Mark the SM is not just a human being—a power is at work in Jesus which sets him apart from the rest of humanity.[44]

A helpful starting point might be found in the scribes's response to Jesus' pronouncement of forgiveness in which they question "Who can forgive sins but God alone?" (τίς δύναται ἀφιέναι ἁμαρτίας εἰ μὴ εἷς ὁ θεός, v. 7b). According to Joel Marcus, the use of εἷς highlights the oneness of God and echoes the *Shema*: ἄκουε Ισραηλ κύριος ὁ θεὸς ἡμῶν κύριος εἷς ἐστιν (LXX: Deut 6:4).[45] The *Shema* was and still is Israel's pivotal affirmation of monotheism.[46] In light of Dan 7, Marcus argues that the apparent breach of Jewish monotheism is solved through Jesus functioning as the exalted danielic SM.[47] In this way, the SM is not acting on his own apart from God, but yet is the one "who can forgive sins" (2:6). According to Marcus, "the Son of Man has authority to forgive sins *on earth*, acting as the earthly

---

forgive sins" ("Son of Man," 374).

43. Guelich, *Mark*, 91.

44. Demurrals of interpreting the SM as someone more than mere "man" include Hurtado, *Mark*, 38 and Hay, "Son of Man," 72. The latter interprets the SM as "man" in 2:10 on the basis of Matt 9:8, which is a flawed methodology for one who is seeking what Mark meant by his use of the term.

45. Marcus, "Forgive," 196.

46. Marcus cites Reif, *Judaism and Hebrew Prayer*, 83–84 ("Forgive," 196 fn. 2).

47. Ibid., 202–5.

Chapter 4: The Son of Man's Divine Authority on Earth

plenipotentiary of the one who forgives them *in heaven* (see Mt. 18:18)."[48] Marcus is heading in the right direction, particularly in light of Dan 7 and subsequent Jewish interpretations of the "one like a son of man" contemporaneous with Mark.

Unlike the passive danielic SM who is brought into Yahweh's presence and is given authority, Mark's SM demonstrates his ἐξουσία in tangible ways ἐπὶ τῆς γῆς.[49] A similar movement is evident in the *Parables* of Enoch and *4 Ezra* which, as we have seen, reuse and modify the danielic figure. In the evocations of the danielic SM in these texts, he appears to be elevated to the status of Yahweh, executing his tasks and sharing in his authority. In the *Parables*, the SM continues to dwell in the heavenly temple (46:1–2) but now judges Israel's enemies (46:4–8; 62:5) and himself sits upon Yahweh's throne (62:5). Reminiscent of depictions of Yahweh as warrior, a destructive stream of fire flows from the SM's mouth in *4 Ezra* 13 while situated upon a cosmic temple mount from which he destroys the adversaries of faithful Israel and to which the persecuted ones come for deliverance (vv. 10–13). In Mark, however, the SM does not initially manifest his authority in a celestial, other-worldly realm but, rather, "upon the earth." Given the celestial settings in which the SM appears both in Daniel and the *Parables*, Mark's use of "upon the earth" suggests such a contrast between heaven, in which the SM is thought to reign, with this new, unexpected realm in which he forgives sins; otherwise, the use of this phrase by Mark is meaningless.[50] By means of Mark's interpretative rendering of the danielic "one like a son of man," Yahweh's divine authority is now the possession of the SM who uses it to forgive a paralytic's sins in Galilee, not unlike the development evident in the *Parables* and *4 Ezra* which strengthens the *historical probability* of my proposal. But, yet, a tension still remains as the crowds respond by giving glory to God and not to Jesus in v. 12. Marcus concludes: "our passage thus evidences a characteristic Markan ambiguity about whether Jesus himself is acting [as seems to be the case in v. 10] or whether God is acting through him; in Mark's view both perspectives contain aspects

---

48. Ibid., 204; Gundry, *Mark*, 120. Hooker suggests that the idea is not wholly foreign to Dan 7 as forgiving sins is related to the overthrowing of evil (*Son of Man*, 93).

49. The placement of ἐπὶ τῆς γῆς varies in the manuscripts. In P88, ℵ, C, D, L, the phrase occurs before ἀφιέναι ἁμαρτίας while in A, K, Γ, it is placed in between ἀφιέναι ἁμαρτίας, and in B and Θ, it follows ἀφιέναι ἁμαρτίας. Marcus suggests that the *lectio difficilior* is the one reflected in P88, ℵ, C, D, L and puts more emphasis on the sphere of the SM's authority (*Mark*, 218).

50. Gundry, *Mark*, 120; Watts, "Mark," 138.

of the truth."[51] I believe the ambivalence is mitigated when we consider Mark's evocation of the danielic SM such that now Jesus as SM possesses Yahweh's divine authority to execute Yahweh's prerogatives. Already in Mark 1, the Spirit of Yahweh is at work in Jesus as the Holy One of God who exorcises an unclean spirit and purifies an unclean man defiled by leprosy. Mark wants his readers to see on the basis of the crowd's response that this forgiveness has ultimately come from Yahweh but the means by which it comes is unexpected, a difficult reality for the Galilean scribes. Arguing that Mark's Jesus evokes Dan 7 in this manner brings a high level of *thematic coherence* to the narrative as it coheres with Mark's presentation of Jesus in chapter 1 and accounts for the connection between the SM and the forgiveness of sins.

The Son of Man's Authority Over the Sabbath

The next appearance of the SM phrase is occasioned by the Pharisees who question Jesus on the "unlawful" activity of the disciples who pluck heads of grain on the sabbath. Plucking heads of grain, presumably to eat, constitutes work which the law prohibits (Lev 23:3). According to Hooker, in Deut 23:25, one is permitted to pluck the ears of a neighbor's grain with one's hands on the sabbath but not with the use of a sickle. From this, she concludes that the disciples are not actually working and that "it is only according to the scribal view that the disciples's action in plucking a few ears can be understood as work and so be said to contravene the Torah" (see *m. Šabb.* 7:2).[52] However, the injunction of Deut 23:25 does not appear to have anything to do with sabbath but rather with protecting fellow Israelites from exploitation.[53] Possibly, the Pharisees's opposition could derive from Exod 34:21 which prohibits "reaping" on the sabbath.[54] Even though the disciples are technically not harvesting the grain, they are still working when they pluck the heads of grain in order to eat. The work of gathering manna, for example, on the sabbath is prohibited where the Israelites are not to reap their crops: "Six days you shall gather it; but on the seventh day, which is a

---

51. Marcus, *Mark*, 224.
52. Hooker, *Mark*, 103. See also her similar assessment in Hooker, "Mark," 225.
53. McConville, *Deuteronomy*, 353.
54. France, *Mark*, 145; Guelich, *Mark*, 120–21; Westerholm, "Sabbath," 717. Exod 34:21: "Six days you shall work, but on the seventh day you shall rest; even in plowing time and in harvest time you shall rest."

Chapter 4: The Son of Man's Divine Authority on Earth

sabbath, there will be none" (Exod 16:26). The sabbath is to be "a day of solemn rest" (Exod 16:23a). The latter text from Exodus provides a scriptural warrant to make the accusation that Jesus' disciples are doing that which is unlawful on the sabbath, in addition to any halakhic teaching of the Pharisees. Rabbinic tradition, which might provide some insight into Pharisaic jurisprudence during the time of Jesus, contains a variety of prohibitions for sabbath activities in *m. Šabb.* 7:2.[55] In the end, however, we must be content with Richard France's observation that "the Pharisees do not specify in what way the sabbath regulations are being broken, nor does Jesus argue the point," but suffice it to say that sabbath law has been breached.[56]

Jesus gives two responses to the objection of the Pharisees. The first, in vv. 25–26, is a very brief reference to David entering the "house of God" and consuming the bread of the presence based on the account found in 1 Sam 21:1–6 and the second response, in vv. 27–28, is a statement that sabbath was made for "man," so the SM is Lord of the sabbath (2:27–28).[57] There are a number of difficulties and inconsistencies that plague the tradition history and final form of this text. John P. Meier opines that "there are almost as many opinions about this story as there are exegetes."[58] Part of the difficulty is found in Jesus' account of David and his companions unlawfully eating the holy bread reserved for the priests which does not appear to be immediately relevant to the disciples's breach of sabbath law. Meier notes that "Jesus stresses that David's violation involved *what* David did—eating food that only priests should eat—and not *when* he did it."[59] Further, it is not clear how vv. 27–28 relate to the preceding two verses about David consuming the bread in the sanctuary at Nob, assuming that Mark wants his readers to see a connection. However, a number of scholars do agree upon a basic moral that this text teaches—human need takes precedence over obedience to the law.[60]

---

55. Lohse, "σάββατον," 12–14.

56. France, *Mark*, 145.

57. Dewey notes that the two answers are distinct from each other by means of καὶ λέγει αὐτοῖς found at the beginning of both vv. 25 and 27 which has provided much fodder for form critics over the years (*Public*, 99).

According to Wenham, the bread of presence likely derives its name from the fact that it was placed in the presence of the Lord in the tabernacle (see Exod 25:30) (*Leviticus*, 309 n. 4).

58. Meier, "Historical," 563.

59. Ibid., 576.

60. Schottroff and Stegemann, "Sabbath," 124–26. These authors claim that Mark's

The syntax of v. 28, in which the SM phrase appears, recalls the structure of 2:10 which may imply a thematic connection between the ways in which the SM functions in the two passages. Some scholars claim that καὶ τοῦ σαββάτου in v. 28, translated as "*also* of the sabbath," harkens back to the first appearance of the SM in which he demonstrates authority to forgive sins.[61] Joanna Dewey analyzes the texts of vv. 10 and 28 and points out a parallel rhetorical structure: ἐξουσίαν/ κύριός comes first, then the verbs ἔχει/ἐστιν, the subject, ὁ υἱὸς τοῦ ἀνθρώπου, and finally the object of the SM's authority/lordship: forgiving sins on earth and dominion over the sabbath.[62] The SM, then, not only has authority "to forgive sins upon the earth" but also has authority over sabbath. Given that these two SM passages share a structural relationship, the following analysis of this second SM saying and the pericopé in which it is found seeks to determine if there is a thematic connection as well which would satisfy Hays's criterion of *recurrence*. That is, is the SM once again manifesting Yahweh's divine authority now in a Galilean grain field and does Dan 7 form the background for this connection? If so, how does it function in its narrative context forming a response, along with vv. 25–26, to the Pharisees's accusation?

Solidarity between Jesus and His Disciples

One thing that is abundantly clear at the beginning of this passage is that a close bond is developing between Jesus and his followers. Mark begins with an emphasis on Jesus who is making his way through the grain fields in v. 23a and then refers to the disciples as well: "as they made their way his disciples began to pluck heads of grain" (v. 23b). The Pharisees, who seem to be stalking the group appear out of nowhere and confront the leader about the actions of his followers that they deem "unlawful" (v. 24). Meier

---

Jesus rejects sabbath observance completely: "In Mark's view, the dispute of Jesus with the Pharisees over sabbath is a dispute that, joined to other conflicts with the Pharisees, leads to the decision that Jesus must die. Mark 2:27, taken in connection with 2:28 and 3:1–6, means that the Pharisees make the sabbath more important than human beings and their needs, whereas Jesus gives them priority over the sabbath, which the followers of Jesus now have no reason for observing" ("Sabbath," 122). However, the language of 2:27–28 points in the direction of the restoration of God's intent for sabbath versus complete abrogation, as we will see.

61. Kuhn, *Ältere Sammlungen im Markusevangelium*, 73, 76, 87, cited in Dewey, *Public*, 99 fn. 132; Lane, *Mark*, 120; France, *Mark*, 148.

62. Dewey, *Public*, 99; Gundry, *Mark*, 144.

Chapter 4: The Son of Man's Divine Authority on Earth

claims that Mark introduces a pattern of "distinction-yet-connection" in vv. 23–24.[63] He comments that "the disciples are performing the objectionable action, but Jesus, as their teacher, is considered responsible for it—a common view in the ancient world, both Jewish and pagan."[64] This bond is first evident in the preceding passage in which an undefined group in 2:18 questions Jesus about σοὶ μαθηταὶ who do not fast like the disciples of John and the Pharisees. The use of μαθηταὶ to describe Jesus' followers in this context (2:18–20) over against other groups of disciples indicates that these ones who do not fast are a defined group (see 2:15).[65]

According to Meier, the pattern of "distinction-yet-connection" continues in v. 25 in Jesus' account of David and his companions. At the beginning of his response, Mark's Jesus emphasizes the singularity of David similar to Jesus himself who goes through the grain fields. He asks them if they have read what *David did* (ἐποίησεν) when *he had* (ἔσχεν) need and when *he was hungry* (ἐπείνασεν). This also extends to his companions: καὶ οἱ μετ' αὐτοῦ. Paralleling v. 25, in v. 26, David alone *entered* (εἰσῆλθεν) the house of God, *ate* (ἔφαγεν) the bread of the presence, and *gave* (ἔδωκεν) it to his companions (καὶ τοῖς σὺν αὐτῷ οὖσιν).[66] Although Jesus highlights the actions of David alone, the hunger and need he experiences extends to his companions (v. 25) along with the consumption of the bread that satisfies first David and then his followers (v. 26). This pattern in vv. 25–26 demonstrates that the unique relationship between Jesus and his disciples needs to be viewed in terms of the relationship that existed between David and his companions. Specifically, the disciples's abrogation of sabbath law is permitted by virtue of their relationship to Jesus just as David's companions eat the bread reserved for the priests because their leader has also done so.[67] But what exactly is it about David and his unlawful activity that provides

---

63. Meier, "Historical," 568–70.

64. Ibid., 569; Dewey, *Public*, 97. For a similar conclusion, see Daube, "Responsibilities," 4–5; Pesch, *Markusevangelium*, 1:180–81.

65. France, *Mark*, 137.

66. Many translations of v. 25 bring οἱ μετ' αὐτοῦ forward and translate the singular verbs ἔσχεν and ἐπείνασεν as plural which distorts the literary pattern of distinction-yet-connection.

67. Dewey, *Public*, 97; Pesch, *Markusevangelium*, 1:182. Hooker argues that the analogy turns on the idea that David and his companions did not follow the laws guarding the holiness of the bread which parallels the disciples's abrogation of the sabbath laws which protect its holiness (*Mark*, 97–98). However, the emphasis seems to fall on the close connection between the leaders and their respective followers.

a paradigm for Jesus? Given the nuanced ways in which Jesus recounts the story of David, which I discuss below, it must be functioning as more than just an instance of law-breaking spearheaded by an authoritative figure which generically applies to the situation of the disciples.[68]

A number of scholars argue that Jesus' account of David entering the temple and consuming the bread highlights his royal authority that then warrants the disciples's breach of sabbath law. For instance, Larry Hurtado claims that "in both cases we have a band of men who represent a new, as yet unrecognized, 'regime' in emergency circumstances."[69] Joel Marcus, from his analysis of these verses, suggests that they link Jesus with the "Davidic Messiah".[70] For others, such as France, Francis Moloney, and Hooker, the story communicates that Jesus has an authority tantamount to David's.[71] Finally, Collins argues that Jesus points to the David incident at Nob as he was one who overrode a law by virtue of human need, and so the disciples can legitimately do so as well due to their hunger and need.[72] However, in all of these proposals, little attention has been given to the modifications that Mark's Jesus makes to 1 Sam 21:1–6, and how this relates to his defense of the disciples's "unlawful" sabbath activity. A quick comparison reveals that Jesus does not give a very accurate summary of the account! Rikk Watts's assessment that they are "legitimate inferences from the narrative" of 1 Sam 21 is certainly a helpful starting point, but why does Mark's Jesus make these particular inferences and what is the exegetical impact of his modifications of this OT text?[73]

There are a number of differences. In Mark, Jesus says that David enters "the house of God" while in 1 Samuel, the priest comes to meet David (21:1). In Mark, David eats the bread of the presence likely while in the sanctuary along with "those who were with him" (2:26b). In 1 Samuel, it is not mentioned that he and his companions ever eat the bread mentioned

---

68. This line of reasoning is evident in the statement of Westerholm: "a precedent is cited from Scripture (1 Sam 21:1–6) for an activity which, on the strict application of scriptural commands, was [also] 'not lawful'" ("Sabbath," 717). See also Hooker, *Son of Man*, 98.

69. Hurtado, *Mark*, 48.

70. Marcus, *Mark*, 245. See also Collins, *Mark*, 205.

71. France, *Mark*, 145; Moloney, *Mark*, 69; Hooker, *Mark*, 104. See also Gnilka, *Das Evangelium*, 122. However, Gundry claims that David has no relevance for Jesus because the account in v. 26 is occasioned by an action of the disciples, not Jesus (*Mark*, 141).

72. Collins, *Mark*, 202–3.

73. Watts, "Mark," 140.

Chapter 4: The Son of Man's Divine Authority on Earth

in 2:26b and, in fact, David travels to the sanctuary alone (1 Sam 21:2b). The only legal matter in the original account concerns the purity of David's companions (1 Sam 21:4b–5) while in Mark, Jesus highlights that David eats what is lawful only for the priests to eat and then shares it with his compatriots (2:26). Mark's Jesus refers to the high priest Abiathar while his father, Ahimelech, actually officiates in the sanctuary.[74] By means of these modifications, with the exception of the last one, Jesus highlights that David and his followers execute a task reserved only for the priests. Mark's placement of the clause in v. 26, οὓς οὐκ ἔξεστιν φαγεῖν εἰ μὴ τοὺς ἱερεῖς, between a reference to David eating the bread and giving it to his companions draws out this idea. In fact, verse 26 is replete with terminology associated with priests: "house of God," "Abiathar the high priest," "bread of the presence," and "priests." Clearly something more is going on here than Jesus holding up a well-known OT figure and his compatriots as precedent for breaching Mosaic laws that get in the way of satisfying human need. Rather, the emphasis on the unlawful priestly action of David and his companions as well as the way in which David and his cohorts mirror the close relationship that exists between Jesus and his disciples provide a lens through which to view the disciples's action in v. 23. However, further consideration of the relevance of vv. 25–26 for the disciples's plucking heads of grain must be held in abeyance until a discussion of vv. 27–28 which contain Jesus' second response to the Pharisees.

The Son of Man is Lord of the Sabbath

The saying in vv. 27–28 seems to addresses the behavior of the disciples more clearly than the material in vv. 25–26, as a number of scholars recognize.[75] The statement of Jesus in v. 27 is not a novel one. His claim that "the sabbath was made for humankind, and not humankind for the sabbath" is clearly reflected in Exod 16:29a: "See! The Lord has given you [Israel]

---

74. Gundry makes the appealing suggestion that this difference is intentional because Abiathar was a priest in the Jerusalem temple (2 Sam 15:24, 35; 17:15; 19:11) which may serve to connect this narrative in Mark with the second temple (*Mark*, 141). Abiathar also was also closely related to David (1 Sam 23:6–11; 2 Sam 20:25) which could explain the confusion. France suggests that the error may stem from the inconsistency in the OT itself because in 2 Sam 8:17 and 1 Chron 24:6 Ahimelech is reported to be the son of Abiathar (*Mark*, 146).

75. This has prompted some scholars to dismiss the authenticity of vv. 25–26, for example, Hooker, *Mark*, 104 and Haenchen, *Der Weg Jesu*, 120.

the Sabbath." A text in *Jubilees* expands on this: "And he gave us a great sign, the sabbath day, so that we might work six days and observe a sabbath from all work on the seventh day" (2:17). It is to be a day of "blessing and sanctification, and glory" (2:32). At the foundation of these texts is Gen 1:1—2:4a in which God rests from his creative work on the seventh day after having labored the previous six days. Humanity is to model the work and then rest rhythm of God himself and so in the fourth commandment, Yahweh commands Israel to honor the sabbath by ceasing from all labor because it is "a sabbath to the Lord your God" (Exod 20:10). These subsequent references to sabbath, beyond the creation account, also indicate that sabbath is for Israel. Again, in *Jubilees*, Yahweh pronounces, "Behold, I shall separate for myself a people from among all the nations. And they [the separated people, Jacob-Israel] will also keep the sabbath" (2:19). A little later the author states, "he [Yahweh] did not sanctify any people or nations to keep the sabbath thereon with the sole exception of Israel" (2:31). The exclusivity of the sabbath for Israel is also evident in Exod 31:13, 17 and Ezek 20:12.[76] Jesus' aphoristic response in v. 27 captures the essence of all of these texts which highlight that sabbath belongs to Yahweh which he gives to *his* people for their wellbeing.[77] The referent, then, of ὁ ἄνθρωπος in v. 27 is Israel as sabbath is a gift given to the nation by Yahweh and also because the verse addresses a criticism of the Pharisees directed at Jewish disciples which centers on obedience to sabbath law, a distinctly Jewish concern. Their criticism undermines the goodness of this day by their *halakhic* concerns which, in this case, prohibit the disciples from finding sustenance.[78]

Verse 28 is connected to the preceding one with the conjunction ὥστε: "*so that* the SM is lord even of the Sabbath." It is not immediately clear how the inference of the SM being lord of the sabbath follows from ὁ ἄνθρωπος/ Israel being made for the sabbath. Casey argues that behind ὁ υἱὸς τοῦ ἀνθρώπου is an idiomatic Aramaic phrase (בר אנש(א)) by which Jesus is

---

76. For instance, the Lord says to Ezekiel, when reminding the prophet of all he has done for the nation, "moreover I gave them my sabbaths, as a sign between me and them, so that they might know that I the Lord sanctify them" (20:12).

77. Hooker, *Son of Man*, 96. This is reflected in rabbinic thought as well: "The sabbath is given over to you and not you to the sabbath" (*m. Exod.* 109b). See, Lohse, "σάββατον," 14.

78. Collins, in her recent commentary, only refers to the creation account in her discussion on the background of v. 27 concluding that ὁ ἄνθρωπος is generic (*Mark*, 203). This is an inadequate interpretation because of how sabbath is understood in Jewish tradition and Jesus' use of v. 27 as a response to the Pharisees's accusation.

Chapter 4: The Son of Man's Divine Authority on Earth

referring to himself or a group of his compatriots.[79] In this reading, Jesus is deducing from the general principle of v. 27 that he and his disciples are lord or master of the Sabbath. Aside from Casey's often criticized methodology of reconstructing an Aramaic text from which he then interprets Mark, this is an underwhelming interpretation of a climactic statement of Jesus which essentially renders vv. 27 and 28 an instance of synonymous parallelism. Given the structural and thematic connections between this verse and v. 10, which I described above, this statement is not making a claim that applies solely to a certain segment of humanity.[80] Mark's ὁ υἱὸς τοῦ ἀνθρώπου has already demonstrated an "authority" that transcends mere humanity/Israel. Further, in this passage, Jesus is the one who leads his disciples, takes the criticism from the Pharisees elicited by the disciples's actions, and then makes a defense for them. A careful consideration of the phrase "lord of the sabbath" will make clear that the SM is Jesus who exercises, once again, an authority that is exclusively Yahweh's which drives home the point that ὁ υἱὸς τοῦ ἀνθρώπου is not a circumlocution for "man." It is quite unlikely that Mark is advocating that Israel herself is in a position of dominion over the sabbath, something which is clearly Yahweh's.[81]

Given that sabbath is under Yahweh's dominion, the designation κύριός might recall the "Lord/Yahweh" from the OT which becomes convincing when we see that terminology from v. 28, specifically, κύριός and τοῦ σαββάτου, echoes a series of passages from the Pentateuch which contain the phrase "a sabbath of/to Yahweh" expressing that the sabbath day belongs to Yahweh and is under his dominion.[82] This construction is evident in Exod 16:25: γὰρ σάββατα σήμερον τῷ κυρίῳ, 20:10: σάββατα κυρίῳ, Lev 23:3: σάββατά ἐστιν τῷ κυρίῳ, and Deut 5:14: σάββατα κυρίῳ. These terminological correspondences as well as the way they complement the thematic connection between the SM here and in v. 10, which the syntax of both verses already indicates, makes a convincing case that Mark's Jesus is echoing this often repeated construction—σάββατα κυρίῳ. While Mark is not ontologically identifying Jesus as Yahweh, his application of κύριός to him in this context reveals another prerogative of Yahweh that

---

79. Casey, *Solution*, 124; Ibid., "Culture and Historicity," 18–19.

80. Responding to those who argue that ὁ ἄνθρωπος and ὁ υἱὸς τοῦ ἀνθρώπου are synonymous, Hooker rightly points out that "it is difficult to see how the nation as a whole could be regarded as lord of the sabbath" (*Son of Man*, 97). See also, Gundry, *Mark*, 145.

81. France, *Mark*, 147.

82. Ibid., 147; Gundry, *Mark*, 148.

the SM now exercises. Already in 2:10, Jesus as the SM has done that which only Yahweh can by forgiving sins. We have also seen that key narratives in Mark 1 demonstrate that Jesus has a distinct relationship with Yahweh as his son and that he is at work through Jesus himself, and now, in v. 28, the SM exercises Yahweh's dominion over sabbath as "Lord of the Sabbath."

This coheres with a danielic understanding of the markan SM which I have argued is quite evident in 2:10 and now seems to extend to v. 28. In light of these two intertextual backgrounds, Dan 7 and a series of passages from the Pentateuch, the SM in v. 28 exercises Yahweh's authority over the sabbath day restoring it to its intended purpose as a day of blessing and restoration, which the Pharisees have undone. Yahweh has always intended that sabbath function for the good of Israel, that is, be subservient to the nation, as Jesus indicates in v. 27, *and so* (ὥστε) the SM, who possesses Yahweh's authority, is Lord also over the sabbath.[83] Although the absence of the term ἐξουσία weakens the *volume* of the danielic allusion in v. 28, the phrase "Lord of the sabbath," which Jesus uses to describe the SM's authority, suggests a thematic correspondence with the danielic figure. Essentially, the SM in v. 28 is another expression of the danielic SM's authority upon the earth first displayed in v. 10 and, therefore, is an allusion which effects a high degree of *thematic coherence* not only in both passages but also between them.[84] Regarding the latter—the SM forgiving sins—on the one hand, and restoring sabbath, on the other, both actions are specifically associated with Yahweh which the SM is now entitled to perform. The criterion of *recurrence* is also satisfied as we have two similar allusions to Dan 7 in close proximity with one another. Finally, the *historical probability* of this allusion is strong for the same reasons as it was in 2:10. The SM in both the *Parables* and *4 Ezra* behaves a lot like Yahweh: judging sinners and restoring the faithful in the former and destroying adversaries in the latter. The markan SM also executes prerogatives of Yahweh but just different ones.

Now that we have considered Jesus' two responses in turn, we now ask how they relate to each other. That is, how does the emphasis on David and his friends executing duties reserved for the temple priests in vv. 25–26 go together with his teaching on ὁ ἄνθρωπος and ὁ υἱὸς τοῦ ἀνθρώπου in vv. 27–28 so that both passages together form a coherent refutation of the

---

83. Gundry rightly argues that Jesus goes beyond the sentiment of v. 27 which is expressed by the conjunction ὥστε (*Mark*, 144).

84. Note also that these two verses correspond with one another syntactically, as I described earlier, which associate the SM's authority in v. 28 with that of v. 10.

Chapter 4: The Son of Man's Divine Authority on Earth

Pharisees? This is a reasonable and necessary question to ask in a narrative-critical treatment of Mark as I discussed in chapter 1. I have already established that, according to Jesus' narration, David and his companions carry out a task lawful only for the priests—consuming the bread of the presence. However, it is clear that the disciples are not consuming bread and are nowhere near the temple, but they do "work" on the sabbath, something which is likewise lawful only for the priests throughout the first- and second-temple periods. Further consideration of the bread of the presence might be the link that connects this story, as it is briefly recounted in vv. 25–26, with its narrative context. Technically, the temple priests's preparation of the bread on the sabbath (Lev 24:5–9; 1 Sam 21:6b) constitutes work that appears to breach sabbath law: "you are not to do any work; wherever you live, it is a sabbath to the Lord" (Lev. 23:3b).[85] However, in light of passages such as Lev 24:8, which reads, "every sabbath day Aaron shall set them [the loaves] in order before the Lord regularly as a commitment of the people of Israel, as a covenant forever," work is permitted in the tabernacle and, later, in the temple. In addition to preparing and arranging the bread on the sabbath, God commands Israel to present an additional burnt offering (Num 28:3–10). According to Bruce Chilton and Jacob Neusner, these temple activities only to be performed on the sabbath indicate that "what was not to be done outside of the Temple, in secular space, was required to be done in holy space, in the Temple itself."[86] Fletcher-Louis maintains that this work is acceptable because "the temple is a time and space with an ontology that transcends that of the world outside."[87] The priests, then, do not breach sabbath when preparing the sacred bread in the tabernacle/temple despite Yahweh's command that on the Sabbath "all work" (כָּל־מְלָאכָה, Lev. 23:3) is prohibited. This is not obscure, background information. Mark and his audience would be well aware of this as other authors subsequent to him reveal. In Matthew's account of this sabbath controversy, Jesus himself acknowledges that the work of the temple priests desecrates (βεβηλοῦσιν) the sabbath, but yet they remain guiltless (Matt 12:5). The rabbinic texts also acknowledge the unique status of the temple priests: *b. Šabb.* 132b; *m.*

---

85. For a helpful discussion of the "bread of the presence offering" (Lev 24:5–9), see Gane, "Bread," 179–203.

86. Chilton and Neusner, *Judaism,* 142. See also a similar assessment by Milgrom, *Leviticus 23–27,* 3:2099.

87. Fletcher-Louis, "High Priest," 44.

ʿ*Erub.* 10:11–5; *m. Pesaḥ.* 6:1–2. According to *b. Šabb.* 132b, "temple service takes precedence over the sabbath."

This is a crucial piece of background information which connects the priestly actions of David and his companions in vv. 25–26 as well as the statements about the SM and the sabbath in vv. 27–28 with the work the disciples are accused of doing on the sabbath. Just as David and his companions did that which was lawful only for the priests, consuming the bread of the presence, which Jesus emphasizes in v. 26, the disciples likewise do that which is lawful only for the priests, work on the sabbath, by virtue it would appear, of their connection to the authoritative SM who enables his disciples to be guiltless on this holy day. We know that through the pattern of distinction-yet-connection, evident in vv. 23–26, the disciples have a bond with Jesus, just as David did with his companions for whom David provided, a point that Jesus expresses in his account in v. 26b. Because of the SM, whose authority is incomparable with any other character thus far in Mark, his Lordship over the sabbath has direct implications for his followers. As "Lord also of the sabbath", the SM essentially redefines Torah, namely, the exemption which applies to the temple priests is now broadened and, consequently, the sabbath is restored for the good of Israel such that now the disciples can tend to human need with impunity. Because of the SM's dominion, doing work which is unlawful on the sabbath and heretofore permitted only in the temple and to be performed only by the priests, is now lawful for the disciples in his presence. This continues in the next scene, when Jesus himself as Lord of the sabbath takes center stage and works on this most holy day by healing a man with a withered hand (3:1–6).

Conclusion

This examination reveals that Mark, like the authors of the *Parables* and *4 Ezra*, has transformed the danielic SM from a passive symbol for faithful Israel to an active individual who utilizes the authority and dominion bequeathed to him in Dan 7 to execute prerogatives of Yahweh, not in heaven, but on earth. The close connection between the SM and Yahweh does not begin with the first appearance of the markan figure. The divine presence is already in Jesus in three key narratives in Mark 1. The first one, the baptism (vv. 9–11), reveals that the Spirit of Yahweh now indwells him. Accordingly, the last two demonstrate how Yahweh is now at work through his Son when he, as the "Holy One of God," casts out an unclean spirit (vv. 21–28)

Chapter 4: The Son of Man's Divine Authority on Earth

and then when he miraculously heals a leper by his contagious purity (vv. 40–45). Continuing this theme, the SM manifests Yahweh's divine authority first in his home in 2:1–10 and then in a Galilean grain field in 2:23–28. In the former, Jesus declares that a paralytic's sins are forgiven (v. 5) and then demonstrates that as the SM he has "authority on earth" to offer forgiveness by dramatically healing him. While many ponder a precedent for the connection between the SM and the forgiveness of sins, a consideration of the danielic SM's investiture of dominion and authority and how this figure is reinterpreted in similar ways in two first-century CE Jewish texts, the *Parables* and *4 Ezra*, reveals that the markan SM in his first two appearances is one who exercises Yahweh's prerogatives, not in heaven, but "on the earth."

In 2:28, two intertextual backgrounds come together—Dan 7 and a series of passages from the Pentateuch—in a complementary way expressing that the SM is exercising yet another prerogative of Yahweh: authority over the sabbath. Through this, Jesus repudiates a sabbath defined by onerous *halakhic* laws and restores it, as Yahweh intended, to be a day of restoration and blessing (see *Jubilees*). As Jesus himself says in v. 27, "the sabbath was made for man, not man for the sabbath" and it is apparent that the Pharisees had lost sight of this in their denunciation of the disciples's sabbath work for personal sustenance. An analysis of Jesus' creatively unrestrained account of 1 Sam 21:1–6 in its markan context, which focuses on an activity lawful only for the priests, reveals that the disciples likewise do that which is lawful only for the priests, in this case, work on the sabbath. The temple priests work without breaching the law because Yahweh has provided an exemption for those who carry out his ordained duties in the temple's sacred space. In his second response to the Pharisees, Jesus reminds them that sabbath serves the need of Israel as it was created for her benefit, and so the SM, who is endowed with Yahweh's authority in light of Dan 7, is also Lord of the sabbath and as such redefines the laws which safeguard its holiness so that those under his authority may do that which is lawful only for the priests, just as David and his companions had done centuries earlier. Those laws that once applied only to the priests now apply to his faithful followers who can now work on the sabbath to satisfy human need and enjoy the day as one made for the sake of the nation.

Chapter 5: The Son of Man's Suffering and Death

Introduction

AS WE HAVE SEEN, the first two SM sayings in Mark highlight his authority to engage in prerogatives of Yahweh which is evident in his ability to forgive sin and redefine sabbath law. This chapter examines another group of sayings that occur in the middle section of Mark in which Jesus teaches his disciples about the imminent suffering and rejection of the SM at the hands of the temple leaders in Jerusalem.[1] For Mark's audience, this should not be completely unexpected as Jesus refers to himself as the SM in the context of developing hostility in Mark 2. In both instances, Jesus responds with a statement about the SM to address accusations raised by the scribes in 2:6–7 and then by the Pharisees in 2:24. Mark has placed these sayings in two narratives that belong to a series of conflict stories beginning in 2:1 and ending in 3:6. Confrontation between Jesus and various religious leaders intensifies through each of the accounts climaxing with the desire of the Pharisees and Herodians to destroy him in 3:6.[2] Very early in Mark's Gospel, the teachings and miracles of Jesus, including the SM's demonstration of authority, are narrated in such a way that they will eventually prove fatal for Jesus himself, and specifically, as the second section of the Gospel reveals, for the SM (8:31; 9:31; 10:33–34) and potentially for his followers (8:34–37).

---

1. The three major sections in Mark are 1:14—8:21, 8:27—10:45, and 11:1—16:8. Cook suggests that the most notable breaks in the narrative occur at 8:27 and 11:1 (*Structure*, 17).

2. Kingsbury, *Conflict*, 67–72; Dewey, *Public*, 118–19.

CHAPTER 5: THE SON OF MAN'S SUFFERING AND DEATH

There are a number of studies on Mark's presentation of the Jewish leaders that indicate he has intentionally organized these characters to form an almost unified rejection of Jesus.³ The scribes, elders and chief priests, along with their scribal counterparts in Galilee, emerge as the dominant force who reject the SM (2:6-7; 8:31; 9:12, 31; 10:33-34, 45; 14:41).⁴ Michael J. Cook argues that Mark weaves the scribes, one component of the "Jerusalem triad," early into his narrative to connect the Galilean conflicts with the ultimate rejection of Jesus in Jerusalem by the "chief priests, elders, and scribes."⁵ On a literary level, then, Mark portrays the Galilean scribes and their Jerusalem counterparts united in their resistance toward Jesus; see especially 3:22 and 7:1 in which scribes come down from Jerusalem. Although literary-critical treatments of Mark's religious leaders rightly identify the Pharisees, Herodians, chief priests, scribes, elders, and Sadducees "as characters [united] by their active opposition to the Markan Jesus,"⁶ almost no attention has been given to the consistent predictions of the SM's rejection specifically by the temple leadership in the second half of Mark and the significance that this has for Mark's understanding of the SM (8:31; 9:12, 31; 10:33-34). For instance, Hooker claims that the SM will suffer if "men," whom she later generically labels "Jewish leaders," resist God and his agent.⁷ However, Jesus names the SM's adversaries as "the elders, the chief priests, and the scribes"—those specifically associated with the temple. In the last third of his Gospel, Mark refers to the chief priests more

---

3. Kingsbury, "Religious Authorities," 42-65; Ibid., *Conflict*, 63-88. Unfortunately, Kingsbury's generic, oft-repeated phrase, "religious leaders," to designate the differing groups of authorities in Mark renders his study less useful than it might have otherwise been. In the passion predictions, it is those specifically associated with the temple that reject the SM and so must be identified, as I am arguing, as the "temple leadership." The same is true for certain passages in Mark's third section when two or three members of the temple triumvirate plot Jesus' arrest and death (11:18, 27; 12:12; 14:1). See also Malbon, "Jewish Leaders," 259-81; Bond, "Caiaphas," 183-87. For historical considerations of Mark's religious leaders, see Cook, *Treatment*.

4. Mark 10:45 is included in this list because it is the climax and corollary of Jesus' predictions of the SM's suffering and death. For a detailed treatment of which temple leaders resist Jesus and where in Mark's text, see Malbon, "Jewish Leaders," 267-68.

5. Cook claims that Mark gained his knowledge of the scribes from a "special collection of scribe pericopae" (9:11-12a, 13ab; 12:28-34a [Cook incorrectly cites v. 18 instead of 28]; 12:35-45) (*Treatment*, 62-63).

6. Malbon, "Jewish Leaders," 270; Kingsbury, *Conflict*, 86-88.

7. Hooker, *Son of Man*, 109.

than any other group as the ones who reject Jesus, seek his arrest, and desire to condemn him to death all out of jealousy (see 15:10).[8]

In light of the foregoing, there may be a connection between the claims and actions of the SM in his first two appearances, which conceivably encroach upon the Jerusalem temple as I will suggest presently, and the predictions of his suffering at the hands of the temple leaders. In the narrative following 2:1–12, Jesus dines with "sinners and tax collectors" (v. 15) and Mark's audience learns that Jesus *has come* (ἦλθον) to call "sinners" (v. 17) which corresponds with the SM who *has come* (ἦλθεν) to provide the means by which they will be redeemed (10:45).[9] In this chapter, I will argue that the passion-resurrection predictions and the culminating statement in 10:45, along with a further explanation of the SM's service in 14:24, imply that his suffering, rejection, and death renders the temple cult redundant as a new covenant community is formed by Jesus' shed blood and not by the blood of animals. So the SM who forgives sins in 2:1–12 is a suitable introduction for the same one whose vocation is sacrificial service through the giving of his own life (10:45), all of which undermines the legitimacy of one of the major functions of the temple. As for 2:23–28, Mark may be hinting at a redefinition of the temple around the SM since work on the sabbath, heretofore permitted only for temple priests serving in the temple, is now permissible in his presence. I do realize that it is not the temple leaders who are the first ones to actually witness the SM's authority in 2:10 and 28, but Jerusalem scribes appear while Jesus is still in Galilee and level serious accusations against him on two occasions (3:22; 7:1) suggesting that his Galilean ministry poses a serious concern for these ones from the Holy City.

Predictions of the Son of Man's Suffering, Death, and Resurrection

The first prediction of the SM's passion and resurrection occurs at Caesarea Philippi, the locale from which Jesus begins his ominous journey to Jerusalem to face the fulfillment of that which he will predict. After asking the disciples who others say that he is and hearing a variety of responses (8:27–28), he directs the question to his disciples (v. 29a). Peter declares σὺ

---

8. Gundry, *Mark*, 431–32; Pesch, *Das Markusevangelium*, 1:51. See 8:31; 10:33; 11:18; 11:27; 14:1, 10, 55; 15:3, 10, 11.

9. France, *Mark*, 135.

Chapter 5: The Son of Man's Suffering and Death

εἰ ὁ χριστός (v. 29b) whereupon Jesus commands them to tell no one about him (v. 30). Then he begins to teach them that "the SM must (δεῖ) undergo great suffering (πολλὰ παθεῖν), and be rejected (ἀποδοκιμασθῆναι) by the elders, the chief priests, and the scribes, and be killed, and after three days rise again" which has the effect of qualifying for the disciples the type of messiah that he will be—a messiah who suffers.[10] Jesus' use of δεῖ expresses the divine necessity of his suffering and death, in other words, that this is God's will for the SM (see 14:36).[11] This idea is synonymous with the phrase "according to the Scriptures" or, as we will see later, "*how is it written* about the Son of Man" (9:12b; 14:21a).[12] France comments that "the basis for this 'necessity' (δεῖ) is not spelled out here, but in 9:12; 14:21, 49 it [the suffering] is traced explicitly to what 'is written', and the same thought surely underlies this and Jesus' other predictions of his passion."[13] Although there is no extant Jewish literature which speaks explicitly of a son of man who suffers, this passage and the following passion-resurrection predictions along with 10:45 reflects a pastiche of OT terminology and figures which Mark's Jesus draws together to indicate, with the same level of authority as an OT quotation (see 1:2–3), that it is God's will that he as the SM experience suffering and death. However, it is not uncommon to find scholars advocating one OT text or figure to the exclusion of others as that which provides *the* interpretative framework for the SM's lowly vocation, as I will discuss below.

As in 2:10 and 2:28, one clear piece of OT terminology is the SM phrase itself. However, there are a couple of significant difficulties with establishing an allusion to Dan 7 in this and the other predictions. First, there is no explicit lexical correspondence with the text of Dan 7 other than υἱὸς ἀνθρώπου in 8:31 whereas with 2:10 the term ἐξουσία is found in both Greek versions in close proximity to υἱὸς ἀνθρώπου (Dan 7:13–14).

---

10. Hooker, *Mark*, 203. Evans, *Mark*, 16. Gundry does not believe that the passion predictions are in any sense corrective teaching as the Gentile audience has no awareness of messianic nationalism but rather serve an apologetic purpose of "defanging the crucifixion of Jesus" (*Mark*, 503). However, if they are not corrective teaching, why would Mark include the ensuing controversy between Peter and Jesus in 8:32–33 which appears to suggest an incongruity between Jesus' affirmation that he is the messiah and the subsequent prediction of the SM's suffering?

11. Bolt, *Distance*, 49.

12. Ibid., 49, cites Smith, "Darkness," 332; Evans, *Mark*, 16. For a brief survey of debate surrounding δεῖ and γέγραπται, see Moo, *Old Testament in the Gospel*, 87 fn. 2.

13. France, *Mark*, 334.

Second, the "one like a son of man" does not appear to suffer in Daniel. He symbolizes the holy ones in vindication but not in suffering; for this reason, France argues that Dan 7 is not in the intertextual makeup of any of the passion-resurrection predictions.[14] Others, however, suggest that a link does exist on the basis of the persecuted "holy ones" with whom the SM is associated.[15] Hooker contends that when the figure first appears in v. 13, "he has not yet been glorified: his human form may mark him out as destined for dominion, but this has not yet been given to him, so that it would seem that the Son of man represents the saints of the Most High before their glorification as well as after."[16] As tempting as it is for me to adopt Hooker's reading because it coheres so well with my argument, it is very difficult to defend. Another possibility for linking the suffering of the markan SM with the danielic one is advanced by Watts. Although he argues that the isaianic servant is the key background of the SM's suffering, he proposes that the obverse side of the vindication of the SM, vis-à-vis, his suffering is implied in the vision of Dan 7: "Since the first four symbols in Dan 7 relate to both the success and downfall of their referents, it might be that the reader is being encouraged to bring the same 'reversal' paradigm to the fifth, i.e. the SoM, even if the emphasis lies on the SoM's exaltation."[17] This pattern is evident in the passion-resurrection predictions in which the markan SM will suffer and die but after three days will be raised from the dead which is a moment of vindication for one who was rejected and condemned to death by his adversaries. The problem still remains that the SM does not explicitly suffer in Daniel, but only the holy ones prior to the coming of the Ancient of Days. When he comes, he judges in their favor leading to their reception of the Kingdom as "one like a son of man" (see Dan 7:21–22). It is important to interpret Daniel on his terms and not on those of the Gospel tradition of which some proposals, such as Hooker's, are guilty.

There is another feature of the vision and its interpretation that Mark develops, along the same lines as the authors of the *Parables* and *4 Ezra*. While I am not attempting to draw exegetical conclusions in Mark's Gospel on the basis of what the authors of these texts have done, this material does

---

14. Ibid., 334. In a strongly worded statement, France contends that "it seems little short of perverse to look for a source of Jesus' passion-predictions in a passage [Dan 7] where suffering is not predicated of the Son of man" (*Old Testament*, 128).

15. Hooker, *Son of Man*, 108–9; Wright, *Victory*, 599; Barrett, "Background," 14; Schaberg, "Daniel 7, 12," 212.

16. Hooker, *Son of Man*, 28.

17. Watts, *New Exodus*, 260 fn. 152.

Chapter 5: The Son of Man's Suffering and Death

provide other instances of what I will propose Mark has done with Daniel 7 in the passion-resurrection predictions and hence satisfies the criterion of *historical probability*. I have argued in chapter 2 that the SM is a symbol for the saints of the Most High. Faithful Israel is relieved of her suffering when the Ancient of Days comes and they as "one like a son of man" receive authority, glory and power (see Dan 7:14, 27). We have also seen that in subsequent interpretations of the danielic figure in the *Parables* and *4 Ezra*, he is no longer a corporate symbol but an individual who performs tasks associated with Yahweh. However, in these texts, the SM is still related to the nation of Israel, in some way, which finds its basis in Dan 7, albeit there the relationship between the SM and faithful Israel is one of identity.[18] In the *Parables*, he is associated with the holy, righteous and chosen because he will one day save them. In a variety of instances, the terms "Righteous One" and "Chosen One" appear in tandem with "righteous ones" and "chosen ones." For example, at the great judgement, "the Righteous One appears in the presence of the righteous . . . and light appears to the righteous and chosen who dwell on earth" (38:2; see 38:3; 51:2) and in 45:3 "on that day, I shall make my Chosen One dwell among them . . . and I shall transform the earth and make it a blessing. And my chosen ones I shall make to dwell on it, but those who commit sin and error will not set foot on it" (45:4a, 5b; see 40:5).[19] According to Kvanvig, the Chosen One is a heavenly representative and as such the text "indicates the common fate of the Chosen One and the chosen ones, and identifies the Chosen One as a warrant for the salvation of the chosen ones."[20] Although the term SM is not mentioned in the above passages, SM, Righteous One, and Chosen One are interchangeable referring to the same figure as a number of scholars recognize.[21] Further, the SM is a "staff for the righteous," "a light for the Gentiles," and "the hope of those who are sick in their hearts" (48:4). The "wisdom of the Lord of Spirits"

---

18. See Hooker, *Jesus and the Servant*, 145.

19. Manson makes the dubious claim that the appearance of the titles, "the Elect One," "the Righteous One," and the "Anointed One" in tandem with "the (my) Righteous Ones" and "the (my) Elect Ones" indicates that the singular terms are in fact plural designations (*Teaching of Jesus*, 228). This, however, is to read too much of Daniel into the *Parables* because the SM, as I have established in chapter 3, is clearly distinct from the earthly righteous, chosen, and holy whom he will one day deliver. It is important to realize, however, there is still a strong association between the two.

20. Kvanvig, "Son of Man," 188.

21. Chialà, "Son of Man," 161; Kvanvig, "Son of Man," 188; VanderKam, "Righteous One," 185.

reveals the SM "to the righteous and holy ones" (48:7a), and the persecuted righteous and chosen ones "with that son of man they will eat, and they will lie down and rise up forever and ever" (62:14b). When the adversaries of the earthly faithful ones see the SM, they shall at that point be judged (62:5–6), but also at that time "the congregation of the chosen and the holy will be sown; and all the chosen will stand in his presence on that day" (62:8; see 53:6). Whereas in Daniel the SM was a symbol for the "holy ones," an association between the SM and the faithful continues in the *Parables* in which he will secure their eschatological salvation and overthrow their adversaries.[22] The SM in *4 Ezra* is also associated with a faithful group. After coming down from the mountain, he calls and gathers to himself a "multitude that was peaceable" (13:12) that is composed of those who are joyful, sorrowful, bound, and of those who bring others as "offerings" (13:13a). All of these are likely victims of the oppressors destroyed by the SM, and now their deliverance has come.[23]

What is clear in these texts is that the SM is connected with faithful Israel. Similarly, in Mark's Gospel, the suffering of the SM is not limited to Jesus himself but implicates the disciples. After Peter takes no small issue with Jesus' predictions that the SM will suffer much (vv. 32–33), he then calls his disciples to likewise participate in his impending fate: "If any want to become my followers, let them deny themselves and take up their cross and follow me. For those who want to save their life will lose it, and those who lose their life for my sake, and for the sake of the gospel, will save it. For what will it profit them to gain the whole world and forfeit their life? Indeed, what can they give in return for their life" (vv. 34a–37)? The only intertextual background that reflects an association between the SM and a group of faithful ones is Dan 7 in which the figure symbolizes the latter. Mark modifies this, of course, as he has done with the SM in 2:10 and 28, so that the he is more than a symbol now being distinct from the nation as an individual figure, just as is the case in the *Parables* and *4 Ezra*. However, a connection is still maintained as the SM's plight and experiences have implications for his disciples. Later, in our examination of the future SM sayings, we will see that the resurrection of the SM, which Jesus clearly predicts, also directly affects the disciples and other faithful followers. These

---

22. Chialà, "Son of Man," 161.

23. Myers, *1 and 11 Esdras*, 314. Stone argues that the "sorrowful" are the Gentiles but there is nothing in the vision or in the interpretation that suggests this (13:39–50) (*Fourth Ezra*, 387).

Chapter 5: The Son of Man's Suffering and Death

passion-resurrections predictions are a knife which cuts both ways: just as the SM will experience suffering and rejection at the hands of his enemies, so will those who seek to follow him (see 13:9–13) and just as he will be resurrected after three days, so the disciples will gather to meet him in Galilee, but more on this latter point anon.

This proposed link with Dan 7 is also evident earlier in the Gospel. We have already seen that the authority of the SM has implications for his followers in 2:23–28 in which the exercise of Yahweh's dominion over sabbath by the SM leads to a redefining of sabbath law so that now the exemption which applies to the priests enabling them to work without guilt now applies to the disciples. The solidarity between the SM/Jesus and the disciples at which Mark hints in this passage is evident in the appointment of twelve apostles. In 3:15, Jesus prepares to send them out to preach and to have ἐξουσία to cast out demons. As many scholars recognize, Jesus' calling of twelve is symbolic given that Israel was originally constituted as a nation of twelve tribes. For Jesus to call twelve indicates that he is about the business of restoring the nation around himself as true and faithful Israel (see LXX Isa 49:5–6; 11QTa LVII, 2–15).[24] Mark tells his audience that Jesus went up on a mountainside to appoint them which echoes the Mount Sinai event where Israel became a nation (3:13; see Exod 19—20). The bestowal of authority on Jesus' followers is reminiscent of the danielic "holy ones of the Most High" (TH: ἁγίοις ὑψίστου/LXX: λαῷ ἁγίῳ ὑψίστου (7:27) who also receive "authority." Prior to the calling of the twelve, the term ἐξουσία has been only a characteristic of Jesus and the SM (1:22, 27; 2:10) but has had implications for the disciples in the last SM saying in 2:23–28. Now, he is conferring it upon them, ἔχειν ἐξουσίαν ἐκβάλλειν τὰ δαιμόνια, an activity heretofore exclusive to Jesus himself (see 1:25, 34, 39; 3:11–12).[25] When he sends the disciples out, Mark indicates that ἐδίδου αὐτοῖς ἐξουσίαν τῶν πνευμάτων τῶν ἀκαθάρτων (6:7). In light of the SM's authority demonstrated in 2:10 and 28, Mark's use of ἐξουσία in 3:15 and later in 6:7 becomes significant in light of Dan 7. That is, an evocation of Dan 7 highlights the unique bond that is developing between Jesus and the disciples at this early point in Mark. Since we only have this one lexical correspondence with Dan 7 in 3:15 and 6:7, satisfaction of the criterion of *volume* is weak, but when we consider the unstated correspondence among these passages as well as 2:23–28, this proposed reading reveals a high degree of *thematic*

---

24. Wright, *Victory*, 300; Collins, *Mark*, 216.
25. France, *Mark*, 160.

Daniel's Son of Man in Mark

coherence—the authority of the SM is not limited to Jesus himself, just as in Dan 7 the exalted SM and those whom he symbolizes both have authority. Many years ago, Moule insightfully noted that it is misguided to limit one's investigation of the danielic background of the SM to the occurrences of the phrase itself: "one has to take into account also the passages where other features in the Danielic scene are recalled, even without the phrase."[26] This is one of those places where a fruitful reading results. Mark 3:15 and 6:7, when read in light of Dan 7, highlight the solidarity between Jesus and his faithful followers who have obediently responded to his call in 3:13 and, prior to this, followed him through the grain field. This close association continues in the second section of Mark in which Jesus invites the disciples to share in his plight of suffering, which is a relinquishment of authority, following each of the passion-resurrection predictions (8:34–37, 9:35–37, and 10:39b–44).

My proposal is inspired by a slightly different version advanced by T. W. Manson some sixty years ago but is quite instructive for perceiving the close connection between the SM and the disciples in the passion-resurrection sayings. In his study, *The Teaching of Jesus*, he argued that the notion of a "saving remnant" is fundamental to a more complete understanding of the gospel.[27] The SM in the Gospels, for Manson, is one such instance of remnant theology and as such is "an ideal figure and stands for the manifestation of the Kingdom of God on earth in a people wholly devoted to their king."[28] A problem arises, however, when he foists this on the Gospel SM by arguing that he is a symbol for faithful Israel as in Dan 7. This is overdrawn because the markan figure is clearly a distinct individual in keeping with subsequent, first-century interpretations.[29] When it comes to the passion-resurrection

---

26. Moule, *Origin*, 21.

27. Manson rightly bases his understanding of the remnant on the concept that Israel is Yahweh's chosen nation and as such he commands unwavering devotion to him (*Teaching of Jesus*, 175). However, "as the standard of loyalty and obedience is raised, the number of people who may be expected to attain it decreases. It ceases to be an ideal for the nation and becomes an ideal for an elect few within the nation. So the doctrine of the Remnant emerges."

28. Ibid., 227.

29. Manson recognizes this as a potential difficulty because of the SM in the *Parables* and *4 Ezra* who is a "personal Messiah" (*Teaching of Jesus*, 228). His defence that the titles "Elect One," "Righteous One," "Anointed One" and "Son of Man" are all ways of referring to the nation is indefensible because the titles refer to an individual in the text. Nonetheless, others have supported Manson's unqualified corporate reading. See, for example, Moule, *Origin*, 16 and Dodd, *According to the Scriptures*, 96.

Chapter 5: The Son of Man's Suffering and Death

predictions, Manson rightly indicates that Jesus calls his disciples to participate in his fate. While many recognize this, not least because it is self-evident in the text, not many relate the call to Jesus' role as the SM. Hooker, however, recognizes the connection in her comment: "It was to the twelve that Jesus explained what lay before the Son of man, and once again the term 'Son of man' is clearly associated with the disciples, and could even be interpreted as including them: the destiny of the Son of man extends beyond Jesus himself to those who follow him."[30] After each of Jesus' three predictions in 8:31, 9:31, and 10:33-34, the disciples respond with incomprehension (8:32-33; 9:32; 10:35-41), followed by his invitation to follow the way of suffering and service (8:34-37; 9:35-37; 10:39b-44). Hooker is correct: what is true for the suffering SM should also be the case for those who profess to be his followers, as is the case with the authoritative SM earlier. In the end, Jesus is the only one who suffers because the disciples have chosen to save their lives instead of lose them in the moment of crisis (14:43-50), but they will still be the beneficiaries of his sacrificial death which preserves the connection between the SM's suffering and his followers.

As I have mentioned above and as others have recognized, there are a few OT texts and figures that are at play in 8:31 in addition to the danielic background. When we consider the terminology of v. 31, a number of possible backgrounds emerge. To begin, there are those who argue for the servant of Yahweh from Isa 53 on the basis of πολλὰ παθεῖν.[31] For Watts, the verb חָלָה is important because its root is used three times in Isa 53, v.3: חֳלִי (infirmity), v.4: חֲלָיֵנוּ (infirmities), v. 10: הֶחֱלִי (to make sick) which parallels the notion of πάσχω. The difficulty with this view is that in the LXX, חָלָה is not translated as πάσχω, but rather μαλακίαν in v. 3, τὰς ἁμαρτίας in v. 4, and τῆς πληγῆς in v. 10. However, as we will see, there are explicit terminological correspondences with Isa 53 in 9:31, 10:45, and 14:24 leaving only a thematic parallel in 8:31 with the servant, which is still important.

Other studies consider the stories of the maccabean martyrs in which the term πάσχω actually appears. In 2 Macc 7:18, just before the sixth of the seven martyrs undergoes torture and eventual death for refusing to eat

---

30. Hooker, *Son of Man*, 139. Hooker makes a concluding statement that this could be related to the corporate status of the danielic SM but does not develop the idea as I have here. See also Schaberg, "Daniel 7, 12," 217.

31. Watts, *New Exodus*, 265; Ibid., "Jesus' Death," 125-51. See also France, *Mark*, 335; Ibid., *Old Testament*, 125-28; Lane, *Mark*, 300. For a seminal work on the servant background of the passion-resurrection predictions, consult Jeremias, *Menschensohn-Logien*," 167.

swine, he exclaims to the king: "Do not deceive yourself in vain. For we are suffering (πάσχομεν) these things on our own account, because of our sins (ἁμαρτόντες) against our own God" (see 7:32). This recalls the "servant" who bears the "iniquity" (LXX: τὰς ἁμαρτίας) of the nation (Isa 53:11). This movement is evident in 4 Maccabees in which πάσχω also expresses the suffering of faithful Israel at the hands of her adversaries (4:25; 10:10).[32] A bit later, in the same writing, Eleazar's suffering leads to redemption: "Be merciful to your people, and let our punishment (δίκη) suffice for them (ὑπὲρ αὐτῶν). Make my blood (τὸ ἐμὸν αἷμα) their purification (καθάρσιον), and take my life (τὴν ἐμὴν ψυχήν) in exchange for theirs (ἀντίψυχον αὐτῶν)" (6:28-29; see 17:21-23). The term καθάρσιον recalls the suffering of the wise/holy ones in Dan 11:35 and 12:10: "Some of the wise shall fall, so that they may be refined, purified (LXX: καθαρίσαι), and cleansed, until the time of the end" (11:35a). Wright claims that "in Dan 12, as in 4 Macc ... we are witnessing the transference to the sphere of human suffering a theology which properly, or at least originally, belongs within the world of Temple and cult."[33] This transference begins with the sacrificial suffering of the servant of Isa 53 where he bears iniquities as opposed to animal sacrifice providing redemption.

Caution must be exercised with studies that prioritize one OT background over another as seen in the attempt of Watts, for example, to determine *the* background of πάσχω. This is supported not least by the allusive nature of Mark's use of the OT.[34] Although I would not endorse the following assertion of Tom Hatina for every instance of Mark's use of the OT, I think that it does describe the way Mark evokes the OT in his passion-resurrection predictions: "if Mark is taken seriously as narrative art, a search for *the* meaning and hence *the* echo, is reductionistic because it potentially excludes other layers of meaning which would have been open to the earliest audiences (and should remain open to the modern literary critic)."[35]

---

32. According to Hengel, 4 Maccabees dates from the first or even second century CE which needs to temper considerations of its usefulness as a background source for Mark, but it at least it provides a trajectory for the usage of πάσχω (*Atonement*, 4). Recently, however, Nickelsburg suggests the period between 20 and 54 CE due to the reference to Apollonius as "governor of Syria, Phoenicia, and Cilicia" (4:2), the period when Cilicia and Syria shared the same Roman administration (*Jewish Literature*, 258).

33. Wright, *Victory*, 585.

34. See, for example, the discussion in Kee, "Function of Scripture," 166. See also Watts, *New Exodus*, 259.

35. Hatina, "Embedded Scripture Texts," 147.

Chapter 5: The Son of Man's Suffering and Death

Instead of favoring one Hebrew root, for example, as in the arguments of Watts, particularly when there is clearly no verbal correspondence between Mark 8:31 and the LXX of Isa 53, πολλὰ παθεῖν likely has a composite background which includes, on a conceptual level, the servant of Yahweh and the maccabean martyrs (see 2 Maccabees). Although 4 Maccabees does not inform Mark's understanding of πολλὰ παθεῖν due to its late date, it is valuable because the writing attests to the movement of redemption deriving from the temple's sacrificial system to that effected by human suffering. In Mark, then, this phrase points to the idea that redemption is to be found in the suffering of the SM, which will become clearer in our study of 10:45 and 14:24 below.

Jesus also predicts that the SM "will be rejected" (ἀποδοκιμασθῆναι) by the elders, chief priests and the scribes. In the LXX of Jeremiah, Peter G. Bolt observes that this verb refers to God's rejection of Israel for her sin and corruption (6:30; 7:29; 14:19).[36] For instance, the prophet receives this word from the Lord because of Judah's unfaithfulness: "Shear your head, and throw away, and take a lamentation on your lips because the Lord has discarded and rejected (ἀπεδοκίμασεν) the generation that did these things" (NETS: 7:29). This is not unrelated to the maccabean martyrs, albeit over three centuries later, who suffer as a result of "their sins" (2 Macc 7:18) and the servant who is "despised and rejected by others; a man of suffering and acquainted with infirmity" (Isa 53:3b; see v. 4). This jeremianic background also supports the idea, as in Isa 53 and the maccabean writings, that Mark's SM is now being rejected for the sin of the nation and hence experiences God's judgement. To deal with Israel's sin is why the SM has *come* (10:45; see 2:17). However, Mark is most likely not consciously alluding to these texts but rather he is echoing a series of texts, including Jeremiah, which furnish his mind on the theme of suffering rejection for sin.

Ps 118 is one background text that deserves careful consideration because Jesus concludes his parable about the wicked tenants in Mark 12 with a quotation of Ps 118 [LXX 117]: 22–23 in which ἀποδοκιμάζω also occurs. Further, the ones who reject the SM in 8:31 and then the stone in 12:10 are clearly the leaders in charge of the temple. As I will demonstrate below, this is one of the most insightful and relevant OT passages which points to a specific dimension of the SM's rejection that dovetails with the sacrificial significance of his death which Jesus will explain in 10:45 and 14:24.[37] This

---

36. Bolt, *Cross*, 50–51.
37. Amongst those who favour Ps 118:22, see Moo, *Passion*, 89; Watts, *New Exodus*,

Psalm was sung by a king triumphant in battle who praises Yahweh for his faithfulness (118:5–18). In v. 19, the warrior king requests to enter the temple and then proclaims, "the stone that the builders rejected has become the chief cornerstone" (v. 22). Wright suggests that in vv. 19–27 the focus is on temple-building, which corresponds to the ancient pattern of temples being established for kings who are victorious in battle and, hence, the king in the Psalm becomes the "chief cornerstone."[38] In Wright's words, Ps 118:19-27 "is all about building the Temple, celebrating the Temple, and ultimately sacrificing in the Temple."[39] This last statement of Wright overdraws the significance of the temple. Rather, the focus is on the return of the king to the temple who came perilously close to destruction save for the faithfulness of Yahweh.[40] The imagery of the king becoming the chief cornerstone, which was a stone once rejected, describes his restoration and vindication, which in the context of the Psalm does not describe temple building *per se*. Mark's placement of this quotation on the heels of a parable which denounces the temple leaders and whose vineyard will be given to others does, however, suggest that some type of temple building might be in view as far as Mark's appropriation of the text is concerned (v. 9b). Although Mark uses ἀποδοκιμάζω in 8:31 to describe the SM's rejection, we will see that there is an implicit note of promise and hope in this ominous prediction because his rejection has a temple-building significance, in light of the quotation of Ps 118 [LXX 117]: 22-23 in the parable, which coheres with the redemptive implications of his suffering and eventual death which he describes in 10:45 and 14:24. This proposed evocation of Ps 117:22 in Mark 12:10 and, by implication, 8:31 establishes a high degree of *thematic coherence* between the two passages both of which center on the rejection of Jesus and that which results from it.

Although the parable in 12:1–8 alludes to Isaiah's song of the vineyard in Isa 5:1-7, there is less concern in Mark with the vineyard itself but rather with the tenants who are hoarding its produce to the point of killing the owner's slaves and even his son. The slaves represent Israel's prophets who have almost continually been rejected by the religious establishment and

---

265; Evans, *Mark*, 17; Gundry, *Mark*, 446; Hooker, *Son of Man*, 114; Pesch, *Das Markusevangelium*, 2:50.

38. Wright, *Victory*, 498.
39. Ibid., 498.
40. See Kraus, *Psalms*, 399–400.

Chapter 5: The Son of Man's Suffering and Death

the now the son experiences the same.[41] For Mark, the tenants/temple leaders will soon face destruction whereupon the owner/Yahweh will give the vineyard to others, likely referring to a new leadership devoted to Jesus.[42] In Isa 5:7, the vineyard symbolizes the nation of Israel, which is still the case in Mark, despite attempts by some to link the vineyard with the temple.[43] At some future point, God will entrust the nation to those who are devoted to Jesus Messiah, but as we have seen in the calling of the twelve, this is a redefined nation, a new Israel. After having been a rejected stone, which parallels the rejected son, Jesus will become the vindicated cornerstone of this faithful nation at his resurrection (v. 10).[44] Mark, as is the case in Peter's sermon in Acts 4:11, uses this quotation to speak of the suffering, rejection and eventual resurrection of Jesus.[45] In contrast, Craig A. Evans contends that it is simply referring to vindication after rejection. In his opinion, interpretations that claim that Mark's Jesus is speaking of his crucifixion and resurrection in v. 10 is "to read a post-Easter nuance into the meaning of the quotation."[46] In my opinion, this is a needlessly flat reading especially because the temple builders who reject the stone, parallel the wicked tenants in the parable who kill the son, ultimately pointing to the temple leaders's complicity in effecting Jesus' sentence of death in Mark 15.[47] Also, there is little else in the Gospel narrative that could be considered vindication, which follows from rejection, suffering, and death, other than resurrection.

Further reflection on the imagery of Jesus as a capstone in v. 10 provides more insight into this restored nation, namely, that it will be a new temple community because of the application of temple architecture or language associated with the temple to Jesus.[48] This is a theme that will come up again in the false accusation in which Jesus allegedly predicted that

---

41. Wright, *Victory*, 498; Collins, *Mark*, 547.

42. Collins, *Mark*, 547; Evans, *Mark*, 237.

43. See, for instance, Gray, *Temple*, 62–63 and Wardle, *Jerusalem Temple*, 187–88.

44. There is little evidence to know for certain whether κεφαλὴν γωνίας refers to a base stone or a capstone at the top of a structure but it is a moot point as the metaphorical meaning is clear—Jesus will be in a position of prominence. See France, *Mark*, 463.

45. Collins, *Mark*, 549; Hooker, *Mark*, 276–77.

46. Evans, *Mark*, 228.

47. As a number of scholars recognize, the connection between the son and the stone is strengthened with the consonance of the Aramaic or Hebrew terms בן and אבן, which would likely be lost on Gentile Greek speaking Christians.

48. See Wright, *Victory*, 499–501, Kim, "Jesus – The Son of God," 135–38, Heil, "Narrative Strategy," 59–60, and Marcus, *Way of the Lord*, 121.

he would "destroy this temple that is made with hands, and in three days ... build another, not made with hands" (14:58). The notion of a temple composed not of bricks and mortar but rather faithful ones is clearly paralleled in the Qumran literature. The *Rule of the Community* uses the phrase "precious cornerstone" (פנת יקר, 1QS VIII, 7), along with other temple terminology, in its description of the community as a metaphorical temple. Further, Mark's placement of the quotation and what it connotes about the construction of a non-physical temple coheres well with the parable which expresses that the keepers of the physical temple will soon meet their end for treachery.[49] Likewise, when Jesus overturns the tables of the money changers denouncing the temple as a σπήλαιον λῃστῶν when it should be οἶκος προσευχῆς in Mark 11, the future of the temple becomes quite uncertain particularly in light of the cursing of the fig tree which brackets this episode (11:13–14, 20–21).[50] Tracing temple-themes throughout Mark 11 and into 12, Francis J. Moloney comments that "the traditional way to God, by means of the temple cult, has been brought to an end (11:12–21), and faith, prayer, and forgiveness provide a new way to God (11:22–25). But there is also to be a new temple, and the cornerstone of that temple is the *rejected* beloved Son of God [emphasis mine]."[51] It is little wonder that the chief priests, scribes and elders realize "that he had told this parable against them" (v. 12a) and that they now seek to arrest him (v. 12b) as Jesus has predicted the abolishment of their oversight of the nation and has hinted at the construction of something new which does not involve them.[52] It is not unwarranted to read into 8:31 the more developed significance of ἀποδοκιμάζω from 12:10 because the SM, who is the object of the temple

---

49. Mark's appendage of Ps 118:22 to the end of the parable might be an example of the rabbinical *nimshal*, a citation of Scripture, placed at the conclusion of a *mashal*, a parable, to accord the latter with scriptural authority. See Wardle for the secondary literature he cites (*Jerusalem Temple*, 185 fn. 69).

50. Wardle insightfully argues that Jesus is condemning both temple leaders and the institution itself in 11:15–18, in response to those scholars who argue that Jesus' primary target are the overseers (*Jerusalem Temple*, 175). See also Watts, *New Exodus*, 328–29 and France, *Mark*, 437.

51. Moloney, *Mark*, 234. See also, Collins, *Mark*, 548.

52. Gnilka, *Das Evangelium*, 2:15; Pesch, *Das Markusevangelium*, 2:51; Wardle, *Jerusalem Temple*, 189. Marcus appeals to a rabbinic text, *m. Cant.* 1:5 to argue that the "builders" in v. 10 are specifically the scribes (*Way*, 124). Despite the dubious methodology of allowing a rabbinic text to inform one's interpretation of the "builders," Mark clearly indicates that Jesus told the parable (12:1–10) against them, that is, the chief priests, scribes, and elders who confront him in 11:27.

Chapter 5: The Son of Man's Suffering and Death

leaders's rejection as predicted in 8:31, will become, figuratively, the most important aspect of the new temple's architecture—the chief cornerstone—when he is raised from the dead after his suffering and death. This term is a "verbal thread" for Mark's listening audience that links 8:31 with the parable and would help them realize that vindication will come following his rejection![53]

The next prediction of the SM's suffering and resurrection occurs while three disciples and Jesus descend the mountain upon which he is transfigured. These SM sayings, in 9:9 and 12, are unlike the similarly structured passion-resurrection predictions of 8:31, 9:31 and 10:33–34 each of which belong to coherent literary units. In the first saying, Jesus warns the three not to tell anyone about what they have seen until the SM has risen from the dead (v. 9). The injunction indicates some type of connection between what has happened on the mountain with the SM's resurrection. According to Marcus Öhler, the command to silence protects Jesus from the rest of his disciples making known that he is the Son of God to "die Öffentlichkeit" which Yahweh declares only to three of them (v. 7).[54] However, not to diminish the importance of what they have heard, Jesus does emphasize that the disciples are not to tell *what they have seen* (ἃ εἶδον) until the SM has risen from the dead, which would entail describing the luminescent appearance of his clothes, the presence of Moses and Elijah, and a cloud which settles upon the mountain from which comes the voice of Yahweh (vv. 2b–7).[55] Given the context in which this injunction occurs, Jesus does not want this prefiguring of his glory to detract from the call of suffering and rejection he, as the SM, extends to his followers.[56] As we have seen following 8:31, and will see after each passion-resurrection predic-

---

53. For a short but helpful discussion on the literary value of verbal threads in Mark, see Rhoads et al., *Mark as Story*, 47–48. Evans comments that the quotation of Ps 118:22 in Mark 12:10 connects 8:31 with the location of the prediction's fulfilment, Jerusalem, where Jesus tells the parable (*Mark*, 17). I think the association needs to be pressed further.

54. Öhler, *Elia im Neuen Testament*, 41; Kim, *The 'Son of Man'*, 1.

55. Kee argues that Jesus' clothing, which undergo a supernatural whitening, is inspired by Moses' face which shone radiantly after his encounter with Yahweh on Sinai (Exod 34:29) ("Transfiguration in Mark," 143). This allusion finds support in the appearance of the cloud and the voice that comes from it in v. 7 which recalls the way in which God spoke to Moses while on Mount Sinai (see Exod 24:15–17). For more on this, see France, *Mark*, 355; Hooker, *Mark*, 218; Chilton, "Transfiguration," 641; Zeller, "Bedeutung," 312.

56. France, *Mark*, 356.

tion in 9:31 and 10:33–34, the disciples do not understand the nature of Jesus' messiahship and that they must embrace a cruciform vocation. In the meantime, however, a select few are given a foretaste of his glory and exaltation, but suffering must come first.

Not understanding "what the rising from the dead could mean," the disciples discuss the issue amongst themselves (9:10). They are specifically talking about the SM's rising from the dead, not just a general resurrection, which is apparent in the disciples's question in v. 11.[57] Jesus' first prediction in 8:31 that the SM will be resurrected from the dead in a very short period of time, "after three days," appears to be at odds in their minds with the scribal teaching about Elijah: "why do the scribes say that Elijah must come first" (v. 11)? In some 2TJ texts, resurrection is associated with the dawning of a new age and does not refer to an individual resurrected in the current age.[58] In light of this, the disciples could be confused because they perceive that Jesus will be resurrected within history and Elijah has not yet come.[59] Jesus responds with a statement and then a question of his own, which for many interpreters introduces additional confusion: "Elijah is indeed coming first to restore all things. How then is it written about the Son of Man, that he is to go through many sufferings and be treated with contempt (v. 12)? Öhler comments that Elijah coming first "to restore all things" (ἀποκαθιστάνει πάντα) alludes to Mal 4:6 [LXX: 3:23] in which the prophet will restore familial relationships (3:23: ἀποκαταστήσει).[60] Further references to his preparatory work are seen in Mal 4:5: the sending of Elijah precedes the "great and terrible day of the Lord" and in 3:1: Elijah "prepares the way before me" in which he is to make Israel ready for the Lord's coming to his temple who will draw near in judgement (3:5). He does so by purifying the Levites (v. 3) until they offer pleasing sacrifices (v. 4). Then the presence of the Lord will return (v. 7). Sirach 48:10 also refers to Elijah who will restore (καταστῆσαι) not just the tribe of Levi as in Mal 3:3 but all the tribes of Jacob. It is not until the next verse, v. 13, that Jesus clarifies that Elijah has in fact already come (Ἠλίας ἐλήλυθεν).[61]

---

57. Gundry claims that the τί is anaphoric and refers to the Son of Man's rising from the dead (*Mark*, 463).

58. For two very helpful discussions on resurrection in ancient Judaism and how Christ's resurrection relates to 2TJ thought, see Brown and Coenen, "Resurrection," 259–79 and Wright, *Resurrection*, 85–208.

59. France, *Mark*, 357; Collins, *Mark*, 428.

60. Öhler, *Elia*, 42.

61. Elijah himself is not unacquainted with resistance and hardship which is evident

CHAPTER 5: THE SON OF MAN'S SUFFERING AND DEATH

In Mark, the preparatory work of Elijah manifests itself in the preaching and deeds of John the Baptist, whose clothing recalls the ninth-century prophet (1:6, see 2 Kgs 1:8).[62] In light of Mark's conflated quotation of Mal 3:1 and Exod 20:23 in 1:2, it is John, a returned Elijah, who prepares the Lord's way. In preparing the way, "all" the country of Judea and "all" the people of Jerusalem respond to Elijah-John's proclamation of a baptism of repentance *for the forgiveness of sins* (1:4–5) which most likely accounts for Jesus' statement that Elijah restores "all things" in 9:12.[63] Not everyone heeds Elijah-John's call to a baptism of repentance. Although King Herod "liked to listen to John," he made an oath with the daughter of Herodias to have him beheaded (6:17–29). In his coming to restore all things, Elijah-John encounters rejection which could explain the seemingly unrelated, subsequent question that Jesus poses in 9:12b (compared with the statement in 9:12a that Elijah has come first) about the SM who will πολλὰ πάθῃ and ἐξουδενηθῇ. In 9:13, it becomes clear how the two parts of the verse relate: the SM's suffers because Elijah-John has suffered too: "Elijah has come, and they did to him whatever they pleased, as it is written about him" (9:13).[64] Just like Elijah-John, Jesus as the SM will experience suffering and rejection but through this will complete the task which John began by establishing a new people of God.[65]

In 9:12, the terms πολλὰ πάθῃ and ἐξουδενηθῇ clearly recall the SM's plight in 8:31 who will πολλὰ παθεῖν and ἀποδοκιμασθῆναι by the elders, scribes, and chief priests. As I have argued there, the phrase "suffer much" has a composite background recalling the isaianic servant and the maccabean martyrs whose deaths serve a redemptive purpose and this same intertextual background should apply here as well. The term ἐξουδενηθῇ has the same meaning as ἀποδοκιμασθῆναι which occurs in 8:31, although

---

in his dealings with Ahab and Jezebel in 1 Kgs 19:2–14.

62. To claim as Gundry does that Elijah-John cannot be viewed as the restorer of all things because he clearly did not do so, i.e., he himself was imprisoned and killed, is to miss Mark's use of hyperbole in 9:12, just as "all" the region of Judea and the city of Jerusalem did not submit to John's baptism (1:5) (*Mark*, 484). Rather, John's work of restoration is preparatory as is evident in Mark 1:7–8.

63. Brower, "Elijah," 87. In light of the preparatory work of John as Elijah in 1:2–5, the assertion of Marcus that "Mark does not see John the Baptist/Elijah as a restorer" is the result of erroneously concentrating only on 9:11–13 for Mark's understanding of John (*Way*, 99 fn. 26).

64. Öhler, *Elia*, 44–45; France, *Mark*, 358; Evans, *Mark*, 44.

65. Collins, *Mark*, 432.

it is more difficult to argue that Ps 117:22 is in the background since it does not occur in the LXX version of the Psalm. However, Gundry suggests that ἐξουδενέω is "a non-Septuagintal alternative to ἀποδοκιμάζω."[66] This becomes especially compelling when one considers Acts 4:11 in which Ps 117:22 is quoted using ἐξουδενέω instead of ἀποδοκιμάζω.[67] If indeed these two terms are interchangeable, Mark's Jesus may once again be alluding to the temple-building effects of the SM's rejection in 9:12, which becomes apparent in light of the function of Ps 117:22 at the conclusion of the parable of the wicked tenants. However, in the absence of ἀποδοκιμάζω, this proposal remains only a possibility.

The influence of Dan 7 on the saying about the SM's resurrection in v. 9 and his suffering and rejection in v. 12, in contrast with the other SM passages I have examined thus far, is quite minimal. Unlike 8:31, 9:31 and 10:33–34, these two SM sayings, although very much related to the three predictions, do not teach about the suffering and resurrection of the SM in same way. That is, there is not any subsequent teaching about the implications of the SM's suffering for Jesus' followers. Here Mark's Jesus refers to himself as the SM for other purposes: the reference to the SM's resurrection in v. 9 serves as a marker indicating when the disciples may share what they have witnessed on the mount of transfiguration while the teaching of his suffering and death in v. 12 relates to the plight of Elijah-John—just as the one who prepared the way for Jesus experienced suffering, rejection, and even death, so too will the SM. Despite the insignificance of Dan 7 in the background, these two passages underscore an important aspect of the SM's role in Mark. As we will see in our analysis in the following chapter, the SM is at the center of the restoration of his followers at his resurrection. This is very much related to his suffering and death as described at this point because it completes the work that Elijah-John began of "restoring all things" which involves the formation of a new people of God.

In the next passion-resurrection prediction, the SM "is to be betrayed into human hands (παραδίδοται εἰς χεῖρας ἀνθρώπων), and they will kill him, and three days after being killed, he will rise again" (9:31). Unlike the passive ἀποκτανθῆναι of 8:31, Mark identifies the subject as "the hands of men" which will destroy (ἀποκτενοῦσιν) the SM. The phrase "hands of men" replaces the triumvirate of 8:31 and broadens the conspirators of Jesus

---

66. Gundry, *Mark*, 485. He also cites Seitz, who claims that, in the LXX, both of these terms often occur as translations of מאס, "rejected" ("Future Coming," 478–94).

67. France, *Mark*, 360.

Chapter 5: The Son of Man's Suffering and Death

who will eventually include the Gentiles in 10:33. In 10:33, however, Mark once again names the chief priests and the scribes as the ones to whom Jesus will be delivered (παραδοθήσεται) but the agent who will actually "deliver up" Jesus is one of his own, Judas (14:10, 21, 41). Isa 53 appears, once again, this time in discussions of the OT background of παραδίδωμι not least because this verb appears three times in the chapter (vv. 6, 12 [2x]).[68] In v. 6, "the Lord gives him up for our sins" (κύριος παρέδωκεν αὐτὸν ταῖς ἁμαρτίαις ἡμῶν); similarly in its last occurrence, the servant "was delivered up because of their sins" (v. 12b: διὰ τὰς ἁμαρτίας αὐτῶν παρεδόθη). The first instance of the verb in v. 12 in which the servant is "delivered to death" (παρεδόθη εἰς θάνατον) parallels the sequence in 9:31 of the SM being "delivered up" and then killed.[69] This isaianic background highlights the sacrificial significance of the SM's death. Some, however, demur because there is only this one terminological reference to Isa 53 in v. 31.[70] After our study of 10:45 and 14:24, it will become apparent that the servant background plays a role in Mark's interpretation of the death of Jesus and so passages like 9:31, where the evidence is limited to one term, need to be considered in light of more overt allusions that we will see later.

In an attempt to trace some of the terminology of the passion-resurrection predictions to Dan 7, Jane Schaberg proposes that the background of 9:31, specifically, παραδίδωμι, εἰς χεῖρας and μετὰ τρεῖς ἡμέρας, is Dan 7:25: "And he shall speak words against the Most High and shall wear down the holy ones of the Most High and shall expect to change seasons and the law, and everything shall be delivered into his hands for a time and times and until half a time" (NETS).[71] According to Schaberg, the first term,

---

68. Collins, *Mark*, 441. See also her discussion of παραδίδωμι in Mark's passion narrative in Collins, "Noble Death," 492-93.

69. Caragounis, *Vision*, 197. Mark employs παραδίδωμι in 14:10 and 14:21 to describe the agency of Judas in "delivering up" Jesus. In 14:41, Jesus labels both the temple leaders, the ones who sent the armed crowd, and Judas as "sinners" for handing him over. I do not discuss the references to the SM in 14:21 and v. 41 as they are restatements of passion predictions and do not add any information other than what is already communicated by Jesus in the middle section of Mark.

70. France, *Mark*, 372; Marcus, *Way*, 188-89. France rules out the influence of Isa 53 in the passion-resurrection predictions because "there is no verbal echo of Isa 53," which is inaccurate in the case of 9:31, 10:33, 14:21 and 14:41 (*Mark*, 335). However, in the next breath, he asserts that "Mark expects his readers to be aware that Jesus understood his mission as the Son of Man in terms derived from these OT pointers toward messianic suffering, with Isa. 53 as probably the most influential" (*Mark*, 335).

71. Schaberg, "Daniel 7, 12," 209-11.

παραδίδοται and, for that matter, παραδοθήσεται in 10:33, corresponds to παραδοθήσεται in Dan 7:25b (LXX), εἰς χεῖρας in 9:31 to εἰς τὰς χεῖρας (LXX: Dan. 7:25b) and μετὰ τρεῖς ἡμέρας to ἕως καιροῦ καὶ καιρῶν καὶ ἕως ἡμίσους καιροῦ (LXX: Dan. 7:25c). The last proposed allusion is not at all convincing as there is no terminological correspondence and Schaberg attempts to overcome this by appealing to Rev. 11:11–12 where a phrase indicating a timeframe of μετὰ τὰς τρεῖς ἡμέρας καὶ ἥμισυ appears which she suggests is inspired by the one in Dan 7:25. She proposes that in Rev 11 "there may be an application of the time frame of Daniel (three and a half years) to the period between death and assumption to heaven (three and a half days), an application that may occur with further shortening in the passion predictions."[72] This line of reasoning, however, is quite indefensible. A more convincing background of μετὰ τρεῖς ἡμέρας is Hos 6:2, a text which speaks of the restoration of Israel ἐν τῇ ἡμέρᾳ τῇ τρίτῃ, which technically is one day shorter than the time frame Jesus provides in Mark. The parallel in Matt 17:23 on the timing of the resurrection (Luke does not refer to it at this point) uses the phrase τῇ τρίτῃ ἡμέρᾳ that reflects more accurately the time Jesus was in the tomb (see 1 Cor 15:4). Jesus' point in Mark is that after a set time, he will be raised from the dead.[73]

The first two correspondences, παραδίδωμι and εἰς χεῖρας, should give pause for consideration especially since the little horn of the fourth beast persecutes faithful Israel and now it is the markan SM, the one closely associated with his followers, who will soon be delivered over to his adversaries. The danielic beasts and the temple leaders parallel one another in their aggression toward those faithful to Yahweh.[74] This parallel, in addition to the *volume* of the lexical agreements of παραδίδωμι and εἰς χεῖρας between Mark and Daniel, strengthen the case for an allusion. As I have already indicated, nowhere is the danielic SM said to suffer or, in this case, is he delivered into the hand Antiochus Epiphanes. However, this allusion continues to reveal the *thematic coherence* of the passion predictions because it implies the solidarity that exists between the markan SM and his followers, for which I have argued above. A closer reading of the two Greek versions of Dan 7:25 indicates that the ἅγιοι are not actually named as the subjects of παραδοθήσεται in the LXX or δοθήσεται in Theodotion. Rather, "everything" (LXX: πάντα) or "it", the grammatical subject of δοθήσεται in Theo-

---

72. Ibid., 210.
73. See Evans, *Mark*, 18; Gundry, *Mark*, 430; Casey, *Solution*, 201.
74. Evans, *Mark*, 57.

Chapter 5: The Son of Man's Suffering and Death

dotion, is delivered into Antiochus's hands (LXX)/hand (Theod). At the same time, in the LXX, the substantival adjective πάντα would include the saints whereas in Theodotion the antecedent of the unexpressed subject of δοθήσεται is likely νόμον. In Mark's allusion to Dan 7:25 in 9:31, and likely to the LXX text as both contain παραδίδωμι, he has replaced πάντα with ὁ υἱὸς τοῦ ἀνθρώπου. This change is another way by which he expresses the corporate significance of the SM. Mark's audience would know that in Daniel it is faithful Israel who will be handed over, but now, it is the SM. This modification still fits the danielic context because the disciples must be prepared to embrace the unenviable experiences of the markan SM, just as faithful Israel underwent persecution for their devotion to Yahweh by those opposed to his saving purposes. By replacing "holy ones" with the SM in the context of the call of Jesus to share in the SM's suffering, the corporate significance of the figure is once again evident. The faithful followers of Jesus are to bear their cross (8:34), serve all (9:35), and drink the cup of suffering (10:39), all of which will become a reality for the SM at the cost of his life (10:45).

Of the three predictions, the third one in 10:33–34 is the longest and most detailed indicating that the SM will not only "be handed over" (παραδοθήσεται) to the chief priests and scribes but also that this group "will condemn him to death" (κατακρινοῦσιν αὐτὸν θανάτῳ) and "will hand him over to the Gentiles" (παραδώσουσιν αὐτὸν τοῖς ἔθνεσιν). This two-stage handing over is reflected in Mark's passion narrative in which Jesus is "handed over" (παραδοῖ) to the temple leaders by means of Judas (14:10; see vv. 21, 41) and then, in 15:1, the chief priests, elders and scribes "handed him over to Pilate" (παρέδωκαν Πιλάτῳ) who shortly "handed (παρέδωκεν) him over to be crucified" (v 15). In v. 34, Jesus describes the mockery he will undergo in his trial before Pilate, which is recorded in 15:15–20, before concluding that he will be killed but will rise again after three days.[75]

The corporate dimension of the SM, which we have seen in the first two predictions, appears again. The influence of Dan 7:25 continues in 10:33 in which παραδίδωμι occurs but this time χεῖρας ἀνθρώπων found in 9:31 is replaced by two specific groups, the scribes and the priests. The SM remains the subject of the two passive forms of παραδίδωμι, although now the verb is in the future tense whereas in 9:31 it is in the present. Although there is only one linguistic correspondence with Dan 7:25 in 10:33,

---

75. France, *Mark*, 413.

the SM is still handed over to hostile foes who seek his destruction which recalls the oppressive tyrant, Antiochus IV Epiphanes. As I have argued above, Mark has replaced Daniel's πάντα, which includes the "holy ones of the Most High," with ὁ υἱὸς τοῦ ἀνθρώπου attributing a corporate dimension to the figure which is supported by Mark's text. The first half of this third prediction, in v. 33, in which Jesus declares that ὁ υἱὸς τοῦ ἀνθρώπου παραδοθήσεται τοῖς ἀρχιερεῦσιν καὶ τοῖς γραμματεῦσιν is similar to the one he gives to his disciples in 13:9 in which he predicts that their adversaries will παραδώσουσιν ὑμᾶς εἰς συνέδρια which includes going before synagogues (Jews) and pagan kings (Gentiles), not unlike the experience of Jesus himself in the passion narrative. France comments that "the choice of this verb [παραδίδωμι], with its echoes of 9:31 and 10:33, suggests a link between their treatment and that of Jesus himself."[76] For the third time, Mark's Jesus makes it known that the disciples will emulate him in his ordeal of suffering and reproach. Mark's observation that "those who followed were afraid," in v. 32, may imply that the disciples are starting to realize, now that they are about to enter Jerusalem, that the fate of the SM might have implications for them as well, something Jesus has taught them beginning in Caesarea.[77] Although it is impossible to know for sure what has elicited this fear, it is at the very least associated with the destination of this journey and what Jesus will undergo while in Jerusalem in fulfilment of the predictions of his passion. The last two references to "Jerusalem" in Mark are found earlier in the Gospel where scribes from the Holy City challenge Jesus on the legitimacy of his exorcisms (3:22) and the ritual purity of his disciples (7:1–5). According to Evans, "with these hints of trouble to come, the attentive reader of Mark is not surprised that the passion of Jesus will take place in the Holy City."[78]

---

76. Ibid., 514.

77. Collins, *Mark*, 484. Evans argues that φοβέομαι "should be understood in the OT sense of awe that overwhelms humans in the presence of the divine" and supports this with examples of prior cases where a miraculous act of Jesus elicits fear on the part of the disciples, e.g., 4:41, 5:15, etc. (*Mark*, 108). However, Jesus has not performed any miracles since arriving in Judea, but instead is about to enter Jerusalem where the predictions of his suffering, rejection, and death come to fruition. The healing of blind Bartimaeus follows after the last prediction of Jesus (10:45–52).

78. Evans, *Mark*, 107.

Chapter 5: The Son of Man's Suffering and Death

The Purpose of the Son of Man's Suffering and Death

The passion predictions of Mark culminate in 10:45 in which Jesus expresses the purpose of the SM's imminent suffering, rejection, and death in Jerusalem.[79] In 10:45, Jesus teaches that "the Son of Man came not to be served but to serve (διακονῆσαι), and to give his life a ransom for many (δοῦναι τὴν ψυχὴν αὐτοῦ λύτρον ἀντὶ πολλῶν)." There is a substantial amount of debate on the OT background of 10:45. While some scholars, once again, wish to elevate the influence of one OT text or figure over others, it is highly probable that more than one scriptural passage is operative, similar to the background of passion-resurrection predictions. In this case, the debate centers on whether Isa 53 is the definitive intertext of 10:45 or the danielic SM. Examining arguments in favor of the servant of Yahweh, Watts appeals to the Septuagint for the background of 10:45a and then to the MT for 10:45b.[80] According to Watts, δουλεύοντα πολλοῖς in Isa 53:11 is echoed in Jesus serving many. However, a clear allusion to Isa 53 is limited to πολύς because the LXX has δουλεύω, not Mark's διακονέω. C. K. Barrett levels a number of convincing criticisms against attempts to ground the latter in this text not least of which is that the root עבד is never translated as διακονέω.[81] Undeterred by this, Watts conveniently argues that the semantic fields of words shift over time.[82] At any rate, Mark's πολύς may be sufficient in itself to establish an evocation of the "servant" because this is not the first time that there is a potential allusion to Isa 53 when speaking of the SM as we have seen.[83] As I have set out in the introductory chapter, *recurrence* is an important element is establishing proposed allusions.

---

79. Watts, "Death," 136. See also France, *Mark*, 415.

80. Watts, "Death," 138–47. Although Watts argues for the "primary influence of Isa 53 on Jesus' predictions of his suffering and death," he does not wish to exclude a place for Dan 7 or other OT references (*New Exodus*, 285). For others who advocate the isaianic servant background of 10:45, see Evans, *Mark*, 120–23; Pesch, *Das Markusevangelium*, 2:163–64; Collins, *Mark*, 500.

81. Barrett, "Background," 4. See also France, *Mark*, 419–20.

82. Watts, "Death," 138 fn. 45.

83. Watts remarks that some criticize an isaianic allusion because the "servant" serves Yahweh in Isaiah while it appears that Mark's SM serves the "many" (*New Exodus*, 138 fn. 45). Watts responds that "the two types of service are merely facets of the one servant calling: to be Yahweh's 'servant' means 'to serve the many' [as in Isa 42:1b–4, 6b; 49:6] and thus διακονέω in 10:45 could happily be a nuanced allusion to this fact [as Jesus is obedient to God in 14:36]" (*New Exodus*, 138 fn. 45).

Daniel's Son of Man in Mark

Probably the most difficult challenge for Watts is the attempt to ground 10:45b in Isa 53, which is precisely the reason why Hooker and Barrett rejected the servant background almost fifty years ago.[84] For Watts, δοῦναι τὴν ψυχὴν αὐτοῦ echoes the MT of Isa 53:10: "you made his life a sin offering" (תָּשִׂים אָשָׁם נַפְשׁוֹ) and 53:12: "he poured out his life to death" (הֶעֱרָה לַמָּוֶת נַפְשׁוֹ).[85] It would seem to me, however, that the LXX of 53:12, παρεδόθη εἰς θάνατον ἡ ψυχὴ αὐτοῦ, is a more compelling intertext for δοῦναι τὴν ψυχὴν αὐτοῦ. Watts appeals to the MT of Isa 53:10 to argue that the derivation of λύτρον for Mark is אָשָׁם. However, there does not appear to be a connection between these two terms because λύτρον in the LXX has to do with the equivalent price paid for a person, such as a slave, while אָשָׁם is a sin offering.[86] For this reason, Barrett argues that אָשָׁם and λύτρον do not even refer to the same realities, and, further, the LXX never translates אָשָׁם as λύτρον.[87] One also wonders if Mark's audience, particularly his listening audience, would be able to detect an intricate shift from one version of Israel's Scriptures to another since Watts does argue that διακονῆσαι of 10:45a alludes to the LXX and δοῦναι τὴν ψυχὴν αὐτοῦ of 10:45b refers to the MT. Hooker, on the other hand, separates Mark's SM from the sin offering and sacrificial suffering associated with the servant's work. She maintains that suffering and death leading to atonement is foreign both to the danielic figure and Mark's SM.[88] For her, "λύτρον and its cognate verb λυτρόω are used especially of God's acts of deliverance by which he freed his people from bondage, both at the Exodus and at the long-awaited Return from Exile."[89] Watts counters this dissociation by indicating that Hooker herself realizes that λυτρόω translating גָּאַל in Isa 52:3 expresses

---

84. Barrett, "Background," 1–18; Hooker, *Servant*, 74–79.

85. Watts, "Death," 139–47. See also, France, *Mark*, 420, and his discussion of verbal echoes of Isa 53:10–12 in *Old Testament*, 110–32.

86. For the significance of אָשָׁם in the context of Isa 53, see Janowski, "Bore," 62–70.

87. Barrett, "Background," 5–6.

88. Hooker, *Servant*, 158–63. See also Hooker, *Not Ashamed*, 55–56. However, this could be a false dichotomy. For example, the death of the maccabean martyrs, such as the high priest Eleazar in 4 Macc 6:16–30, suffer for the salvation of others by "giving their lives in exchange for theirs" (6:29b; see 4 Macc 17:21–22). Experiencing death has a sacrificial significance which appears to be the pattern of Mark 10:45. Could the text in 4 Maccabees be a re-application of Dan 7, i.e., suffering death at the hands of one's adversaries, and Isa 53, i.e., the sacrificial suffering of the servant, so that the suffering martyrs atone for the many? In light of recent work on the complex nature of intertextuality, this at least seems possible.

89. Hooker, *Son of Man*, 144.

Chapter 5: The Son of Man's Suffering and Death

the *redemption* of Israel. He argues that this passage needs to be seen in the context of Isa 53 and 54.⁹⁰ Isaiah 52 calls Israel to prepare for the departure from Babylon while Isa 54 highlights the success of the second Exodus or the return to the Land in which case Isa 53 and, in particular, the sacrificial function of the servant as a "sin offering" (אָשָׁם) reveals the means by which Israel, "the many," will be "redeemed" (גָּאַל).⁹¹ Watts concludes that "this relationship is significant not only because it represents an apparently new synthesis of two commonly used restorational concepts – redemption (גָּאַל) and compensation (אָשָׁם)—but also because the oft-stated hard and fast distinction between the two is frequently cited as the basis for rejecting an allusion to Isaiah 53 in Mark 10:45."⁹² According to Barrett, however, there are sufficient uses of λύτρον and its cognates in the LXX, as opposed to Isa 53, to help clarify its use in Mark 10:45. On the basis of the term's usage in Exod 21:30, 30:12, and Ps 48:8, Barrett concludes that the basic meaning of λύτρον is the giving of something, which can be a ψυχή.⁹³ When one examines these passages, they are not actually as relevant as Isa 53. For instance, the use of λύτρον in Exod 21:30 is about retributive justice—the giving of a ransom in order to maintain social order—and, further, none of the contexts of these texts relate in any way to the suffering vocation of the markan SM, which cannot be said of the servant. Taken on its own, the allusion to אָשָׁם, for which Watts argues, is found wanting. However, the other verbal and thematic correspondences of Isa 53 in 10:45 and in the passion-resurrection predictions strengthens the probability that the isaianic background plays an important role in defining the death of the SM as an atonement for sin. France comments that verbal allusions become more compelling "when it is recognized that the whole thrust of Isaiah 53 is to present the servant as one who suffers and dies for the redemption of his people, whose life is offered as a substitute for their guilt. It would be hard to construct a more adequate short summary of this concept than the clause δοῦναι τὴν ψυχὴν αὐτοῦ λύτρον ἀντὶ πολλῶν."⁹⁴

Finally, the author of 2 Maccabees uses terminology, which appears in 10:45, to interpret the suffering of those who willingly submit to the

---

90. Watts, "Death," 141; Hooker, *Servant*, 76–77.
91. Ibid., 142.
92. Ibid.
93. Barrett, "Background," 6. The concept appears in 2 Kgs 10:24 LXX: ἡ ψυχὴ αὐτοῦ ἀντὶ τῆς ψυχῆς αὐτοῦ.
94. France, *Mark*, 420–21.

persecutions of Antiochus IV Epiphanes. Because of this, Barrett derives his understanding of 10:45 from the maccabean martyrological traditions in which the deaths of individual Jews result in the deliverance of the nation.[95] In 2 Macc 7:37, the martyr claims, "I, like my brothers, give up body and life (σῶμα καὶ ψυχὴν προδίδωμι) for the laws of our ancestors, appealing to God to show mercy soon to our nation and by trials and plagues to make you confess that he alone is God" (see 4 Macc 6:27–29). Barrett claims that this tradition is echoed in the willful giving of Jesus himself (see Mark 14:36) and employs the same terms as Mark 10:45. He concludes that "it would not be an exaggeration to say that the martyrs are here described as λύτρον ἀντὶ πολλῶν."[96]

Are the proponents of Isa 53, on the one hand, and the martyrological traditions, on the other, needlessly refuting one another's arguments that results in a potentially one-sided understanding? Is it reasonable to prioritize one OT passage or figure over another given the creative ways in which Mark combines OT allusions in other places? Watts may very well have become hoist on his own petard by focusing the following comment exclusively on the servant background of Mark 10:45: "insufficient attention has been paid either to the hermeneutical framework provided by Mark's Gospel as literary whole or to those indications which the Markan Jesus offers as to the provenance of his descriptions of his future sufferings."[97] Although Watts is primarily concerned with the role that the "servant" motif plays in 10:45 and feels that inadequate attention has been paid to this, he is not justified in favoring Isa 53 over other traditions. Interpreters need to be attuned to a variety of texts in passages as brief as 10:45 where it is difficult to establish the prominence of one over another. As I have mentioned earlier, Hooker attempts to ground the suffering vocation of the markan SM on what is an assumed experience of suffering of the danielic "one like a son of man" which I do not believe reflects a careful treatment of Dan 7.[98] However, the relevance of the danielic background is evident, as it has been in the preceding passion-resurrection predictions, in the corporate significance of the suffering SM. While it is quite clear that what is true of the SM

95. Barrett, "Background," 12. See also, Hengel, *Atonement*, 60–61.

96. Barrett, "Background," 12; Marshall, *Last Supper*, 89. Hengel claims that ἀντίψυχον is a later Greek variant of the earlier Semitic term λύτρον (*Atonement*, 35).

97. Watts, "Death," 126.

98. Hooker, *Son of Man*, 27–28. Evans suggests that the danielic and isaianic backgrounds are not mutually exclusive because the servant recasts the role of the "one like a son of man" from a symbol of vindication to one of suffering (*Mark*, 123).

in terms of his suffering is to be embraced by his disciples, we see in 10:45 that his redemptive, sacrificial suffering has implications for others as well. Hooker insightfully indicates that "in some way the events in Jerusalem are the means whereby others (in Luke the twelve, in Mark the many) are given a share in Jesus' kingdom."[99] But it cannot be overlooked that in the context of the pronouncement about the SM's service (διακονῆσαι, v. 45), Jesus calls the disciples to follow him by being a servant (διάκονος) as well (v. 43).[100]

Any study of Mark 10:45 must include some discussion of 14:24 which reveals additional information about the redemptive significance of the SM's service.[101] Comparing the two passages, Mark replaces τὴν ψυχὴν αὐτοῦ of 10:45 with τὸ αἷμά μου in 14:24. The terms ψυχή and τὸ αἷμά are virtually identical in meaning along with, of course, ἀντὶ πολλῶν (10:45) and ὑπὲρ πολλῶν (14:24). It is not unwarranted, then, to keep Mark's SM in the foreground of 14:24 because he is the one who not only gives his life as a ransom for many but also whose blood is "poured out." In this passage, Mark's Jesus employs distinctly sacrificial language when he explains the significance of the cup: "This is my *blood of the covenant which is poured out for many.*" Many agree that the first part of v. 24, "blood of the covenant," alludes to Exod 24:8 in which a covenant is established between Yahweh and Israel though a blood ritual forming them into God's holy people.[102] Half of "the blood of the covenant" (τὸ αἷμα τῆς διαθήκης, 24:8), Moses dashes on the altar (24:6b) and the other half he dashes on the people of Israel (24:8a). According to E. W. Nicholson, this ritual is primarily concerned with communicating holiness through blood and so constitutes Israel as a "kingdom of priests and a holy nation" (Exod 19:6).[103] This is reflected in the consecrations of Aaron and his sons whom Moses touches with sacrificial blood (Exod 29:20; Lev 8:22–30).[104] Taking Exod 24:3–8 as the confirmation of 19:3b–8, Nicholson concludes that Israel becomes "a holy nation, obedient to God's holy will and functioning among the nations in the manner that a

---

99. Hooker, *Son of Man*, 146.

100. Evans, *Mark*, 120.

101. Grey, *Temple*, 160; Evans, *Mark*, 394; France, *Mark*, 571.

102. Watts, *New Exodus*, 351; France, *Mark*, 570; Marshall, *Last Supper*, 45; Hengel, *Atonement*, 42.

103. Nicholson, "Covenant Ritual," 83.

104. Ibid., 83. Note the explicit language of Exod 29:21: "Then you shall take some of the blood that is on the altar, and some of the anointing-oil, and sprinkle it on Aaron and his vestments and on his sons and his sons' vestments with him; *then he and his vestments shall be holy, as well as his sons and his sons' vestments.*"

priesthood functions in a society."[105] In addition to "blood of the covenant language," there are other significant allusions to Exod 24 in Mark's last supper: twelve disciples (14:17) recall the twelve pillars (Exod 24:4c), and the last supper meal (14:17–25) recalls the meal consumed by the leaders of Israel (Exod 24:11).[106] Just as Israel, represented by the twelve pillars, becomes "a kingdom of priests and a holy nation," through "the blood of the covenant," so too do the twelve disciples. This is not the first time that Mark portrays the disciples as a new Israel or a new people of God. As we have seen, the mountain from which Jesus calls his disciples in 3:13–15 is theologically significant recalling Mount Sinai in Exodus 19–20 from where God creates the nation of Israel. Jesus also calls twelve "apostles" reminiscent of the twelve tribes of Israel (see Gen 49) and so reconstitutes the nation around himself serving as its leader.

Debate ensues once again as to the OT background of the second phrase, τὸ ἐκχυννόμενον ὑπὲρ πολλῶν. Continuing her defense of a non-isaianic background, Hooker denies that "poured out" blood is a sacrificial category and so is unrelated to Isa 53:12: "he poured out his life to death" (הֶעֱרָה לַמָּוֶת נַפְשׁוֹ).[107] Rather, according to her, a more appropriate background is שָׁפַךְ דָּם/ἐκχέω αἷμα generically meaning "bloodshed" (LXX: Gen 9:6; Deut 19:10; Is 59:7; Ezek 22:3–12; Prov 1:16; Ps 106:38).[108] In response, Watts indicates that sometimes this supposed non-sacrificial terminology does indeed have sacrificial/atoning implications. In Lev 8:15, as part of the sacrificial ritual that purifies the altar, Moses pours out blood at its base (τὸ αἷμα ἐξέχεεν ἐπὶ τὴν βάσιν τοῦ θυσιαστηρίου).[109] It is also an important component in the consecration of priests (Exod 29:12: αἷμα ἐκχεεῖς; see 29:21) and, of course, of Israel herself (Exod 24:8), although here Moses "sprinkles/dashes" (κατεσκέδασεν) the blood.[110] Blood is also poured out in the sin offering ritual which effects atonement both for the priests and Israel in Lev 4:18, 25, 30, 34. Although it is tempting for Watts to argue that the "poured out blood" is in effect an אָשָׁם from Isa 53:10, he realizes the complexity of the sacrificial system, not to mention the less than clear evidence that Mark understands Jesus to be functioning solely as the servant in

---

105. Ibid., 84.
106. Watts, *New Exodus*, 353.
107. Hooker, *Servant*, 82.
108. Ibid., 82. Watts, *New Exodus*, 357, lists the above examples of ἐκχέω αἷμα.
109. Watts, *New Exodus*, 358.
110. Ibid., 358.

Chapter 5: The Son of Man's Suffering and Death

10:45 and 14:24, and so suggests "that something along these lines [servant imagery] is in view in Mark 14:24."[111] Certainly, the sacrificial imagery of Jesus' poured out blood is by no means incongruous with אָשָׁם. Others also see an allusion to "the many" in Isa 53:12: וְהוּא חֵטְא־רַבִּים נָשָׂא, particularly the πολλῶν of the LXX: αὐτὸς ἁμαρτίας πολλῶν ἀνήνεγκεν.[112] Given the terminological correspondences with Isa 53 in the predictions and 10:45, as well as the parallel between the vocation of the SM and the servant, the likelihood of an allusion at this point to the last section of Isa 53 is strong. Isaiah 53:12 contains the most explicit statement of the vicarious suffering of the servant highlighting that his abuse and rejection will be for the many. Likewise, Jesus' words on the significance of his death, at the last supper, make absolutely clear that he is sacrificially dying for "the many" as well.[113]

Probably the most prominent OT background of "poured out" is Exod 24:8 in which Moses "dashes" on the people "the blood of the covenant," despite the lack of terminological correspondence between the LXX's κατεσκέδασεν and Mark's ἐκχυννόμενον.[114] However, Mark's ἐκχέω must be seen in relation to passages which refer to formalized sacrificial rituals, as evident in Exodus and Leviticus, all of which harken back to the great inaugural covenant event of Exod 19-24.[115] Exodus 24 is a covenant ceremony which is also echoed in Mark's presentation of the last supper in which it becomes apparent that the giving of the SM's life and his poured out blood establishes the disciples as a new people of God, a new kingdom of priests and a holy nation. Heretofore, this status of Israel was maintained by the sacrificial system of the temple, but through the SM's atoning death the existing temple cult becomes redundant. In light of the clear anti-temple theme that runs through Mark 11-13 and the sacrificial terminology Jesus employs to elucidate the significance of his imminent death, it appears that the locus of redemption is no longer the sacrifices offered in the temple but the death of the SM.

Until the discovery of the DSS, there was little by way of parallel in the literature of 2TJ which depicts a community of Jews who finds redemption

---

111. Ibid., 359.

112. Bolt, *Cross*, 105; Evans, *Mark*, 392-93; France, *Mark*, 570-71.

113. France, *Mark*, 570-71.

114. Evans, *Mark*, 392-93; Pesch, *Das Markusevangelium*, 2:358; Grey, *Temple*, 160; France, *Mark*, 570.

115. Marshall, *Last Supper*, 92, cites Pesch, who refers to the Targum's emphasis on the atoning significance of the blood which Moses throws against the altar in Exod 24:7-8 (*Das Abendmal*, 95).

outside of the second temple and who have not constructed an alternative, such as the Oniad temple in Egypt and the Samaritan one on Mount Gerizim.[116] Since their discovery, however, several publications have attempted to demonstrate that the ecclesiology of the NT, namely, the application of temple terminology to early Christian communities, is not vastly different from the self-perceptions of the sectarians at Qumran.[117] A clear example is Paul's pronouncement to the church in Corinth: "Do you not know that you are God's temple and that God's Spirit dwells in you? If anyone destroys God's temple, God will destroy that person. For God's temple is holy, and you are that temple" (1 Cor 3:16-17). Similarly, the *Rule of the Community* clearly reflects the application of temple language to the sectarians:

> The Community council shall be founded on truth, *Blank* to be an everlasting plantation, a holy house (בית קודש) for Israel and the foundation of the holy of holies (קודש קודשים) for Aaron, true witnesses for the judgement and chosen by the will (of God) to atone for the land and to render the wicked their retribution. *Blank* This (the community) is the tested rampart, the precious cornerstone (פנת יקר) that does not *Blank* /whose foundations/ shake or tremble from their place. *Blank* (It will be) the most holy dwelling for Aaron with eternal knowledge of the covenant of justice and in order to offer a pleasant /aroma/; and it will be a house of perfection and truth in Israel (1QS VIII, 5-9).

The leaders of the sect, "the community council," ascribe to themselves temple language: "holy house" and "foundation of the holy of holies."[118] Likewise, the rest of the community is "the tested rampart, the precious cornerstone" and "a house of perfection and truth." The next column indicates that the prayers and holy living of this group will atone for the sins of the land and not the "flesh of burnt offerings" and the "fats of sacrifice" (1QS IX, 4-5). The result of this piety is "a holy house for Aaron, in order to form a most holy community" (1QS IX, 6).[119] In what is left of another scroll, the fragment 4Q164, which is a pesher on Isa 54:11-12, depicts a restored and

---

116. Wardle, *Jerusalem Temple*, 99-139.

117. The most recent publication on this topic is by Wardle, *Jerusalem Temple*. For a couple of seminal studies, see Gärtner, *Temple and the Community* and McKelvey, *New Temple*.

118. Wardle, *Jerusalem Temple*, 157.

119. Wardle indicates that prayer and praise function as surrogates for temple sacrifice which is evident in CD XI, 20-21 and 11QPsa XVIII, 9-12 respectively (*Jerusalem Temple*, 156).

glorious temple composed of a variety of stones which symbolize members of the community.[120] Collins point out that the sectarians also referred to themselves as a living Zion in 11QMelch II, 23–24.[121]

The Qumran depiction of believers as a metaphorical temple is not that far removed from Mark's application of temple language, specifically that which is associated with its cult, to Jesus in 14:24. The sectarians make it quite clear in 1QS that the temple cult no longer atones for "the guilt of iniquity and for the unfaithfulness of sin" but rather the community itself through prayer and holiness (1QS IX, 4). We also see a reference in column 8, quoted above, where the council is chosen by God's will "to atone for the land." I have demonstrated above that Jesus' explanation of his death in which he proclaims that τοῦτό ἐστιν τὸ αἷμά μου τῆς διαθήκης τὸ ἐκχυννόμενον ὑπὲρ πολλῶν derives from sacrificial rituals which in the 2T period are carried out in the Jerusalem temple. Mark's audience would know that the slaughtering of animals to effect atonement would be performed in the temple, whether it is still standing or not at the time of the Gospel's composition. This transference of cultic language to Jesus expresses that the locus of Yahweh's redemptive activity has been transferred from cult to cross forming a new covenant community through Jesus' shed blood and not through that of animals.

Conclusion

For each of the three passion-resurrection predictions, I contend that the propensity of scholars to argue for one intertextual background is misguided not least because these are brief descriptions about the SM's suffering, rejection and death. That is, other than Dan 7:25 and Mark 9:31, these sayings do not contain phrases of two or three terms which one can trace to a specific OT or extra-biblical text and thereby argue that this or that text is *the* intertext. Folks such as Watts, Hooker, and Barrett focus much of their energies on seeking *the* background of individual terms, a method that in itself should temper their proposals. Rather, we must be attentive to a variety of figures and texts including the maccabean martyrs, the servant of Isaiah, and the "one like a son of man." In 8:31, there are allusions to the sacrificial suffering of the "servant" and the oppressed maccabean martyrs who willingly give their lives and suffer intensely on behalf of the nation's

---

120. Ibid., 160.
121. Collins, *Mark*, 548.

sin so that God will show his mercy (2 Macc 7:37). One of the prominent verbs in the last two predictions, 9:31 and 10:33, is παραδίδωμι which appears three times in the LXX of Isa 53. The servant is "delivered up" on account of the sins of Israel which contributes to the sacrificial significance of the SM's suffering and rejection.

Despite what I think are misguided attempts by Hooker and others to argue that the suffering of the markan SM is inspired by the alleged suffering of the "one like a son of man", the danielic background still makes a formative contribution. Of all the proposed figures and texts for the background of the suffering SM in Mark, only in Daniel is υἱὸς ἀνθρώπου associated with a group of faithful ones who are oppressed by a hostile adversary. It is quite clear in the literary context of each prediction that Jesus expects his disciples, this new Israel which he has inaugurated, to share in the unenviable plight of the SM, which strengthens the *thematic coherence* of the predictions and the saying in 10:45. This proposal is also *historically probable* because the association between the SM and his faithful is also evident in the *Parables* and *4 Ezra* where the SM delivers those who remain devoted to the Lord of Spirits in the former and calls to himself those who have been affected by the temple's destruction in the latter. After teaching the disciples about the suffering and betrayal of the SM in each prediction, Jesus calls them to embrace his plight by bearing a cross, serving others, and drinking the cup of suffering. The corporate significance is also evident in 10:45, the culmination of the passion-resurrection predictions, in which the SM will serve by giving his life to redeem "many," the sacrificial significance of which Jesus explains in more detail in 14:24. As with the passion-resurrection predictions, I have argued that the intertextual meaning for the SM who serves and gives his life as a ransom for many in 10:45 has a composite background including the servant and the maccabean martyrs which together draw attention to the sacrificial giving of the SM's life for others.

Regarding 14:24, I have argued, as do others, that Jesus' "blood of the covenant" recalls the blood ceremony in Exod 24:3–8 through which Israel becomes a royal priesthood and a holy nation (Exod 19:6). Although the imagery of the poured out blood may allude to the "servant" who sacrificially poured out himself to death and the sacrificial system more generally, the pouring out of blood in the covenant ritual of Exod 24:3–8 seems more relevant not least because of the terminological correspondences and the similar contexts of a covenant ceremony in Exodus 24 and Mark 14:17–25. However, the reference to "many" at the end of Jesus' statement

Chapter 5: The Son of Man's Suffering and Death

likely recalls the culminating statement about the servant in Isa 53 whose atoning sacrifice is likewise for many. The sacrificial service of the SM that results in his blood being "poured out," establishes Jesus' faithful followers as a new people of God, or in the words of Exod 19:6: "a priestly kingdom and a holy nation."

I have also argued in this chapter that the rejection, suffering, and consequent death of the SM, as an act of sacrificial service, renders the temple cult redundant. The SM clearly dies for a purpose—to redeem "the many." At the beginning of this chapter, I have suggested that the resistance that the scribes and then the Pharisees manifest toward Jesus in Mark 2, which in both cases elicits a statement about the authority of the SM, might be related to the predictions of the SM's suffering and death at the hands of the Jerusalem leadership because of the ways in which the pronouncements of the SM appear to encroach upon the temple: he forgives sins and redefines the laws governing its priests. This infringement upon the temple continues in Jesus' teaching about the sacrificial import of the SM's suffering, rejection, and death as well as in his comments about his own poured out blood which effects a new covenant outside of temple sacrifices. The transference of sacrificial service from cult to cross and the resultant redundancy of the former also dovetails with Mark's use of ἀποδοκιμάζω in 12:10 where the rejection of the "stone," which will become the "capstone," hints at the formation of a new temple. Mark and other early Christians are not the first to apply terminology associated with the temple's architecture or its sacrificial system to people. We have a clear precedent for this at Qumran and is an argument which I will develop more fully in the following chapter.

Chapter 6: The Coming of the Son of Man in the Heavenly Temple

Introduction

THE LAST SERIES OF SM sayings I will investigate are the future sayings that depict the SM as an exalted figure coming in a celestial context to exercise judicial action. I argue that Mark evokes the heavenly temple setting of Dan 7 in which the markan SM comes as a judge to deal with those who have been opposed to him and the gospel. In 8:38, he comes in the heavenly temple to settle the score with would-be followers who have been ashamed of him and his call to live cruciform lives for the sake of the gospel. In 13:26, Jesus comes on the clouds with great power and glory for the purpose of judging the terrestrial Jerusalem temple for its corruption. At the same time, he sends his holy angels to gather those faithful to him which signals the vindication of a new covenant community, which is, as we have learned, founded not on the temple cult but on the sacrificial suffering and death of the SM. Finally, in 14:62, Jesus predicts that the Sanhedrists, who have been at the center of resistance toward him in the passion narrative, will see the SM seated at the right hand of Yahweh and coming with the clouds. Based on the evocations of Dan 7:13 and Ps 110:1, Jesus casts his adversaries as enemies of Yahweh who will be judged by the exalted SM. In the final section of the chapter, I argue that the new covenant community is beginning to take shape in light of the rending of the temple veil at Jesus' death which signals Yahweh's judgement in a proleptic manner on the temple and in light of the command of Jesus that the disciples meet him in Galilee after his resurrection which distances this group from that institution.

Chapter 6: The Coming of the Son of Man in the Heavenly Temple

The Coming of the Son of Man in 8:38

Prior to this SM saying, Jesus warns his disciples not only about the cost of following him but also the cost of not doing so: to save one's life is to lose it (v. 35) and to gain the whole world is to give up one's soul (v. 36). The warning becomes explicit in v. 38 when Jesus warns his disciples that ὁ υἱὸς τοῦ ἀνθρώπου will be ashamed of the one who is ashamed of him and his words when he comes in the glory of his father and with the holy angels. His "words" almost certainly refer to the admonitions in vv. 34–37.[1] For Mark's Jesus, it is absolutely crucial that the disciples not only realize the type of messiah he will be, one who suffers at the hands of his enemies, but also that they personally join him inaugurating a reign which will only come about through suffering and death. As I have argued in the last chapter, Jesus' depiction of ὁ υἱὸς τοῦ ἀνθρώπου in 8:31, as one who will suffer much and be rejected, has a corporate dimension in light of Dan 7 and, after putting Peter in his place in v. 33, he calls his disciples to share in his fate. The very next SM saying makes clear, however, that a day of reckoning will come for those who refuse to heed his call.

Then, in 9:1, Jesus predicts that "some standing here will not taste death until they see that the Kingdom of God has come in power." Scholars debate exactly what event Jesus describes here. Various options include the *parousia*, transfiguration, resurrection, destruction of Jerusalem, Pentecost, or the growth of the early church.[2] In a number of these interpretations, 8:38 usually refers to the *parousia* while 9:1 describes one of these events which transpired during the lifetime of those standing there with Jesus.[3] Others such as Norman Perrin claim that 8:38—9:1 describes the second coming of Christ but that 8:38 is a message of judgement while the following words about the Kingdom of God having come in power functions positively as a promise of hope.[4] I will argue in this section that an analysis of the imagery in both

---

1. Although a few MSS omit λόγους, in which case ἐμοὺς could refer to the disciples, it is more likely that the shorter reading is due to the accidental omission of the former because it has the same ending as the latter. See Metzger, *Textual Commentary*, 84.

2. Bird, "Crucifixion," 23–24. See also the helpful discussion in Brower, "Seeing," 18–26.

3. For example, Nardoni argues that 9:1 refers to the transfiguration ("Redactional," 365–84). See also Lane, *Mark*, 314; Gundry, *Mark*, 457; and, most recently, Adams, "Coming," 48–52. Hurtado is a proponent of 9:1 describing the resurrection (*Mark*, 142).

4. Perrin, "Composition," 68; Bird, "Crucifixion," 32; Hooker, *Mark*, 213; Collins, *Mark*, 413. Bird cites Brower, "Seeing," 34, as supporting the judgement/promise dichotomy of 8:38/9:1 respectively ("Crucifixion," 32 fn. 50). However, Brower also realizes

verses in pre-Christian Jewish literature, not the least of which is the status of the cloud riding SM in Dan 7 in subsequent first-century Jewish interpretation, reveals that 8:38 describes the manifestation of God's heavenly temple from which the SM judges those ashamed of him and that 9:1 refers to an historical event, in the lifetime of some of those hearing Jesus' words, which is also associated with judgement. I will not, however, attempt to argue what event in Mark's Gospel or early Christian history is a reflection of the Kingdom of God having come mainly because the prediction is too imprecise to draw any type of convincing conclusion. The fact that we have a variety of proposals offered by scholars is a symptom of this imprecision.

A helpful starting point is the function of 8:38—9:1 in its literary context, on which I have already commented briefly. It is quite reasonable to assume that 9:1 forms the conclusion of a literary unit that begins in 8:34, a view that a number of scholars endorse.[5] Hatina claims that the verses leading up to 9:1 gradually focus on the theme of judgement. Jesus contrasts "potential insiders with potential outsiders in v. 35, and [ends] with a fuller statement concerning potential outsiders in vv. 36–38."[6] He even goes as far as claiming that the "ashamed" of 8:38 and the "some" of 9:1 are synonymous with each other as it is they who do not embrace the radical call of cross bearing and losing life for the sake of Jesus and the gospel.[7] I am unconvinced of this because there is no indication in the text that those who witness the Kingdom of God having come in power are the objects of judgment in the way that those who are ashamed of Jesus and his words, but this does not mean that 9:1 does not depict some form of judicial ac-

---

that 9:1 sounds a note of judgement ("Seeing," 34).

5. Hatina, "Kingdom," 23. On the literary unity of 8:34—9:1, see Lane, *Mark,* 312; Gundry, *Mark,* 440; Lührmann, *Das Markusevangelium,* 153; Hooker, *Mark,* 211; Adams, "Coming," 48–49; France, *Mark,* 343; Collins, *Mark,* 412. However, Kilgallen argues that 9:1 is unrelated to vv. 35–38 largely because the section begins with γάρ while 9:1 starts with καὶ ἔλεγεν αὐτοῖς (Kilgallen, "Conclusion," 81–83). However, the latter phrase in Mark connects preceding material with what follows. Hatina lists the following examples: 2:27a; 4:2b, 11, 21, 24; 6:4, 10; 7:9; 8:21; 9:31; 11:17 ("Who Will See," 21).

6. Hatina, "Who Will See," 23.

7. Alternatively, France argues that the "some" are a special group for whom the expectation of "tasting death" is "something to look forward to before that death comes" (*Mark,* 343). However, as will be argued below, "in power" carries a strong tone of judgement not unlike the message of 8:38. See also Lane, *Mark,* 313. In an original but unconvincing approach, Chilton argues that those who will not taste death are the immortals Elijah and Moses ("Transfiguration," 115–24). For criticisms, see Evans, *Mark,* 28 and France, *Mark,* 344 fn. 1.

Chapter 6: The Coming of the Son of Man in the Heavenly Temple

tion which those standing with Jesus will witness. These verses are clearly related to one another which is evident in the following thematic and structural parallels.⁸ Mark uses the verb ἔρχομαι, although in two different morphological forms, of which both the SM and the Kingdom of God are grammatical subjects. The adverbial phrases ἐν τῇ δόξῃ τοῦ πατρὸς αὐτοῦ and μετὰ τῶν ἀγγέλων τῶν ἁγίων indicate the manner by which the SM comes (ἔλθῃ) and ἐν δυνάμει designates how the Kingdom of God will have come (ἐληλυθυῖαν).⁹ The intertextual background of Dan 7 serves as the link between the dual action of the coming of ὁ υἱὸς τοῦ ἀνθρώπου with that of ἡ βασιλεία τοῦ θεοῦ.¹⁰ In Dan 7:13-14, "one like a son of man" (ὡς υἱὸς ἀνθρώπου) comes (Theod: ἐρχόμενος ἦν/LXX: ἤρχετο) on the clouds of heaven and is presented before Yahweh whereupon he receives a kingdom which will never be destroyed (LXX: ἡ βασιλεία αὐτοῦ ἥτις οὐ μὴ φθαρῇ/ Theod: ἡ βασιλεία αὐτοῦ οὐ διαφθαρήσεται). The LXX also records that πᾶσα δόξα αὐτῷ λατρεύουσα (NETS: "all honor was serving him"). Comparing the LXX with Mark, we have four verbal correspondences: υἱὸς ἀνθρώπου, ἔρχομαι, ἡ βασιλεία, and δόξα and three with Theodotion due to the absence of δόξα in that text.¹¹ These terminological correspondences indicate that Dan 7:13-14 should play a crucial role in our understanding of 8:38—9:1. Given what appears to be a thoroughgoing use of Dan 7 at this point, it is reasonable to ask if Mark is evoking the celestial scene of 7:9-10 and 13-14 in which case these texts form a framework by which to interpret the imagery describing how the SM will come: ἐν τῇ δόξῃ τοῦ πατρὸς αὐτοῦ μετὰ τῶν ἀγγέλων τῶν ἁγίων (8:38b).¹² At the outset of this

---

8. See Trocmé, "Marc 9,1," 261-62; France, *Mark,* 343; Gnilka, *Das Evangelium,* 2:26-27; Collins, *Mark,* 413; Perrin, *Kingdom,* 87.

9. Hatina, "Who Will See," 25.

10. France, *Old Testament,* 139. Lührmann comments that "Das Kommen des Reiches Gottes entspricht dem Kommen des Menschensohns (8,38 13,26 14,62), dessen Wort selber Nähe des Reiches Gottes bedeutet" (*Das Markusevangelium,* 153).

In a once influential publication, Vielhauer claims that the Kingdom of God and the SM are not combined in either the earliest strata of Gospel tradition or in Jewish thought as a whole ("Gottesreich und Menschensohn," 51-79). For a convincing critique of this position, see Tödt, *Son of Man,* 328-47.

11. France suggests that the reference to "holy angels" in 8:38 could derive from Dan 7:10 in which Yahweh is surrounded by heavenly myriads (*Mark,* 342).

12. France advocates that heavenly scene in Dan 7 is the intertextual background for specific imagery such as the reference to glory and angels in Mark 8:38 (*Mark,* 342). However, Adams disagrees with some of the specific exegetical conclusions France draws ("Coming," 49-51). For example, France argues on the basis of his reading of Dan 7

Daniel's Son of Man in Mark

work, I quoted Hays who indicates that "as we move farther away from overt citation, the source recedes into the discursive distance, the intertextual relations become less determinate, and the demand placed on the reader's listening powers grows greater."[13] In this case, although Mark is not citing a text as in a quotation, there are three terminological correspondences with the LXX of Dan 7:13–14 in 8:38 as well as the conceptual parallel between the coming of the SM and the Kingdom of God which provides a high degree of *thematic coherence* between 8:38 and 9:1. I contend that these connections invite more reflection on the danielic background and its relevance for our text. Specifically, I am proposing that the heavenly context of Daniel and also a consideration of the biblical and extra-biblical backgrounds of "glory" and "holy angels" reveals that Mark's Jesus is evoking a heavenly temple scene in which the SM, not Yahweh, comes as the celestial judge. We must bear in mind that this is an evocation, not a complete description as would satisfy the sensibilities of modern readers, of a celestial scene to which Mark alludes with the help of additional terminology quite at home in other heavenly temple contexts. Since 8:38b is an evocation of or an allusion to the scene of a prior text, it is naturally brief which is, as many would agree, the way biblical allusions work. This proposal also finds a considerable amount of *historical probably* when we remind ourselves that the setting of the exalted SM who judges the enemies of Yahweh in the *Parables* is the heavenly temple as well.

The scene in Dan 7:9–10 and 13–14 is a picture of Yahweh judging the adversaries of faithful Israel from his celestial dwelling, not just a heavenly courtroom as many indicate in passing. This setting, as I have argued, is often overlooked by interpreters but it seems clear for a variety of reasons: imagery in Dan 7:9–10 and 13–14 derives from *1 En.* 14, a text which depicts the heavenly temple and, similar to the historical context of the latter, Daniel has this vision which deals with defilement of the earthly temple; the verbs used to describe the heavenly myriads who "stand" before and "serve" Yahweh and then "present" the SM before him is used of the priests

---

that the "language [of 8:38] refers not to a specific event, but to the state of sovereign authority to which Jesus looks forward as the proper destiny of the Son of Man" (*Mark*, 343). To this, Adams responds that Jesus is not referring to a state of exaltation but rather to a particular event in history as indicated by the temporal adverb ὅταν ("Coming," 50). I think that this example illustrates the tendency, at times, of some scholars, in this instance France, to disregard details of NT texts because they have read too much of the evoked text into the NT passage.

13. Hays, *Echoes of Scripture*, 23.

Chapter 6: The Coming of the Son of Man in the Heavenly Temple

in the earthly tabernacle and temple; and Yahweh is portrayed as judging terrestrial corruption from his heavenly dwelling surrounded by a myriad of angelic beings, as in other OT texts, which depict a celestial setting: 1 Kgs 22:19, Ps 82:1, and Isa 6.

As I have mentioned above, there are specific terms in 8:38 that complement the celestial context of Dan 7, which I argue that Mark is evoking, and to these we now turn. The word δόξα is often used to describe Yahweh's presence in both earthly and heavenly temple contexts. At the dedication of Solomon's temple, "the glory of the Lord filled the house of the Lord" (1 Kgs 8:11b LXX: δόξα κυρίου; MT: כְּבוֹד־יְהוָה). Ezekiel witnesses Yahweh's "glory" entering the restored eschatological temple in his vision (Ezek 43:4 LXX: δόξα κυρίου; MT: כְּבוֹד יְהוָה; see 44:4). Comparing the departure of the כְּבוֹד יְהוָה as described in Ezek 1 with its return 43:1–5, von Rad comments that "to this flight of Yahweh from Jerusalem there corresponds his entry into the temple in the great vision of the future (43:1ff.). Both surprise us by the assumption that the true resting place of the כְּבוֹד יְהוָה was and will be again the temple."[14] In Isaiah's vision of the Lord enthroned in the heavenly temple, the Seraphim offer praise proclaiming that "the whole earth is full of his glory" (Isa 6:3b LXX: δόξης αὐτοῦ; MT: כְּבוֹדוֹ).[15] In *1 En.* 14:20, the term is used as a title for Yahweh himself who is enthroned in his celestial dwelling: "The Great Glory sat upon it [a lofty throne, v. 18]; his apparel was like the appearance of the sun and whiter than much snow." Enoch records that "all [the location of his throne] of it so excelled in glory and splendor and majesty that I am unable to describe for you its glory and majesty" (*1 En.* 14:16). In the *Songs of the Sabbath Sacrifice*, כבוד describes both the glory of God in the heavenly temple, e.g., 4QShirShabb[a] 1 I, 4: בדביר כבודו; 4QShirShabb[d] 1 I, 33: ואלוהות כבודו; 4QShirShabb[f] 23 I, 7: הטוהר יגילו בכבודו and the glory of its architecture, e.g., 4QShirShabb[f] 14–15 I, 6: בד]בירי כבוד . . . [; 20 II, 7: הכבוד במשכ[ן]; 20 II, 9: מושב כבודו; see *1 En.* 14:16. In the LXX of Dan 7:14, after the SM/faithful Israel is presented before Yahweh, Daniel claims that πᾶσα δόξα αὐτῷ λατρεύουσα, which is a fitting statement for one in the heavenly temple.

The phrases in 8:38, μετὰ τῶν ἀγγέλων τῶν ἁγίων and ἐν τῇ δόξῃ τοῦ πατρὸς αὐτοῦ, function together to describe how the exalted SM will

---

14. Kittel and von Rad, "δοκέω," 241.

15. As argued in chapter 2, while the earthly temple forms part of this setting, it is more likely that Isaiah witnesses Yahweh in his heavenly abode that appears to include the earthly temple; for example, only the hem of Yahweh's robe fills the terrestrial counterpart. Meanwhile, Yahweh himself is seated on a throne "high and lofty" (Isa 6:1).

come. Edward Adams argues that the former phrase, along with the verb ἔρχομαι of which the SM is the subject in 8:38, alludes to the last half of Zech 14:5: καὶ ἥξει κύριος ὁ θεός μου καὶ πάντες οἱ ἅγιοι μετ᾽ αὐτοῦ.[16] Although ἄγγελοι are not mentioned, the movement of God who comes accompanied by his holy ones is not that far removed from the SM who comes with his holy angels. This line from Zechariah is a prediction of Yahweh's coming to establish his reign over the entire earth, after having judged Israel's adversaries, which is of such a magnitude that creation itself will be altered (Zech 14:6–11). Adams proposes that this text is far more influential in 8:38 than Dan 7 because the SM's "coming [in Mark] is no longer a coming to God, but a coming as God's agent, from heaven to earth, for the purpose of eschatological judgement."[17] From this statement, he abruptly concludes that 8:38 "is about the *parousia* of Jesus."[18] However, he seems to be reading too much of Zech 14:5 into 8:38 because the prophet is actually speaking of Yahweh coming in eschatological *salvation*. Yahweh comes in Zechariah after he has dealt with the enemies of Israel (see vv. 3–5a), at which point "the Lord my God will come, and all the holy ones with him" (v. 5b) which inaugurates his eternal reign over the restored holy city (see vv. 6–11). Although there are two terminological correspondences with 8:38, the verb ἔρχομαι and the substantive οἱ ἅγιοι, this text fails to provide *thematic coherence* for the markan SM coming in judgment on those who fail to confess him and his words. The danielic background fits much better because of its emphasis on judgement and because the language Mark uses coheres with the celestial context of Dan 7.

There are many scriptural echoes which depict angels who attend Yahweh, some of which occurs in the heavenly temple not unlike the myriads in Dan 7:10. In Ps 103 [LXX: 102]: 19–20: "The Lord has established his throne in the heavens, and his kingdom rules over all. Bless the Lord, O you his angels (οἱ ἄγγελοι), you mighty ones who do his bidding, obedient to his spoken word." In another Psalm, a call goes out to all of creation to praise God including all his angels (οἱ ἄγγελοι) and hosts (148:1–2). Echoing Mark's terminology, there are a number of instances in which angelic beings are referred to as "holy ones" or "holy angels" in a celestial context. Eliphaz sardonically questions Job if he can turn to the "holy angels" (ἀγγέλων

---

16. Adams, "Coming," 51.
17. Ibid., 52.
18. Ibid.

Chapter 6: The Coming of the Son of Man in the Heavenly Temple

ἁγίων) who reside in God's presence to come to his defense (5:1; see 4:18).[19] In Ps 89 [LXX: 88], "God is glorified in a council of the holy ones (ἁγίων), great and awesome to all that are around him" (NETS, v. 7[8]; see v. 5[6]). The term "holy angels" (מלאכי קודש) appears in the *Songs of the Sabbath Sacrifice* describing pure angelic beings who offer praise in the inner sanctuary of the heavenly temple (4QShirShabbf 19, 7; 20 II, 9; 23 I, 8). In the *War Scroll*, Yahweh is depicted in his heavenly dwelling in which "there is a multitude of holy ones (קדשים) and host of angels (מלאכים) . . . to [praise] your [truth]" (1QM XII, 1a). The text identifies these ones as assisting the chosen in a victorious battle against "the rebels of earth" (1QM XII, 4–5). In Enoch's vision, "holy angels" appear in the heavenly temple: "the holy angels who (are in) the heights of heaven, were going in and out of that house" (*1 En.* 71:8). On their own, these echoes of Yahweh's glory and his holy angels in the OT and Qumran would not make a compelling case for an evocation of the heavenly temple in 8:38. However, reading Mark against the background of this sampling of celestial uses of δόξα and ἄγγελοι coupled with the heavenly temple scene in Dan 7, with which there are a number of terminological correspondences in 8:38 and 9:1, forms a convincing case that the SM comes in the context of the heavenly temple.[20]

Some may object to my proposed reading because the danielic SM does not function as a judge but rather is a symbol for faithful Israel in vindication after judgement has occurred. Despite this, Wright, for example, attempts to argue that the danielic figure is associated with judicial activities: "the whole scene is precisely forensic, and where the 'one like a son of man' is installed as, so to speak, the executive officer of the central judge."[21] A careful reading of the text indicates, however, that this SM is not an individual but is a corporate symbol and can only be a judicial "executive officer" if one reads into Dan 7 subsequent Jewish interpretations from the first century CE, including the Gospels.[22] Rather, Mark, like his other near-contemporaries, the authors of the *Parables* and *4 Ezra*, have developed this figure such that he now executes judicial prerogatives of Yahweh and is still associated with the celestial context of Dan 7. In chapter 3, I have surveyed two texts in the *Parables* in which the author alludes to the heavenly scene

---

19. Clines, *Job 1–20*, 137–38.

20. Kittel indicates that the "appearance of angels points to his [the SM's] coming from the divine world" ("δοκέω," 2:248–49),

21. Wright, *People*, 514 n. 138.

22. Adams, "Coming," 44.

of Dan 7 when he describes "that Son of Man" (46:1–5; 47:3—48:6) and, in subsequent passages, he exercises judicial action from the heavenly temple (48:10b; 61:8; 62:5). Similarly, after Jesus has suffered and died at the hands of his enemies, he will return as the vindicated SM and will come in judgement by being ashamed of those who are ashamed of him and his words, an instance of *ius talionis*, "justice of equal measure."[23] Matthew is much more explicit about the SM coming as judge in which "he will repay everyone for what has been done" (16:27b) drawing out what is implied in 8:38.

The judicial status of the SM in 8:38 is supported by the usage of ἐπαισχύνομαι and its cognates in the LXX. Bultmann argues that αἰσχύνομαι, ἐπαισχύνομαι, and καταισχύνω are translational variants of בוש and have the sense of "to shame" or "to bring shame" in the context of Yahweh's judgement.[24] Although ἐπαισχύνομαι only occurs three times in the LXX, two of the three instances support Bultmann's observation. In Ps 119 [LXX:118]:6, the speaker finds assurance that he will not "be put to shame" (ἐπαισχυνθῶ) because he has heeded the Lord's commands. In v. 31, he asks that the Lord not put him to shame (καταισχύνῃς) because he has "clung to your testimonies." In light of the context of the Psalm, being put to shame in v. 6 would be Yahweh's judgement for unfaithfulness to his law, e.g., 119:21, 75, 84–85, which this faithful Israelite wants to avoid at all costs. In Isa 1:28–31, the prophet announces Yahweh's judgement on the lawless and sinners of Judah resulting in their destruction. As part of this message, Isaiah declares, "For they shall be ashamed (αἰσχυνθήσονται) because of their idols, which they themselves wanted, and they were embarrassed (ἐπῃσχύνθησαν) because of their gardens, which they desired" (NETS: v. 29). The "gardens" are likely a reference to participation in some type of pagan cult that follows naturally from the reference to "their idols."[25] Yahweh's judgement will manifest itself in the inhabitants of Jerusalem being "put to shame" or "ashamed" for their idolatry. Whereas in the LXX the rebellious will one day experience this for their wickedness, the markan SM warns the disciples that he "will be ashamed," not because of any misdeed of his own, but because of those who have resisted the call to suffer for the sake of the gospel (vv. 34–35). Although Yahweh is never depicted as "being ashamed" of the actions of his people but only those who have been unfaithful in the LXX, the SM "being ashamed" of his would-be followers still

---

23. Evans, *Mark*, 27.
24. Bultmann, "αἰσχύνω," 189.
25. See Blenkinsopp, *Isaiah 1–39*, 188; Watts, *Isaiah 1–33*, 26.

Chapter 6: The Coming of the Son of Man in the Heavenly Temple

fits with this judicial context because of the ensuing separation between himself and the object of which he is ashamed, not unlike the regret and embarrassment that those unfaithful to Yahweh would feel over that which they are ashamed/put to shame when Yahweh judges them. Those who are ashamed in Mark of the call to suffer will thereby align themselves with "this adulterous and sinful generation" (ἐν τῇ γενεᾷ ταύτῃ τῇ μοιχαλίδι καὶ ἁμαρτωλῷ, v. 38a) and will consequently cause the SM to be ashamed of them when he comes from his celestial dwelling.

To sum up, the context of warning and admonition in which 8:38 appears, the Septuagintal background of ἐπαισχύνομαι which is associated with Yahweh's judgement, and the judicial presentation of the danielic SM in a celestial context in the *Parables*, which supports the *historical probability* of this reading, all substantiate my argument that Jesus depicts the exalted SM as a judge whose judicial action, once the prerogative of Yahweh in Dan 7, takes the shape of being ashamed of those who are unfaithful placing these ones, to use Hatina's language, in the "outgroup." In light of the linguistic correspondences with other heavenly contexts, including Dan 7, the setting of the SM's coming in 8:38 is the heavenly temple from which the he judges those who have not responded to his call to embrace his divinely ordained plight of cross bearing.

While many scholars advocate that 8:38 and 9:1 do not refer to the same event, I propose that a keen awareness of the danielic framework, which I have argued is evoked by both texts, at least points to some type of thematic correspondence between the coming of the SM and the Kingdom of God which centers on judgement. The appearance of Yahweh in his heavenly temple to judge the adversaries of his faithful ones marks the coming of his kingdom and the end of Antiochus's pagan kingdom. All of this leads to the former kingdom becoming the possession of the SM/ saints (see Dan 7:22, 26–27). Further, Hatina claims that both 8:38 and 9:1 express the theme of judgement because of terminology they share with 13:26 and 14:62 where it is quite clear, as I will argue later, that the SM comes to judge the temple and those who oversee it, respectively. Hatina begins by indicating that recent studies on the oral/aural transmission of Mark's Gospel warrant a non-linear reading such that later information, as it would already be in the minds of Mark's audience, informs earlier parts.[26] In order to legitimate the method of interpreting 8:38—9:1 by 13:26 and

---

26. Hatina, "Who Will See," 27–32. See Rhoads et al., *Mark as Story*, 48–49, 54–55; Dewey, "Tapestry," 221–36.

14:62, Hatina appeals to "retrospection" which functions "as a unifying narrative thread which clarifies or amplifies earlier events by later events."[27] Specifically, 8:38—9:1, 13:26 and 14:62 function as a "series of three" inviting the audience to make connections amongst each one.[28] In Mark 13:26, the SM will come on the clouds μετὰ δυνάμεως πολλῆς καὶ δόξης. This recalls the coming of the SM ἐν τῇ δόξῃ τοῦ πατρὸς αὐτοῦ and the coming of the kingdom ἐν δυνάμει in 8:38—9:1. Jesus employs the third person plural ὄψονται in 13:26 to denote those who will see the coming of the SM which contrasts sharply with the rest of Jesus' address in the chapter which he directs at the disciples using the second person plural, for example, Βλέπετε (v. 5), ἀκούσητε (v. 7), Βλέπετε (v. 9), πιστεύετε (v. 21).[29] Because of this, Hatina rightly classifies the undefined subjects of ὄψονται as the nebulous "out-group" or "antagonists." Turning to 14:62, it is quite evident that the second person plural subject of ὄψεσθε in the Jewish trial scene is the high priest and the Sanhedrin (see 14:53), those whom Jesus addresses. Mark's Jesus expresses the theme of divine judgement by quoting not only a portion of Dan 7:13 but also some of Ps 110:1 as this chapter will argue later. Applying Mark's use of ὁράω in 13:26 and 14:62 to ὁράω in 9:1, along with the themes of judgement from 13:26 and 14:62, "some of those standing" in 9:1 will witness the coming of the Kingdom ἐν δυνάμει as retribution.[30] As I have pointed out above, it is very difficult to identify the historical event which represents that the Kingdom has come in power, but it appears to be something quite ominous. There are a number of examples of the hostile use of "power" in the OT and DSS directed at human and divine enemies of Yahweh's faithful. In Jer 16:21 LXX, the Lord will teach Israel his power (τὴν δύναμίν) by coming in judgement for her covenantal unfaithfulness (see Jer 16:16–18). In Sir 36:3 [LXX: 2], a petition is offered to Yahweh: "Lift up your hand against foreign nations and let them see your might (τὴν δυναστείαν σου)," and in Ps 21:8–13 [LXX: 20:9–14], Yahweh is extolled for his dominion over his enemies and concludes with the following: "Be exalted, O Lord, in your strength (ἐν τῇ δυνάμει)! We will sing and praise

27. Hatina, "Who Will See," 27.

28. For the "series of three" concept in Mark, see Robbins, "Summons," 119–36. Although Hatina refers to Robbins's work for support, Robbins himself does not actually discuss 8:38—9:1, 13:26, and 14:62. France also advocates that these three passages are uniquely related to each other (*Mark*, 344).

29. Hatina lists seventeen occurrences of the second person plural imperative in Mark 13 ("Who Will See," 29).

30. Ibid., 31–32.

Chapter 6: The Coming of the Son of Man in the Heavenly Temple

your power (τὰς δυναστείας σου)."[31] Likewise, at Qumran, God's power manifests itself in the destruction of those who oppose his faithful ones, specifically in the *War Scroll*. For example, on the various trumpets which represent stages of battle against the "sons of darkness," one such trumpet will have inscribed on it: "God's mighty deeds (גבורות אל) to scatter the enemy and force all those who hate justice to flee" (1QM III, 5b–6a; see I, 14; IV, 4; VI, 2; X, 5).[32] In the LXX, "power" usually appears as δύναμις, δυναστεία, or ἰσχύς which are translated from גבורה, the Hebrew word used in 1QM. In light of the terminological connections evident among 8:38—9:1, 13:26 and 14:62, the danielic background which they all share, and the militaristic/judicial uses of δύναμις, Hatina is justified in his claim that 9:1 speaks of the future coming of the Kingdom of God *in power* as a manifestation of judgement. This coheres well with the image in 8:38 of the SM coming to judge those who have been ashamed of him and his words from his heavenly dwelling. As I have mentioned above, it is, however, very difficult to determine what event will mark the Kingdom having come in power and whether it is the same event in which would-be followers of Jesus will experience separation from the exalted SM because he is ashamed of them. What is clear is that there is a consequence for not sharing in the suffering and rejection of the SM for the sake of the gospel, and, at some point, the exalted SM will come from his heavenly temple to settle the score with those who have chosen not to do so.

The Coming of the Son of Man in 13:26–27

According to Elizabeth Malbon, Mark 11–12 and 14–16 form an interpretative frame around chapter 13.[33] Mark's emphasis on Jesus' rejection of the temple and its leadership is a dominant theme running throughout Mark 11–12.[34] It begins with the prophetic words and actions of Jesus in the temple (11:15–17), which are preceded by him cursing a fig tree (11:12–14) and followed by Peter noticing that the tree is now withered from the roots (11:20–22). This intercalation demonstrates that Jesus judged the institu-

---

31. Ibid., 33.
32. For additional references, consult Hatina, "Who Will See," 33 fn. 40.
33. Malbon, "Literary Contexts," 109.
34. Heil, "Narrative," 77–89. See also the discussions in Dupont, "La Ruine," 223-26; Hatina, "Focus of Mark," 49–50; Gray, *Temple*, 46–93; Kelber, *Kingdom*, 109–28; Donahue, *Are You*, 113–35; Juel, *Messiah*, 127–39.

tion because it is no longer serving Yahweh's saving purposes as a "house of prayer for all the nations" (see Isa 56:7) but rather has become "a den of robbers" (see Jer 7:11).[35] The anti-temple theme continues when Jesus subsequently promises that if the disciples have enough faith to say to "this mountain, 'Be taken up and thrown into the sea,'... it will be done for you" (v. 23). The words τῷ ὄρει τούτῳ almost certainly refer to the temple mount.[36] Beginning in 11:27 to the end of chapter 12, Jesus has a number of verbal exchanges in the temple courts with all of Mark's religious leaders. After refusing to answer the temple leaders' question by what authority he does "these things" (ταῦτα), referring to his temple action (11:27–33), he tells them a parable about wicked tenants, which condemns the elders, scribes, and chief priests (12:1–12). This is a relevant parable in light of the judgement that Jesus has just pronounced on the temple itself (11:12–24) and the temple leaders's subsequent challenge of his authority to act in the way that he has (11:27–33). Not only as the tenants of the vineyard do they keep the harvest for themselves and send the owner's servants away empty-handed, which highlights their misuse of the temple, but also they kill the owner's beloved son, which Mark's passion narrative will describe. Consequently, the owner himself will come and "destroy the tenants and give the vineyard to others" (12:9). Jesus plays a key role in this transition as he is the "son" (v. 6)/"stone" (v. 10) through whose rejection (v. 10; see 8:31; 9:31; 10:33–34) and death (v.7), "the Lord" will make into the "cornerstone" of a new temple.[37]

A scribe poses the last question to Jesus in the temple courts: "Which commandment (ἐντολή) is the first of all" (v. 28b)? He responds by referring to Deut 6:4 for the first commandment and adds a second that "You shall love your neighbor as yourself" (vv. 29–31). The scribe affirms the importance of these commandments and makes the value judgement that these are "much more important than πάντων τῶν ὁλοκαυτωμάτων καὶ θυσιῶν" (v. 33b). Although this phrase occurs at number of times in the LXX, e.g., Isa 1:11; Amos 5:2; Hos 6:6, I have argued elsewhere that Mark alludes to Jer 7:22 where this phrase along with the verb ἐνετειλάμην occurs, a cognate of ἐντολή: "Because in the day that I brought your fathers up out of the land of Egypt, I did not speak to them and did not *command* (ἐνετειλάμην) them concerning whole burnt offerings and sacrifices. But

---

35. Heil, "Narrative," 78. For an in-depth study of the significance of the fig tree in this passage, consult Telford, *Barren*.

36. Marshall, *Faith*, 186; Wright, *Victory*, 422.

37. Heil, "Narrative," 59; Donahue, *Are You*, 125–27.

Chapter 6: The Coming of the Son of Man in the Heavenly Temple

this I *commanded* (ἐνετειλάμην) them, saying, 'Obey my voice, and I will become a god to you, and you shall become a people to me, and walk in all my ways, which I *command* (ἐντείλωμαι) you, that it may be well with you'" (NETS: Jer 7:22–23).[38] As in Jeremiah, Mark's Jesus highlights the importance of obeying Yahweh's commands (v. 31: ἐντολή), in this case, to make loving Yahweh and neighbor top priority over sacrificial ritual. The diminishment of sacrifices, along with Mark's narrative placement of this story following not long after Jesus' denunciation of the temple in 11:12–17 and very close to his prediction of the temple's demise in chapter 13, prompts Hooker to make the claim that "the scribe's words would have been understood as an endorsement of Jesus' condemnation of the worship offered in the Temple as inadequate."[39] Finally, in the last two teachings, Jesus condemns the scribes for oppressing the needy and for pretentious behavior (vv. 38–40), and so this segment of the temple leadership "will receive the greater condemnation" (v. 40b). Jesus illustrates the oppressive temple structure with the example of the poor widow who tithes all of her last resources (vv. 41–44).

In light of the anti-temple theme evident in the two chapters preceding Mark 13, Jesus' words come as no surprise in 13:2: "Do you see all these great buildings? Not one stone will be left here upon another; all will be thrown down" (v. 2).[40] Four of the disciples then ask Jesus "when" will this occur and "what will be the sign that all things are about to be accomplished?" (v. 4).[41] In the following verses until v. 14, Jesus exhorts them to βλέπετε (v. 5, 9) and ἀκούσητε (v. 7) which indicate that the disciples need to be aware of their surroundings but there is no injunction to take physical action.[42] However, this changes in v. 14: "But *when* you see the desolating sacrilege (τὸ βδέλυγμα τῆς ἐρημώσεως) set up where it ought

---

38. Snow, "Understand," 473–74.

39. Hooker, *Mark*, 289.

40. Bolt, in his attempt to argue that Mark's Jesus condemns only people, claims that v. 2 is merely "a passing remark by Jesus" because he is not concerned with the destruction of the physical temple structure ("Mark 13," 20). Jesus, however, seems quite clear that he envisages a physical destruction. Lane, in contrast to Bolt, claims that "the most striking feature of this prophecy is its emphatic definiteness" (*Mark*, 451). See also the similar comments of Geddart, *Watchwords*, 146.

41. Dupont argues that "il semble en tout cas que la seconde partie du verset ne vise plus seulement la destruction du Temple: elle concerne l'ensemble des événements de la fin du monde" ("Ruine," 212). However, as I will argue in this section, there is no indication that Jesus is predicting the end of the space-time universe.

42. Such, "Crux Critecorum," 103.

Daniel's Son of Man in Mark

not to be (let the reader understand), *then* those in Judea must flee to the mountains." When Jesus' followers see this desolating sacrilege, the time for discernment has ended and they are to flee the holy city. The phrase τὸ βδέλυγμα τῆς ἐρημώσεως has given rise to a full debate concerning the historical referent of the "abomination." The options include the Roman army that conquered Jerusalem,[43] an image of a pagan god,[44] or the statue of the Emperor Caligula.[45] The articular phrase, τὸ βδέλυγμα τῆς ἐρημώσεως, corresponds exactly with Dan 12:11 LXX in which it is used to describe the presence of a pagan altar in the temple (see 1 Macc 1:54).[46] However, Dan 9:27 is often proposed as the background. Wright, for example, argues that it "is the crucial reference, with the others being subordinated to it."[47] But Mark's *constructio ad sensum* of a masculine participle of ἵστημι with a neuter subject is not reflected in 9:27 where Daniel uses the indicative form of εἰμί: καὶ ἐπὶ τὸ ἱερὸν βδέλυγμα τῶν ἐρημώσεων ἔσται (Dan 9:27 LXX). Further, applying the background of either 12:11 or 9:27 to Mark is incongruous with his emphasis on the corruption of the temple leadership. Daniel, on the other hand, is concerned with the temple's desecration by a pagan king, aided by a colluding priesthood.[48] Mark's departure from these passages by means of his *constructio ad sensum* "may suggest that [he] envisages something more than a lifeless idol."[49]

While each of the proposals offered by scholars as to the historical referent of "the abomination" has their own merits, it is significant that the terms βδέλυγμα and ἐρήμωσις both occur in Jer 7, the same chapter from which Jesus quotes when he declares that the temple has become σπήλαιον λῃστῶν (Mark 11:17; Jer 7:11 LXX). There is also a strong allusion to Jer

---

43. Beasley-Murray, *Future*, 256; Lührmann, *Das Markusevangelium*, 2:221–22; Pesch, *Das Markusevangelium*, 2:291.

44. Collins, "Apocalyptic Rhetoric," 25; Wright, *Victory*, 251–52.

45. Taylor, "Destruction," 285; Gnilka, *Das Evangelium*, 2:194. For more possible references of the "abomination that causes desolation," see Collins, "Eschatological Discourse," 1134–36.

46. Collins, "Rhetoric," 22–23.

47. Wright, *Victory*, 351; Gray proposes that Mark alludes to three passages: Dan 9:27; 11:31; 12:11 (*Temple*, 130).

48. France argues that τὸ βδέλυγμα τῆς ἐρημώσεως is concerned with the activity of Antiochus IV Epiphanes in maccabean interpretation and so Mark's audience would have interpreted it in a similar way (*Mark*, 520). However, France admits that "the aside ὁ ἀναγινώσκων νοείτω may suggest that it requires some subtlety of interpretation" (*Mark*, 520).

49. Snow, "Understand," 476.

Chapter 6: The Coming of the Son of Man in the Heavenly Temple

7:21–22 in Mark 12:33, as I have argued above. The scribe diminishes the importance of πάντων τῶν ὁλοκαυτωμάτων καὶ θυσιῶν compared with the command to love God and neighbor. Both this phrase and a cognate of ἐντολὴ appear in the text of Jeremiah making this a compelling intertext. Further, I contend that there are allusions to Jer 7 in the parable of the wicket tenants as well. While many rightly argue for an allusion to Isa 5:1–7, Mark's Jesus seems more concerned with the corruption of the tenants, who are the leaders of Israel, than with the vineyard itself. A closer look at both texts reveals that Yahweh in Jeremiah and the owner in Mark repeatedly sends (LXX: ἐξαπέστειλα [v.25]/GNT: ἀπέστειλεν [v. 2, 4–6]) his servants (LXX: τοὺς δούλους μου [v. 25]/GNT: δοῦλον [v. 2, 4–6]) to his people/tenants.[50] In Jeremiah, the servants function as the prophets who call Israel to be obedient to the Mosaic covenant (7:25), but she responds in rebellion: "yet they did not listen to me, or pay attention, but they stiffened their necks. They did worse than their ancestors did" (7:26; see v. 24). This is paralleled in Mark where the slaves are the prophets sent by Yahweh but yet have been resisted by the wicket tenants, a resistance which culminates in their murder of the owner's son. Indeed, Mark's leaders live up to their portrayal in the parable because at its conclusion the chief priests, scribes and elders desire to arrest Jesus (v. 12b) once they perceive "that he had told this parable *against them*" (v. 12a). This is not unlike the response of the same group at witnessing Jesus' condemnation of the temple: "they kept looking for a way to kill him" (v. 18a). It appears that "Jeremiah . . . plays an important role in the inter-textual makeup of this passage [Mark 12:1–10] by highlighting the corruption of Mark's temple leadership who participate in the historic rejection of Yahweh's servants, the prophets, and now even his own son."[51]

Given the *recurrence* of Jeremiah in these three passages, 11:17, 12:1–9, and 12:28–34, all of which are concerned with either diminishing the temple or its overseers in some way and so contribute to Mark's anti-temple theme, it is quite probable that Mark is also alluding to Jer 7 in Mark 13:14 where another reference to the corruption of the temple leaders fits very well. In Jer 7:30, the prophet condemns Israel's leaders for using the temple to house their idols or "abominations" (τὰ βδελύγματα). Consequently, the land shall become "desolate" (ἐρήμωσιν) (v. 34). Later, Jeremiah uses both terms in 44:22 (LXX: 51:22) speaking of the abominable practices of the

---

50. Ibid., 472.
51. Ibid.

Jews in Judah and Jerusalem: "And the Lord could no longer bear up before the evil of your deeds, before the abominations (τῶν βδελυγμάτων) that you committed, and your land became a desolation (ἐρήμωσιν) and something untrodden and a curse, as this day" (NETS).⁵² In Jer 7:9–10, the prophet condemns Israel for a variety of breaches of the Mosaic covenant which he labels "abominations" indicating that this term does not exclusively refer to idolatry. In summary, the preceding anti-temple theme in Mark 11 and 12 and the thoroughgoing use of Jer 7 in three passages preceding 13:14 which contribute to this theme, as well as the terminological correspondence of τὸ βδέλυγμα τῆς ἐρημώσεως with Jer 7:30 and 34 respectively, corroborate my proposal that Mark's Jesus once again has in mind the temple sermon in Jer 7, a text which centers on the corruption of the temple, or more accurately, its leaders—a relevant intertext for the agenda of Mark's Jesus in Mark 13.

Jacques Dupont indicates that Mark's masculine participle "standing" (ἑστηκότα) could point to a personal profaner such as a group of λῃσταί who profaned the temple at some point before its destruction (see 11:17).⁵³ Similarly, for John Paul Heil, Mark's τὸ βδέλυγμα τῆς ἐρημώσεως "became a symbol of the mysterious thing or *person* who would desecrate the temple in the future as a sign of its coming destruction and the beginning of the last days [emphasis mine]."⁵⁴ These readings resonate with a jeremianic understanding of τὸ βδέλυγμα τῆς ἐρημώσεως which ascribes the cause of abomination to *persons* as opposed to an idol or pagan altar as in Dan 9:27.⁵⁵ In Jer 7:10, the prophet describes those who have contravened the Mosaic covenant as ones who come and "stand" before Yahweh in his temple. The prophet questions Israel: "if you came and stood (ἔστητε) before me in the house, where my name has been called on it, and you said, 'We have kept away from doing all these abominations (τὰ βδελύγματα)'—surely my house, there where my name has been called on it, has not become a den of robbers before you?" (NETS: Jer 7:10b–11a). It is seems to me that "the posture of these λῃσταί provides another important point of contact with Mark 13:14 in which the abomination, as a form of defilement stemming

---

52. The term βδέλυγμα also occurs in Ezekiel referring to pagan images that the leaders have erected in the temple courts. See, for example, Ezek 8:6, 9, 13, 15, 17.
53. Dupont, "Ruine," 224–25.
54. Heil, "Narrative," 91.
55. Snow, "Understand," 476.

Chapter 6: The Coming of the Son of Man in the Heavenly Temple

from the corruption of Mark's Temple leaders, is likewise 'standing where he should not be' (ἑστηκότα ὅπου οὐ δεῖ)."⁵⁶

Further, given that Mark's Gospel was likely composed just before the destruction of the temple, during the Jewish-Roman war, or immediately following its destruction, it is unlikely that Mark is referring to its desecration by the Romans, for example. The city was embroiled in a war for four years leading up to the temple's demise, so the need to flee would be self-evident. I argue that "for Mark's audience living outside of the land likely just before or after the Jewish-Roman war, the historical act of profanation, 'the abomination,' and the destruction of the Temple, 'the desolation,' is a foregone conclusion."⁵⁷ Rather, Mark is concerned with the corruption of the temple leadership that he highlights both inner-textually and intertextually and, in consequence, the cryptic phrase, "let the reader understand," could suggest that Mark's readers are not to equate the "abomination" with an obvious historical event. Finally, the genre of Mark 13 has some affinities with Jewish apocalyptic which places some of the burden of proof on literal interpretations of the esoteric phrase.⁵⁸ In vv. 14b–23, Jesus develops the command to flee, warns of suffering, and calls the disciples to beware of false prophets and messiahs, all of which is precipitated by τὸ βδέλυγμα τῆς ἐρημώσεως.⁵⁹ Applying my proposal to these verses, Jesus is warning his disciples in prophetic language not to align themselves in any way with the temple as its desolation is drawing nigh due to the rebellion of its leaders.⁶⁰

In v. 24, Jesus begins with an adversative αλλὰ which contrasts the intense period of tribulation that Mark describes in vv. 14–23 with a great earth-shattering event that implicates even the cosmos (vv. 24–25). Many argue, or even assume, that the event Mark depicts in vv. 24–27 is the "second coming" or *parousia*.⁶¹ According to George R. Beasley-Murray, the SM's coming on the clouds is a theophany (see Isa 19:1; Ps 18:12) so that

---

56. Ibid., 477.

57. Ibid.

58. Dunn claims that the cryptic "abomination of desolation" is not unlike what one would find in the apocalyptic genre (*Unity*, 329). For a helpful discussion of the similarities and dissimilarities of Mark 13 with "apocalyptic," see Hatina, *Search*, 341–44.

59. See, for example, the failed messianic hopes of Simon bar Giora (Josephus, *J. W.* 4.574–78).

60. Gray traces much of the language Jesus uses back to the prophets (*Temple*, 133–35).

61. For example, Lane, *Mark*, 476; Pesch, *Das Markusevangelium*, 2:303; Casey, *Son of Man*, 176; Müller, *Ausdruck*, 91; Evans, *Mark*, 328–29.

the clouds serve as a vehicle for his descent to earth.[62] Gundry comments that "the coming of the Son of man in clouds is almost surely meant to be taken literally (see esp. Acts 1:9–11; 1 Thess. 4:15–17)."[63] Alternatively, Bas van Iersel claims that the familiarity of Mark's audience with Greco-Roman culture would prompt them to interpret these verses as the destruction of all Roman idols.[64] While the latter certainly has its merits, particularly for a Roman audience, van Iersel must account for the larger literary context, i.e., Mark 11–12, which focuses on the corruption of the Jewish temple, not to mention the observation of the disciples in v. 1 about its magnificence which occasions the prediction of its destruction. Similarly, those who argue that Jesus is describing the end of the space-time universe in these verses need to consider that they are a part of a sustained, uninterrupted discourse elicited by questions of the disciples as to when the temple will be destroyed and what the signs of its impending destruction will be (v. 4).

Considering vv. 24–25 first, any examination needs to start not only with this literary context in mind but also the OT texts from which these verses come—Isa 13:10 and 34:4. In both of these passages, the prophet announces the destruction of Israel's enemies, Babylon and Edom respectively.[65] A number of scholars point out the influence of Isa 13:10 on vv. 24b–25a.[66] Likewise, many contend that Mark's Jesus alludes to Isa 34:4 in v. 25b, specifically, αἱ δυνάμεις which appears in Greek versions other than the LXX.[67] The variants Vaticanus and Theodotion read καὶ τακήσόται πᾶσαι αἱ δυνάμεις τῶν οὐρανῶν translated from the Hebrew וְנָמַקּוּ כָּל־צְבָא הַשָּׁמַיִם of Is 34:4a.[68] These prophetic texts and others like them (see Ezek 32:7; Amos

---

62. Beasley-Murray, *Future*, 258. For a short summary of the debate, see Bolt, "Mark 13," 10–32.

63. Gundry, *Mark*, 783.

64. van Iersel, "Sun," 84–92.

65. Gnilka, *Das Evangelium*, 2:200; Grey, *Temple*, 140; France, *Mark*, 532–33.

66. Hatina compares the MT and LXX of Isa 13:10 with v. 24 and concludes that Mark is closer to the MT than the LXX (*Search*, 327–28). However, Verheyden contends that the LXX has a formative influence on vv. 24 and 25 ("Describing," 534). See also Müller, *Ausdruck*, 93. Joel 2:10 has also been suggested as a possible allusion, see Wenham, *Rediscovery*, 309. For criticisms of this option, see Hatina, *Search*, 328–29.

67. See the discussion in Verheyden, "Describing," 536–40 and Watts, "Mark," 225. After a careful discussion of the Greek version(s) and their relationship to the Hebrew text of Isa 34:4, Hatina concludes that "all in all, the eclectic character of Mark 13.25 along with its various omissions make it very difficult to ascertain the source [that is, the Greek or Hebrew of Isa 34:4]" (*Search*, 329–31).

68. Hatina, *Search*, 329.

Chapter 6: The Coming of the Son of Man in the Heavenly Temple

8:9; Joel 2:10), communicate the temporal, earth-shattering significance of national disasters and invests them with theological significance. In the case of Isa 13:10 and 34:4, the imagery depicts the destruction of pagan nations that are objects of Yahweh's wrath.[69] In Mark, Jesus functions, *inter alia*, as one of Israel's prophets and reapplies this imagery to portend the destruction of Jerusalem and its temple for the leaders's rebellion against Yahweh's saving purposes now revealed in his son.[70]

The imagery of the sun being darkened, the moon not giving its light, the stars falling from heaven, and the powers in the heavens being shaken leads to a prediction about the coming of the SM: "Then (τότε) they will see the Son of Man coming in clouds with great power and glory" (v. 26). Mark's use of τότε associates the coming of the exalted SM with the metaphorical description of the temple's destruction. A serious consideration of the danielic background of v. 26 as well as the significance of the imagery that describes the coming of the SM μετὰ δυνάμεως πολλῆς καὶ δόξης indicates that the destruction of the temple occurs as a result of the SM's judicial action against it. Whereas Yahweh was behind the downfall of the pagan cities of Babylon and Edom, now the SM, in the place of Yahweh, judges the temple institution for its internal corruption and resistance toward him as the messiah. Dupont, however, argues that Mark portrays his coming as completely positive because of his role in v. 27 of sending out the angels to gather "the elect."[71] We will see that this interpretation fails to ap-

---

69. Ibid., 358.

70. See Wright, *Victory*, 360–65. Verheyden argues that the imagery of cosmic disruption in vv. 24–25 does not connote judgement or the day of the Lord but rather describes the coming of the SM ("Describing," 543). While Mark's Jesus does predict a temporal judgement of the temple and hence precludes the idea that Jesus is predicting the "Day of the Lord" (final eschatological judgement), the theme of judgement is still dominant particularly in light of its expression in the source texts, Isa 13:10 and 34:4. Verheyden's methodology is tenuous as expressed in his statement regarding the imagery of vv. 24–25: "it is the imagery that is of interest, not the texts from which they are borrowed" ("Describing," 543).

Fletcher-Louis raises the idea that vv. 24–25 actually refer to the literal collapse of the cosmos because the temple, as the meeting place of heaven and earth, is the cosmos's great stabilizer, and if it was destroyed the physical universe would literally come undone ("Dissolution," 117–41). Fletcher-Louis basis much of his interpretation on a literal reading of Joel 2:10 which describes the disruption of heavenly bodies caused by the cessation of "the grain offering and drink offering." One is left wondering why the cosmos has not yet collapsed since the temple has been destroyed.

71. Dupont, "Ruine," 251. See also, Collins, "Rhetoric," 29; Müller, *Ausdruck*, 97; and France, *Mark*, 534.

preciate the literary relationship which exists between 8:38 and 13:26, both of which center on the theme of judgement as well as the intertext of Dan 7.

Many scholars agree that Mark alludes to Dan 7:13 in v. 26 because the *volume* of this intertext is very strong. Mark's Greek conforms with Theodotion's version which uses the present participle ἐρχόμενος (LXX: ἤρχετο) in addition to υἱὸς ἀνθρώπου and νεφέλη which are found in the LXX as well. Mark does not use the phrase μετὰ τῶν νεφελῶν τοῦ οὐρανοῦ in Theodotion but rather ἐν νεφέλαις which still communicates the same idea and so does not call into question the allusion.[72] The precise direction of his coming has been the object of considerable debate: does he descend to earth, ascend to heaven, or merely come to the presence of God for vindication?[73] Recalling the celestial temple scene of Dan 7, another, perhaps more plausible suggestion might be in order. The scene that Mark describes in vv. 26 and 27 builds upon the celestial scene in Dan 7. It is as though Mark assumes that the SM has already received "dominion, glory and kingship" (Dan 7:14a) because now he comes μετὰ δυνάμεως πολλῆς καὶ δόξης and ἀποστελεῖ τοὺς ἀγγέλους καὶ ἐπισυνάξει τοὺς ἐκλεκτούς. This exalted status is foreshadowed in the opening scenes of the Gospel in which Jesus is filled with the Spirit, acts with authority to exorcise as the "Holy One of God," and heals and purifies a leper by means of his contagious purity. I propose that the markan SM neither travels up, down, or even to the Ancient of Days for vindication, but rather is already vindicated, in keeping with the picture in Dan 7, and now acts as an exalted judge who deals with unfaithful Israel from his heavenly temple abode, an obvious development of the danielic scene, just as Yahweh does from the heavenly temple in Dan 7 as well as in Isa 6 and *1 En.* 14. The SM does not come to the Ancient of Days as he does in Dan 7 because now he comes, like Yahweh, to execute judgement.[74]

The prepositional phrase μετὰ δυνάμεως πολλῆς underscores the judicial aspect of his coming. As I have indicated above, δύναμις and its cognates in the LXX and גבורה in the DSS are used to describe Yahweh coming as judge or divine warrior to deal with injustice or unfaithfulness (Jer 16:21;

---

72. France rightfully suggests that the ἐν is similar to עִם of the Aramaic text, ἐπὶ of the LXX, and μετὰ of Theod (*Mark*, 534 fn. 14).

73. Descent: Gundry, *Mark*, 784 (Gundry claims that France argues for ascent when actually France argues that "it is a coming to God to receive power, not a coming to earth" [*Old Testament*, 236]); Beasley-Murray, *Future*, 258; Ascent: Wright, *Victory*, 361; Coming to God: France, *Old Testament*, 236.

74. Hatina, "Focus," 62. See also Lindars, *Son of Man*, 108.

Chapter 6: The Coming of the Son of Man in the Heavenly Temple

Sir 36:2; Ps 20:9-14; 1QM III, 5b-6a; see I, 14; IV, 4; VI, 2; X, 5). The judicial motif communicated by this phrase complements the evocation of Dan 7 where the SM now judges in place of Yahweh. Further, Rudolf Pesch emphasizes the importance of "seeing" in martyrological traditions where oppressors of the righteous who "see" the vindication of those whom they have oppressed, consequently understand themselves to be at that moment judged (Wis 5:2; Rev 11:2; *1 En.* 62:3-5; *Apoc. El. (C)* 35:17).[75] This is an important background for the prediction because Jesus forecasts that "they," which at the very least includes those who oppose him as Jesus himself will make explicit in 14:62, "will see 'the Son of Man coming in clouds' with great power and glory."[76] Enoch is told the following in the *Parables*: "And there will stand up on that day all the kings and the mighty and the exalted and those who possess the earth. And they will *see* and recognize that he sits on the throne of his glory; . . . and pain will seize them when they see that son of man sitting on the throne of his glory" (*1 En.* 62: 3a, 5a). That is, those who have oppressed faithful Israel will one day receive their comeuppance when they see the SM. Similarly, in Mark, those who have refused to recognize the SM's authority and instead brought about his suffering and death will likewise be judged at seeing the vindicated and exalted SM. This passage from the *Parables* specifically parallels Jesus' prediction in 14:62 as we will see below.

The SM not only comes μετὰ δυνάμεως πολλῆς but also with δόξα which amplifies the heavenly temple background of the allusion along with the presence of his angels (τοὺς ἀγγέλους) whom he sends out to gather the elect in v. 27. In my analysis of 8:38, I have demonstrated that "glory" and "angels" are found in a number biblical and extra-biblical texts which depict Yahweh in his earthly and heavenly temples (δόξα: 1 Kgs 8:11b; Ezek 43:4; Isa 6:3b; *1 En.* 14:16, 20; 4QShirShabba 1 I, 4; 4QShirShabbd 1 I, 33; ἄγγελοι: Ps 102:19-20; Job 5:1; Ps 88:8; 4QShirShabbf 19, 7; 20 II, 9; 23 I, 8; 1QM XII, 1a; *1 En.* 71:8). This background, coupled with Dan 7, evokes a celestial scene in Mark from where the SM judges the earthly temple, including those who align themselves with it. It is worth stating again that since this is a biblical allusion, an evocation of an earlier text containing echoes of others as well, it is brief and hence necessarily evocative. It does

---

75. Pesch, *Das Markusevangelium*, 2:439.

76. Gundry suggests that the subject of ὄψονται refers to "all people" in keeping with 13:26 as referring to the *parousia*; meanwhile, Donahue, *Are You*, assumes it is the "faithful" (*Mark*, 745).

not, by any means, include the detail found in, for example, Daniel's description of the heavenly temple in Dan 7.

A consideration of the criterion of *thematic coherence* strengthens this proposed reading. I have already argued, as have others, that in 8:38—9:1 an allusion to Daniel explains the tandem coming of the SM and the KoG and that it also draws out the judicial aspect of both, which entirely fits with Mark's narrative placement of these passages. Likewise, in the verses leading up to 13:26, Jesus warns his disciples in no uncertain terms not to align themselves with the holy city and its temple because it will be destroyed as a result of the SM's judgement. The "abomination that causes desolation" is a veiled reference to the temple leadership who have done nothing but resist Yahweh's messiah since his arrival in Jerusalem, which Jesus highlights in Mark 11 and 12, often evoking Jer 7, and, therefore, they and the institution that they oversee will soon come to an end. Because Daniel supplies the same thematic coherence for the narrative contexts of both 8:38 and 13:26, it also satisfies the criterion of *recurrence*. That is, the SM coming μετὰ δυνάμεως πολλῆς καὶ δόξης in 13:26 parallels the coming (ἔλθῃ) of the SM ἐν τῇ δόξῃ τοῦ πατρὸς αὐτοῦ μετὰ τῶν ἀγγέλων τῶν ἁγίων in 8:38 both of which express the SM's judgement from his heavenly dwelling. In other words, Mark evokes the same aspects of Dan 7 in both of these future SM sayings and will do so again in 14:62. As I have mentioned in the last section, this reading gains a good degree of *historical probability* because of the similar function and location of the exalted SM in the *Parables* who judges those who have rebelled against the Lord of Spirits and does so from the heavenly temple.

Also, under category of *historical probability*, Mark and Daniel are both concerned with some type of corruption or defilement in the Jerusalem temple. Because of the aggressive and despotic Syrian king, Antiochus IV Epiphanes, who turned the temple into a pagan shrine and ordered the cessation of the daily burnt offering, faithful Israel, or "the holy ones of the Most High," have been cut off from Yahweh's dwelling and are now estranged from his presence. Reading beyond Dan 7 and 8, we also see that the temple priests likely aided Antiochus is his profaning actions. Likewise, Mark is addressing a corrupt temple system which no longer functions as a house of prayer but rather has become a σπήλαιον λῃστῶν (11:15) overseen by wicked tenants who wish to hoard the whole thing for themselves and have destroyed the prophets sent to call them back to Yahweh, including his own son. It is little wonder that Jesus predicts its demise. Interestingly,

Chapter 6: The Coming of the Son of Man in the Heavenly Temple

the function of the heavenly temples in both Mark and Daniel deals with the corruption and profanation of the earthly temple, of a divinely ordained establishment that no longer serves its intended purpose. In Dan 7, the heavenly temple manifests itself from which Yahweh judges those responsible for defiling the sacred site of his terrestrial presence and, similarly, in Mark, the heavenly temple appears from which the exalted SM will come "with great power and glory" to judge the temple for housing λῃσταί and representing the center of national resistance against the Messiah. This movement, of the heavenly temple manifesting itself to judge terrestrial temple corruption, has an earlier precedent beginning with the function of the heavenly temple in *1 En* 14. After travelling to and witnessing Yahweh enthroned in his heavenly dwelling, Enoch receives a message of condemnation for the corrupt priests in the Jerusalem temple who, in the vision, are symbolized by heavenly priests having forsaken their priestly duties to fornicate with women on earth (*1 En.* 15:3–4).

In light of my argument above that the SM comes in his celestial dwelling in v. 26, the statement in the second half of v. 25, καὶ αἱ δυνάμεις αἱ ἐν τοῖς οὐρανοῖς σαλευθήσονται, is a fitting segue into v. 26. The term αἱ δυνάμεις often refers to divine beings and certainly their shaking in Isa 34:4 reflects Yahweh's comprehensive judgement of Edom. In 2 Kgs 21:1–9, Manasseh erects pagan altars in the sacred temple courts so that he might worship and serve "all the host of heaven" (2 Kgs 21:5 LXX: πάσῃ τῇ δυνάμει τοῦ οὐρανοῦ; see 21:3). In Jer 19:13 and Zeph 1:5, the word στρατιά is used to refer to pagan gods or "all the host of heaven" which Israel worships. The terms στρατιά and δύναμις appear to be used interchangeably in the LXX to translate צָבָא. According to Verheyden, the "hosts," as objects of worship, also occur with the sun, moon, and/or stars (Deut 4:19 LXX: τὸν κόσμον; MT: צָבָא; Deut 17:3; Jer 8:2), with the worship of Baal (2 Kgs 17:16 LXX: τῇ δυνάμει; 21:3; 23:4), or even with both the heavenly luminaries and Baal (2 Kgs 23:5 LXX: τῇ δυνάμει).[77] However, the "hosts" do not always represent pagan gods but also heavenly beings who worship Yahweh in his heavenly temple such as in Micaiah's vision in 1 Kgs 22:19: "I saw the Lord sitting upon his throne with all the host of heaven (1 Kgs 22:19 LXX: πᾶσα ἡ στρατιὰ τοῦ οὐρανοῦ) standing beside him to the right and to the left of him" (see Neh 9:6 LXX: αἱ στρατιαὶ τῶν οὐρανῶν).[78] Some, such as Verheyden, claim that αἱ δυνάμεις in Mark 13:25 functions more generally

---

77. Verheyden, "Describing," 543 fn. 79; see also Grundmann, "δύναμαι," 292.
78. Verheyden, "Describing," 543 fn. 79.

to refer to the celestial bodies and their disturbance which may explain the use of the plural αἱ δυνάμεις.[79] However, given the repeated use of the phase "hosts of heaven" in the OT to refer to pagan gods or divine beings, "the powers in the heavens" should be seen to stand on their own as such. Functioning as pagan gods, the "shaking" of these heavenly powers, and by implication the pagan cults with which they are associated, highlights the ultimate dominion and power of the SM who comes in the heavenly temple. Additionally, the verb σαλεύω is sometimes used to describe the result of the Lord coming in judgement from his temple which makes it an apt term to depict the effect of the coming of the SM. In Ps 18:6-7, when the Lord becomes angered in his dwelling at those who have oppressed the supplicant, "the earth shook (ἐσαλεύθη) and quaked and the foundations of the mountains were disturbed and were shaken (ἐσαλεύθησαν) (17:8 LXX)" (see Mic 1:2-4 LXX; Isa 64:1-2a Theod.; Ps 96:4-5 LXX).[80] Instead of mountains or the earth trembling at Yahweh's coming, the gods of the heavens will be shaken at the manifestation of the markan SM in his heavenly abode.[81] For a Greco-Roman audience acquainted with the Scriptures of Israel, i.e., Dan 7 and the aforementioned passages, one can conclude, as van Iersel does, that "the house of heaven will be cleared and thus made ready to serve as the dwelling-place of the son of man."[82]

In addition to engaging in judicial activity in the heavenly temple, the SM also sends out angels to gather his "elect (τοὺς ἐκλεκτοὺς) from the four winds, from the ends of the earth to the ends of heaven" (v. 27).[83] Keeping

79. Ibid., 543; Grundmann, "δύναμαι," 307.

80. For additional references where σαλεύω is used in the context of judgement, see Nah 1:2-5; Hab 3:6; Jdt 16:15. See also Bertram, "σαλεύω," 66.

81. This strengthens the argument of van Iersel that Greco-Roman audiences may well see a reference to the deposition of pagan gods ("Sun," 89).

82. van Iersel, "Sun," 90. Caution does need to be exercised with this line of interpretation so that the emphasis does not shift from Mark's concern for the corruption of the temple and its consequent destruction. For example, one is not encouraged to support van Iersel when he concludes that "between 65 and 100 [c.e.] Greco-Roman readers or hearers of Mark 13,24-25 thought *primarily* of traditional divine figures who played a significant role in the Greco-Roman culture of this time [emphasis mine]" ("Sun," 92).

83. Arguing that πᾶσα δόξα αὐτῷ "serves" (λατρεύουσα) the SM in Dan 7:14, M. Stowasser suggests that δόξα in 13:26 could refer to the "angels" in v. 27 whom the SM sends out, but there is little textual evidence for this in Mark ("Mk 13,26f," 248-49).

The pronoun αὐτοῦ is omitted in a number ancient witnesses but is found in ℵ A B C and others which leads many to claim that the pronoun is original. According to France, its omission in some MSS reflects a harmonization with the use of τοὺς ἐκλεκτοὺς in vv. 20 and 22 which occurs without αὐτοῦ; further, τοὺς ἐκλεκτοὺς in v. 20 are identified as

Chapter 6: The Coming of the Son of Man in the Heavenly Temple

Dan 7 still in view, this appears to be another development of that chapter because now the SM no longer symbolizes a faithful group but rather is separate from them, namely his disciples and other faithful followers, and is the agent of their deliverance. Collins points out that the term "chosen" or "elect" appears at numerous points in the corpus of *1 Enoch* to denote those faithful to Yahweh, e.g., 5:7-8; 39:6-7; 93:1-10 and similarly בחיר, "the chosen," is used at Qumran to refer to the members of its own community, e.g., 1QpHab V, 4; IX, 11-12. Similarly in Mark, the term refers to those who remain faithful and persevere until gathered together by the SM.[84] This development of the danielic SM gains a strong degree of *historical probability* when we recall that a similar movement is evident in the *Parables* where the once passive danielic figure is an agent of salvation in which he delivers and restores righteous Israel. He is a "staff for the righteous," "a light for the Gentiles," and "the hope of those who are sick in their hearts" (48:4). Further, these ones are even identified, at times, as "the elect," e.g., 40:5; 45:3-5; 51:3-5; 62:14-15.[85] Enoch sees that "the congregation of the chosen and the holy will be sown; and all the chosen will stand in his [the SM's] presence on that day" (62:8).

Wright argues that the activity of the SM in v. 27 signals a return from exile and one OT passage which echoes this verse and expresses this theme is Deut 30:4: "If your dispersion be from an end of the sky to an end of the sky (ἀπ' ἄκρου τοῦ οὐρανοῦ ἕως ἄκρου τοῦ οὐρανοῦ), from there the Lord your God will gather (συνάξει) you and from there he will take you" (NETS).[86] In v. 27, the SM will gather (ἐπισυνάξει) the elect ἐκ τῶν τεσσάρων ἀνέμων ἀπ' ἄκρου γῆς ἕως ἄκρου οὐρανοῦ.[87] An even clearer echo is found in Zech 2:10 LXX, in which Yahweh gathers the dispersed nation, with which there is more terminological and thematic correspondence. Yahweh promises that "I will gather you from the four winds of the sky" (2:6b NETS; LXX: ἐκ τῶν τεσσάρων ἀνέμων τοῦ οὐρανοῦ συνάξω ὑμᾶς). The purpose of this gathering is so exiled Israel can return to the temple whereupon the Lord will dwell with them (2:14 LXX), which is a

---

the ones Yahweh chose, which supports the authenticity of the possessive pronoun in v. 27 (*Mark*, 536).

84. Collins, *Mark*, 612.

85. Marcus, *Mark*, 909.

86. Wright, *People*, 363; Hatina, *Search*, 370; France, *Mark*, 536.

87. See also Ps 146:2 LXX: "The Lord builds up Jerusalem; he gathers (ἐπισυνάξει) the outcasts of Israel."

particularly tantalizing background given the SM's presence in the heavenly temple to which he gathers his elect.[88] Mark's SM, by sending out his angels to gather his faithful ones, in light of the preceding texts, plays the role of Yahweh bringing those faithful to him into his presence. This coheres with the purpose of the danielic SM, albeit functioning merely as a symbol for the persecuted holy ones, who is associated with the restoration of faithful Israel to the presence of Yahweh.[89] It may also be the case that the SM will draw to himself those outside of the nation and hence will fulfill one of the purposes of the temple to be a house of prayer for all the nations, which it has failed to do. The very next verse following Isa 56:7, a portion of which Jesus quotes in 11:17 (ὁ οἶκός μου οἶκος προσευχῆς κληθήσεται πᾶσιν τοῖς ἔθνεσιν), is an identification of Yahweh as one who not only gathers Israel (ὁ συνάγων τοὺς διεσπαρμένους Ισραηλ) but also will gather others as well (ὅτι συνάξω ἐπ' αὐτὸν συναγωγήν).[90] As the SM, Jesus once again engages in a prerogative of Yahweh by gathering to himself Israel and likely faithful ones from the nations as well, not to the Jerusalem temple, but to his presence in the celestial one.[91] One corollary of this is that the divine presence of Yahweh is now centered in his agent of deliverance to which the elect will be gathered. However, in none of the passages in Deuteronomy or Zecha-

---

88. France, *Mark*, 536. Kee claims that Isa 27:13 functions as a quotation in v. 27 in addition to Zech 2:6, 10 ("Function of Scripture," 169); however, it is difficult to see a quotation of Isaiah especially when there is not one verbal correspondence between the two texts. Thematically there is a parallel that may suggest some type of influence on v. 27 in which the exiles in Assyria and Egypt "will come and worship the Lord on the holy mountain at Jerusalem" (Isa 27:13). Also, Kee suggests Zech 14:5 as one text to which Mark may be alluding ("Function of Scripture," 169). However, πάντες οἱ ἅγιοι accompany Yahweh when he does battle against Israel's enemies, particularly those who attack Jerusalem (v. 12).

Another textual echo, according to Kee, is Ezek 39:27 in which Yahweh will "gather" (συναγαγεῖν) Israel from foreign lands because they have paid the price for their sins (39:29).

89. Hooker suggests that "behind Mark's interpretation ... there may well lie a stage in the tradition in which the coming of the Son of man was understood, as in Daniel, of a judgement scene before God, rather than of a parousia to earth" (*Son of Man*, 158–59). If it were not for Hooker's assumption that 13:26–27 depicts the *parousia*, I think she would have drawn a similar conclusion to mine, on the basis that Mark evokes the larger scene of Dan 7:13, that this is a picture of judgement against the adversaries of the SM and also of his gathering of those who are not ashamed of him (see 8:38).

90. The second half of v. 8 is translated quite literally in NETS: "for I will gather to him a gathering" which in context refers to Yahweh gathering more than just the scattered Israelites to make the temple πᾶσιν τοῖς ἔθνεσιν.

91. Gray, *Temple*, 144.

Chapter 6: The Coming of the Son of Man in the Heavenly Temple

riah do angels participate in the restoration. Whereas in 8:38 the "holy angels" assist the SM in his task of judgement, the angels sent out in 13:27 are assigned the redemptive prerogative of delivering those not ashamed of him and who have endured the trials depicted in 13:9 to the celestial temple now that the earthly one has been judged and destroyed as vv. 24–26 make clear.[92] T. W. Geddart has it right in his claim that "Mark sees the faithful scattered from the old temple at 13:14 and re-gathered fully and finally in the new temple at 13.27."[93]

The Coming of the Son of Man in 14:62

Jesus' predictions of the suffering of the SM and his rejection by the elders, scribes, and chief priests (8:31; 9:31; 10:33–34) finds its fulfilment in the Jewish trial scene (14:53–65). At the beginning of the passion narrative, the scribes and chief priests seek to arrest Jesus "by deceit" (ἐν δόλῳ, 14:1) and Judas conspires with them to betray Jesus (vv. 10–11). The plot is a success when an armed throng commissioned by the temple leadership arrives at the Garden of Gethsemane to arrest him (vv. 41–49). They then deliver him to the palace of high priest where "all the chief priests, the elders, and the scribes were assembled" (v. 53b). A careful reading of the trial reveals the intense desire of the Sanhedrin to destroy Jesus. Its nocturnal setting and location at the palace of the high priest is undoubtedly a departure from Jewish judicial practice in order to condemn Jesus out of view of the crowds.[94] The unsuccessful search for evidence (v. 55), and the many false accusations brought against him, none of which agree, reveal the unabated antagonism of Jesus' opponents (vv. 56–59). Mark portrays this whole scene as completely unfair and is essentially a kangaroo court. At the trial, "all" the chief priests, elders and scribes are assembled (v. 53) and the chief

---

92. France emphasizes the danielic theme of enthronement in his interpretation of v. 26 that contrasts with the negative judgement on the temple in vv. 24-25 (*Mark*, 534). However, this proposal does not adequately capture the judicial action of the markan SM and its danielic background.

93. Geddart, *Watchwords*, 138. See also, Hatina, *Search*, 371.

94. Hooker notes that the nocturnal trial breaches *m. Sanh.* 4:1, and the location at the palace of the high priest breaches *m. Sanh.* 11:2 (*Mark*, 357). Wright rejects mishnaic evidence due to its lateness, i.e., 200 CE, but possibly at this point it could reflect an earlier tradition (*Victory*, 520). Collins also dismisses the relevance of the tractate *Sanhedrin* for historical use ("Blasphemy," 380).

priests and the "whole council" (ὅλον τὸ συνέδριον) seek testimony so that they can put Jesus to death (v. 55).

During the trial, the high priest questions Jesus if he is the Messiah (v. 61b). The question is likely occasioned by the false accusation about his alleged claim that he would destroy the temple and rebuild another in three days (v. 58). Prior to his symbolic act of judgment on the temple, Jesus enters Jerusalem hailed as a Davidic messianic king (11:9b–10), and, following the temple incident, the temple triumvirate questions by what "authority" he does these things (11:28) referring to his words and actions in the temple. The link between messiah and temple is evident in a couple of second-temple texts. In the first-century BCE text, the *Psalms of Solomon*, the messiah is expected to purge Jerusalem and, by implication, her temple from all iniquity (17:21–32). The Qumran text, 4QFlor 1 I, 1–4, which is an interpretation of 2 Sam 7:10 and Exod 15:17–18, demonstrates the connection as well:

> [*Ps 89:23* << Not] [will] an enemy [strike him any]more, *2 Sam 7:10* [nor will] a son of iniquity [afflict] him [aga]in as in the past. From the day on which [I appointed judges] over my people, Israel >>. This (refers to) the house which [he will establish] for [him] in the last days, as it is written in the book of [Moses: *Exod 15:17-18* << The temple of] yhwh your hands will est[a]blish. yhwh shall reign for ever and ever >>. This (refers to) the house into which shall not enter [. . . for] ever either Ammonite, or a Moabite, or a bastard, or a foreigner, or a proselyte, never, because his holy ones are there.

On this passage, James D. G. Dunn comments that "linked with the exposition of 2 Sam 7:12–14 a few lines later [see line numbers 10–13], the expectation seems to be clear: that the Davidic Messiah would fulfil the ancient promise to David and build the eschatological Temple."[95] So the false charge is not without basis as it must in some way refer, however distortedly, to the disruptive temple activity of Jesus (11:15–17) and elicits the question of the high priest.

On a narrative level and in light of the above second-temple texts, the false accusation may actually be a stroke of irony on the part of Mark where the accusers unknowingly declare truth. This trope is evident later in the passion narrative in the titulus that Pilate places on the cross labelling Jesus ὁ βασιλεὺς τῶν Ἰουδαίων (15:26) and the centurion declaring that "Truly

---

95. Dunn, "Messiah," 8.

Chapter 6: The Coming of the Son of Man in the Heavenly Temple

this man was God's Son" (15:39).[96] Mark sandwiches the false charge (vv. 57–58) between two similar statements expressing the inconsistency of the testimonies: ἴσαι αἱ μαρτυρίαι οὐκ ἦσαν (v.56) and οὐδὲ οὕτως ἴση ἦν ἡ μαρτυρία αὐτῶν (v.59), which seems overwhelmingly gratuitous and may indicate that this "false testimony" is not to be taken at face value.[97] Further, the allegation could easily stand on its own without the unusual terms, χειροποίητον and ἀχειροποίητον, which might explain why Matthew drops them (see Matt 26:61) and, hence, they most likely have meaning specifically for Mark.[98] Possibly the inaccuracy of the charge centers on the agency of Jesus: that *he* would both destroy the temple and build another in three days.[99] On this, Gundry argues that it is a distortion of the passion-resurrection predictions and so makes Jesus out to be one who ascribes "to himself the roles of divine destroyer and divine builder of the temple."[100]

A consideration of temple themes in Mark supports my contention that the false accusation is mostly true and that this statement, in turn, contributes to Mark's redefinition of the locus of Yahweh's presence. First, Mark's Jesus uses the verb καταλυθῇ in 13:2 to refer to the temple's destruction which provides a significant basis for affirming the thrust of the first part of the false accusation in which Mark uses the same verb again (14:58a: ἐγὼ καταλύσω τὸν ναὸν τοῦτον) with the difference that the former is in the passive voice and the latter is in the active. Likely the issue of agency, as I have mentioned, is where the inaccuracy of the allegation is found. Mark does not use the term ἱερόν that designates the temple complex, as he does in 13:1, but rather ναός which refers to the sanctuary (see 15:38). This distinction should not be pressed too far as ναός is after all a part of the temple itself.

Second, the phrase διὰ τριῶν ἡμερῶν recalls the passion-resurrection predictions in which the SM, after experiencing suffering, rejection, betrayal and finally death, will rise again μετὰ τρεῖς ἡμέρας (8:31; 9:31; 10:34). Despite that Mark uses two different prepositions, both phrases still

---

96. Gray, *Temple*, 174.

97. Brower suggests that "Mark may be noting that the witnesses are false, not due to the content of their testimony, but because they are testifying against Jesus" ("Reader," 127).

98. Juel contends that they "contribute little to the actual charge but suggest something mysterious about the statement" (*Temple*, 118).

99. Gray, *Temple*, 172–73; Hooker, *Son of Man*, 166. Brown suggests this for the first part of the accusation (*Death*, 447).

100. Gundry, *Mark*, 906; Collins, *Mark*, 701.

communicate a short period of time between the SM's death and his resurrection and, likewise, the destruction of the temple and the construction of a new one in 14:58.[101] I propose that this is an intentional temporal link on the part of Mark that associates the SM's rejection, suffering and death with the accusation that Jesus would destroy the temple, on the one hand, and his resurrection and the claim that he would rebuild the temple, on the other, both of which occur after or in "three days."[102] Regarding the former, I have argued in the last chapter that the suffering and death of the SM has sacrificial and redemptive implications that come to their fullest expression in the last supper narrative. Because the SM essentially creates a new people of God founded upon his sacrificial and redemptive death outside of the temple cult, sacrifices offered in the Jerusalem sanctuary are no longer required. Further, a careful reading of Jesus' condemnation of the temple and its leadership during his final days in Jerusalem, beginning with the temple incident in 11:15–17, implies that the activities of the temple cult have already been nullified as it has become *inter alia* a hideout for insurrectionists against Yahweh's messiah and not a place of prayer for the nations. On the action of Jesus in the temple, Neusner contends that it

> will have provoked astonishment, since it will have called into question the very simple fact that the daily whole offering effected atonement and brought about expiation for sin, and God had so instructed Moses in the Torah. Accordingly, only someone who rejected the Torah's explicit teaching concerning the daily whole offering could have overturned the tables—or, as I shall suggest, someone who had in mind setting up a different table, and for a different purpose: for the action carries with it the entire message, both positive and negative.[103]

Neusner, of course, is linking Jesus' action in the temple with the Passover meal in which Jesus makes known that a new covenant is established

---

101. Juel suggests "diverse origins within the tradition" when accounting for the use of the two different prepositions (*Temple*, 144). Likewise, see Dunn, "Messiah," 5.

102. Collins disagrees with this link because of the different prepositions and concludes that readers should not associate the resurrection to which Jesus refers in 8:31, 9:31, and 10:34 with the construction of a temple "not made with hands" (*Mark*, 702 fn. 32). In response, Mark employs yet a different preposition in the restatement of the false charge by those mocking Jesus while on the cross that he would destroy the temple and build another ἐν τρισὶν ἡμέραις. This reveals that there is a degree of fluidity in Mark's use of prepositions at this point, or in the tradition which he inherited, and, therefore, does not nullify attemps to discern thematic connections between these passages.

103. Neusner, "Money-Changers," 289.

Chapter 6: The Coming of the Son of Man in the Heavenly Temple

through his death. Neusner's assessment of 11:15–17 finds support in Jesus' affirmation of the scribe who claims that loving God and neighbor "is much more important that than all whole burnt offerings and sacrifices" (12:33b), especially in light of Jer 7, as we have seen. So, the sacrificial significance of Jesus' death coupled with the condemnation of the temple serves as another piece of evidence that the first half of the false charge is not a baseless accusation.

The thematic link for resurrection and Jesus building another temple "not made with hands" is found in Mark 12:10. After having been a rejected stone, a plight that the passion predictions describe in detail, Jesus will become a vindicated cornerstone at his resurrection (v. 10). The application of temple architecture, from either the building or cult, to a person is not unique to Mark. The author of the *Rule of the Community* uses the expression "precious cornerstone" (פנת יקר, 1QS VIII, 5–9) to describe the desert community as a metaphorical temple and the phrases "flesh of burnt offerings" and the "fats of sacrifice" (1QS IX, 4–5) to denote their prayers and holy living which deal with the sins of the land.[104] A similar movement is evident in Paul in which he refers to the Corinthian community as "a temple of God:" Οὐκ οἴδατε ὅτι ναὸς θεοῦ ἐστε καὶ τὸ πνεῦμα τοῦ θεοῦ οἰκεῖ ἐν ὑμῖν (1 Cor 3:16), or in Romans in which he exhorts the community "to present your bodies as a living sacrifice (θυσίαν ζῶσαν), holy and acceptable to God" (12:1). The second half of the false charge that Jesus will build a temple ἀχειροποίητον is in coherence with the imagery that Jesus will become the κεφαλὴν γωνίας of a new temple. It is in the trial that Jesus comes face to face with the temple builders of 12:10 and is now the rejected stone as they seek to condemn him to death.[105] If the suffering and rejection of the SM renders the current temple useless, it is fitting, then, that Jesus "in three days" once he has risen from dead inaugurates the construction of another temple, one of a different order, "not made with hands" (14:58b). The idea of a replacement temple for the Jerusalem one, despite the fact that the one described in v. 48 is non-physical, coheres with the Jewish literature both before and after Mark which envisages God constructing an eschatological temple outside of any human agency, e.g., *1 En.* 90:28–29; 11QTemplea XXIX 7–10; *4 Ezra* 10:25; *2 Bar.* 4:2–7; 6:6–9.[106]

---

104. For additional references, see 1QS IX, 6; 4Q164; 11QMelch II, 23–24.
105. Juel, *Temple*, 54.
106. Wardle, *Jerusalem Temple*, 184.

Daniel's Son of Man in Mark

Third, one must consider the significance of the terms χειροποίητον and ἀχειροποίητον since they are unique to Mark which leads some to contend that they make an important contribution to his temple motif.[107] The allegation could easily stand on its own without these unusual terms which might explain why Matthew drops them (see Matt 26:61) and, hence, they most likely have meaning specifically for Mark, as I have mentioned earlier.[108] According to E. Lohse, χειροποίητον in Greco-Roman sources and the LXX refers to that which is built by man, and, in the latter source, that which is constructed is often an idol, e.g., Lev 26:1 and Isa 46:6 LXX.[109] Although it is difficult to know for sure if Mark intends to denigrate the temple by placing this term on the mouth of the false witnesses and hence associate the Jerusalem temple with idolatry, it certainly fits with Jesus' designation that it has become a "den of insurrectionists" who use the temple for their own ends.[110] It is more likely that the term refers to the Jerusalem temple as a man-made structure and in doing so contrasts it with another one, soon to be built "without hands." In Acts 7:48, Stephen refers to the tabernacle and Solomon's temple as that which is made "by humans hands" in which Yahweh does not dwell: ἀλλ᾽ οὐχ ὁ ὕψιστος ἐν χειροποιήτοις κατοικεῖ.

As for ἀχειροποίητον, some argue that the term alludes to Dan 2:34: "And you saw until when a stone was cut from a mountain, without hands (ἄνευ χειρῶν), and it struck the image on the iron and earthenware feet and crushed them" (NETS).[111] Gray suggests that it may even evoke the larger context of Dan 2.[112] However, the terminological correspondence is not strong and this background does not cohere with Mark's critique of the temple that centres on its resistance toward Jesus the messiah and its abuse by the Jewish leadership. Further, the temple is not an embodiment of paganism like the nations symbolized by the gold, silver, bronze, iron, and clay of the great statue in Daniel's vision which is eventually crushed by the cut out stone (2:31–35). Rather, the temple made "without hands" in Mark simply denotes one of a different order and is not a physical building composed of brick and mortar. The use of ἀχειροποίητον to indicate that

---

107. Juel, *Temple*, 208; Brown, *Death*, 1:440; Gray, *Temple*, 174–75.

108. Juel, *Temple*, 118.

109. Lohse, "χειροποίητον," 436.

110. Gray, *Temple*, 175; Collins, *Mark*, 702. Wardle rightly cautions that this reading is not clearly supported by what Jesus says elsewhere (*Jerusalem Temple*, 183–84).

111. Evans, *Mark*, 445; Gray, *Temple*, 176–78.

112. Gray, *Temple*, 176–78.

Chapter 6: The Coming of the Son of Man in the Heavenly Temple

which is non-physical is evident in Paul's statement about Gentiles who "were circumcised with a spiritual circumcision (περιτομῇ ἀχειροποιήτῳ), by putting off the body of the flesh in the circumcision of Christ" (Col 2:11). Here, circumcision functions as a metaphor for leaving behind the sin nature. In 2 Cor 5:1, Paul uses the term to describe the type of body that will replace our earthly ones: "a building from God, a house not made with hands (οἰκίαν ἀχειροποίητον), eternal in the heavens." While the expression does not diminish physicality *per se* (see v. 4), it does refer to a body of a different order that is not of this world. The Pauline uses of ἀχειροποίητος cohere, to a degree, with Mark in which the temple "not made with hands" is definitely of a different type functioning as a metaphor for the new covenant community that finds its redemption not in the temple's cult, but in Jesus' sacrificial work on the cross who becomes the capstone of this new temple following his resurrection.

Returning to the trial scene, Jesus does not respond to this accusation and so the high priest wants to know if he has anything to say about these alleged intentions of his: "Have you no answer? What is this that they testify against you" (v. 60)? Still hearing no response, the high priest asks him, "Are you the Messiah, the Son of the Blessed One" (v. 61b)? As mentioned, the high priest's question is occasioned by the false accusation and so the use of πάλιν (v. 61b) reveals his persistence to determine if Jesus really is a threat to the existing temple establishment and implies, for Mark's audience, that as messiah Jesus has authority over the temple, a connection established in second-temple literature. In response, Jesus affirms that he is indeed "the messiah, Son of God" (v. 62a), and then predicts that "you will see the Son of Man seated at the right hand of the Power and coming with the clouds of heaven" (v. 62b). This statement about the SM, which quotes portions of Ps 110:1 and Dan 7:13, reveals an important dimension of his messiahship much like Jesus' teaching about the suffering SM in 8:31 in response to Peter's declaration in 8:28.[113] Jesus' response in v. 62b highlights that he is an exalted messiah who exercises Yahweh's judicial authority at his right hand in the heavenly temple, which I will argue below by giving careful attention to the intertexts of Ps 110:1 and Dan 7:13.

In Ps 109:1 LXX, the Lord says to the messiah, "Sit on my right (κάθου ἐκ δεξιῶν μου) until I make your enemies a footstool for your feet" (NETS). This imperative is fulfilled in Jesus' prediction that the Sanhedrin will see the SM ἐκ δεξιῶν καθήμενον τῆς δυνάμεως. Concurrent with this

---

113. Brown, *Death*, 494–95.

enthronement is the SM's ἐρχόμενον μετὰ τῶν νεφελῶν τοῦ οὐρανοῦ. Both the phrase μετὰ τῶν νεφελῶν τοῦ οὐρανου and the verb ἐρχόμενος are found in Theodotion's text of Dan 7:13 in addition to the indefinite υἱὸς ἀνθρώπου which is in both Greek versions. On the basis of these terminological correspondences, the *volume* of the allusions both to Ps 110:1 and Dan 7:13 is very strong. As compared with 13:26 where the out-group will see the coming of the SM "in clouds with great power and glory," Jesus directs this prediction specifically at his accusers predicting that "you will see" (ὄψεσθε) the enthroned SM coming with the clouds. At hearing these words, the high priest declares Jesus guilty of blasphemy with the support of the Sanhedrin (vv. 63-64).

There are a variety of views on exactly what provokes this charge, some of which I list here: 1) Jesus' use of ἐγώ εἰμι when he affirms the high priest's question that he is the Messiah, Son of God is tantamount to an enunciation of the divine name;[114] 2) the phrases, "Messiah, Son of God," are in restrictive apposition such that Jesus is guilty of blasphemy for affirming that he is the "Messiah-Son-of-God" referring to a quasi-divine figure who is commensurate with God himself;[115] and 3) Jesus uttered the divine name Yahweh instead of using the circumlocution "the Power" (τῆς δυνάμεως, see *m. Sanh.* 7:5).[116] However, all of these options locate the blasphemy charge in statements other than those about the SM.[117] Raymond E. Brown considers what Jesus says about the SM because sitting at the right hand of Yahweh in conjunction with his prior affirmation that he is the messiah, Son of God, claims for himself a status which is unique only to the God of Israel and, therefore, has demeaned him.[118] Similarly, Hooker argues that Jesus is guilty for claiming that he will sit at the right hand of the Power and will hence share in the authority of God himself (Ps 110:1).[119] Bock asserts that only a privileged few can sit in God's presence and "to equate anyone else with God [e.g., sitting at his right hand] is to risk thinking

---

114. Stauffer, *Story*, 121-28; Hooker, *Mark*, 362. For a critical discussion of Stauffer's approach, see Catchpole, "Heard," 13-17. See also the discussion in Pesch, *Das Markusevangelium*, 2:437-38 fn. 35 and a brief comment in Evans, 450.

115. Marcus, "Mark 14:61," 125-41.

116. Gundry, *Mark*, 916.

117. Bock remarks that "it is this reply [about the SM] in all the Synoptics that sparks the movement to condemn Jesus" ("Son of Man," 186). Collins, "Blasphemy," 381.

118. Brown, *Death*, 531.

119. Hooker, *Son of Man*, 173; Catchpole, "Heard," 17-18; Collins, "Blasphemy," 400.

Chapter 6: The Coming of the Son of Man in the Heavenly Temple

blasphemously."[120] While it is not the purpose of this chapter to engage in the debate as to what elicits a charge of blasphemy, at the end of my analysis of Ps 110:1 and Dan 7:13 and how they apply to the trial scene, I will suggest another alternative.

Psalm 110 contains two oracles, one in which Yahweh calls the king to sit at his right hand (v. 1) and another in which he declares that the king is also a priest (v. 4).[121] To sit at the right hand of a king is to sit in a place of honor (1 Kgs 2:19) and to become a co-ruler or vice-regent.[122] The human king who sits here does not rule on his own authority and strength but rather on Yahweh's and is yet the instrument of his rule. Consequently, "the Lord sends out from Zion your [the king's] mighty scepter" (v. 2a) and he calls the king to "rule in the midst of your foes" (v. 2b). When the king exercises this rule, the nation will support him as "your people will offer themselves willingly on the day you lead your forces on the holy mountains" (v. 3a). The second oracle, as mentioned, identifies the king as a priest: "you are a priest forever according to the order of Melchizedek אַתָּה־כֹהֵן לְעוֹלָם עַל־דִּבְרָתִי מַלְכִּי־צֶדֶק (110:4b MT). This alludes to Gen 14:18, which during the time of pre-Israelite Jerusalem, the king not only possessed a royal status but also a priestly one.[123] Now this is bestowed on Israel's king in the Psalm.[124] Following this declaration, Yahweh reassures his anointed that he is with him by remaining at his right (v. 5a) and that Yahweh will be victorious in battle over all of the king's enemies (vv. 5–6).

We have considered the literary and historical contexts of Dan 7 in detail in chapter 2. I concluded there that the vision of Yahweh enthroned in his heavenly temple reverses the oppressed and persecuted plight of Israel through not only the destruction of their adversary, Antiochus IV Epiphanes whose profaning activities were aided and abetted by a colluding temple priesthood, but also through the presentation of the SM before Yahweh in his heavenly dwelling. His appearance before Yahweh marks the vindication of the persecuted holy ones's God-given dominion over their beastly adversary and their reconnection with the divine presence that is no

120. Bock, *Blasphemy*, 183.
121. For a fairly detailed discussion of this structure, see Allen, *Psalms 101—50*, 113–14. See also, Terrien, *Psalms*, 751.
122. Allen, *Psalms 101–50*, 115.
123. Kraus, *Psalms 60–150*, 351.
124. Kraus cites the following passages which record David and those after him carrying out priestly responsibilities: 2 Sam 6:13–14, 18; 24:25; 1 Kgs 8:14, 62–64 (*Psalms 60–150*, 351).

longer found in the terrestrial temple. One of the most relevant aspects of Daniel's vision for Mark's trial scene is the association of the judgement of the fourth beast with the vindication and exaltation of the SM who comes to Yahweh riding in the clouds. Mark takes it the next step and associates the enthroned and cloud riding SM with Yahweh who now exercises Yahweh's judgement against the adversarial Sanhedrin. As I have indicated several times, texts contemporaneous with Mark, namely the *Parables* and *4 Ezra*, develop Daniel's SM such that he becomes an individual who executes Yahweh's prerogatives of judging Israel's enemies in the former and destroying them in the latter which takes us beyond the passive, albeit exalted, danielic figure.[125] Similarly, I have argued already that the markan SM in the first future saying will one day exercise Yahweh's judicial prerogatives by being ashamed of, which has the effect of severing relationship with, those who have refused to follow in his way of suffering and sacrificial service (see 8:31–38) and, in the second future saying, by overseeing the destruction of the Jerusalem temple for the resistance it symbolized against Yahweh's messiah (see 13:24–26). Now, in 14:62, Jesus predicts that the SM will sit at Yahweh's right, which, in light of Ps 110:1, reveals that he is the "anointed one" who will rule on Yahweh's behalf and have victory over his enemies. This intertext is consonant with Mark's development of the danielic "one like a son of man" who in 8:38 and 13:26 exercises Yahweh's judicial prerogatives over those opposed to him. Mark's portrayal of the high priest and his cohorts who have resisted this anointed king from the time he arrived in Jerusalem leave little doubt that the unstated reference in the Psalm, about the enemies of the Lord's anointed becoming a footstool, now refers to the Sanhedrin and so will be subject to the SM's judgement. There is also an unstated correspondence with the danielic beasts which are also opposed to Yahweh's rule but are destroyed when the Ancient of Days comes.[126] In keeping with the SM in 8:38 and 13:26 and in light of Dan 7 and Ps 110, the markan SM will come enthroned at the right hand of Yahweh exercising his judicial authority specifically over those who have continually resisted him to the point of death.

---

125. Hooker merely argues that the danielic background highlights the exalted status of Mark's SM and does not apply her earlier analysis of the SM in the *Parables* and *4 Ezra* where he is much more than an exalted figure (*Son of Man*, 168). Hooker, however, had advanced the discussion quite significantly as she resisted the common interpretation that Jesus is predicting his *parousia*, a view still held by a number of scholars today.

126. See also Evans, "Blasphemy," 220.

Chapter 6: The Coming of the Son of Man in the Heavenly Temple

In my analysis of 8:38 and 13:26, I have also argued that Mark evokes the heavenly temple of Dan 7 due in part to his use of language that corresponds with descriptions of Yahweh in his heavenly dwelling elsewhere, such as "glory of his father" and "holy angels" in 8:38 and "great glory" in 13:26. Although I have stated this a couple of times already, I do so again: Mark has not, by any means, provided a detailed description of Yahweh's heavenly temple. What I am contending is that Mark is using evocative language which recalls the celestial temple of Dan 7 which is supported by additional terminology associated with it. The abbreviated scene in 14:62 is another such evocation in which the SM is now seated upon a throne, although Mark does not explicit say so, but the intertextual backgrounds certainly point in this direction, as we will see, and the SM is seated. Although the setting of Yahweh's invitation that his anointed sit at his right in Ps 110:1 is not the heavenly temple, the imagery of a throne fits with an allusion to Dan 7 and the heavenly temple scene that I argue Mark evokes. Thrones and particularly the one on which Yahweh is seated is one of the major features in Daniel's description of the heavenly temple. Likewise, the SM in the *Parables* is enthroned in the heavenly temple executing Yahweh's judicial prerogatives against adversaries of the faithful ones, which strengthens the *historical probability* of my proposal. When these hostile opponents see the enochic SM sitting upon his throne, they shall at that point be judged, which is also true for the adversaries of the markan SM in light of Ps 110:1 and Dan 7:13: "And one group of them will look at the other; and they will be terrified and will cast down their faces, and pain will seize them when they see that son of man sitting on the throne of glory" (62:5). We have also seen that, in addition to Dan 7, thrones are a common piece of furniture in Yahweh's celestial dwelling when exercising judicial action, e.g., 1 Kgs 22:19; Isa 6:1b–2a; *1 En.* 14:18, 22–23).

Further, the throne, upon which the SM likely sits, may have an unstated correspondence with the one in both Dan 7 and *1 En.* 14; that is, it may have wheels. In the former, its wheels are "burning fire" (v. 9c) while in the latter they are "like the shining sun" (v. 18). According to Black, the wheeled throne that is surrounded by fire ultimately has its source in Ezekiel's vision of the divine chariot throne (Ezek 1:15–21, 27).[127] In the *Songs of the Sabbath Sacrifice*, Yahweh's throne has "glorious [wh]eels with the likeness of fire, the spirits of the holy of holies" (4QShirShabbf 20 II, 10a; see 4QShirShabbd 1 II 15). In consequence, depictions of Yahweh enthroned

---

127. Black, *Book of Enoch*, 149.

on a wheeled chariot so that it can move is quite at home in heavenly temple contexts and would explain, at the risk of being overly literal, how the SM can be seated but yet still come with the clouds. Further, Daniel's seer indicates that Yahweh himself comes for the purpose of judgement which is possible given that he is seated on a throne with wheels: "As I looked, this horn made war with the holy ones and was prevailing over them, until the Ancient One *came* (LXX: ἐλθεῖν; Theod.: ἦλθεν) then judgment was given for the holy ones of the Most High, and the time arrived when the holy ones gained possession of the kingdom" (7:21–22). In light of this background, Evans rightfully concludes, "it would seem that Jesus has claimed that he will return as the figure depicted in Daniel's vision, seated at the right hand of God in the divine chariot throne, and that he will return in judgement on his enemies."[128]

The intertextual backgrounds of Dan 7:13 and Ps 110:1 provide a substantial amount of *thematic coherence* for the Jewish trial scene making it an appropriate response to his opponents who have rejected him from the time he arrived in Jerusalem as Yahweh's anointed. They will one day "see" the SM coming in the heavenly temple from which he will exercise judicial authority over them. This, of course, is not without just cause. In her careful treatment of the various religious leaders in Mark, Malbon observes that the "chief priests" are the dominant group in Mark's third section who ensure that Jesus is brought to trial and eventually destroyed (11:18, 27; 12:12; 14:1, 10, 43, 53, 55; 15:1, 3, 10–11, 31).[129] This animosity stems from Jesus' prior pronouncement of judgement on them and their temple institution for corruption when he overturned the tables of the money-changers and proclaimed that the house of Yahweh is a den of insurrectionists, and then, through the parable of the wicked tenants, lumped them together with

---

128. Evans, *Mark*, 452. I also wish to add that this reading which focuses on the theological and intertextual meaning of the imagery, in this case the SM sitting upon a throne and coming with the clouds of heaven, saves one from having to solve the dilemma caused by these allegedly separate actions of the SM sitting and then coming. For example, Brown asserts, "while there is a complementarity in the two positions, Mark means us to think of a sequence from one action to another, for obviously one cannot sit and come at the same time" (*Death*, 497). However, if one needs to insist on such literalism, the SM sitting upon a wheeled throne, which is likely given that Yahweh's throne in Daniel likewise has wheels, coheres with the prediction that he will come with the clouds; in other words, the SM is on a throne that moves! Further, as Glasson observed over fifty years ago, it is reasonable to think that the "two participles governed by the same verb [ὄψεσθε] describe simultaneous actions" ("Reply," 89).

129. Malbon, "Jewish Leaders," 267–68.

Chapter 6: The Coming of the Son of Man in the Heavenly Temple

corrupt pre-exilic Israelite leaders who were known for killing Yahweh's prophets and resisting his saving purposes. The trial scene, then, demonstrates a climax in the conflict between Jesus, the truly anointed figure, and the temple leaders, headed by the anointed high priest. Mark's unnamed high priest confronts the soon to be exalted SM for the purpose of condemning him to death (v. 55).[130] However, a great reversal is occurring based on the judicial background of both Ps 110:1 and Dan 7:13. It is the high priest and the whole Sanhedrin now on trial. When they witness the heavenly temple manifesting itself, in which the SM sits at the right hand of Yahweh and comes with the clouds of heaven, they will meet their end being the object of the SM's judgement and, on the basis of 13:26, the earthy temple will be destroyed.[131]

Returning to what in Jesus' response elicits the blasphemy charge, I contend that scholars must take seriously the backgrounds of Ps 110:1 and Dan 7:13. By predicting the judgement of the Sanhedrin because they are enemies of Yahweh by virtue of resisting his anointed one, Jesus defames them, and so they charge him with blasphemy and condemn him worthy of death.[132] This defamation could be taken as an infraction of Exod 22:27 LXX, one of the most notable blasphemy texts in the Torah, according to Bock: "You shall not revile gods, and you shall not speak ill (κακῶς) of your people's rulers" (NETS).[133] Its influence is evident in Luke's Paul who unknowingly insults the high priest after his arrest in the temple and when

---

130. Wright, *Victory*, 523. It is unlikely that Pilate would confer the death penalty on Jesus if he was brought before him on the grounds of being a threat to the temple. Evans comments that "the claim to be seated on God's throne, coming in judgment, would have carried with it . . . political implications [vis-à-vis, a royal Messiah, Son of God]" ("Blasphemy," 222).

131. Both Collins and Gundry claim that there is no reversal (Collins, "Blasphemy," 399; Gundry, *Mark*, 914). Gundry argues that "Mark 14:62 says nothing about judgement by anyone (contrast *1 En.* 62:3, 5; 2 Macc 7:34-38; 4 Macc 10:21; 12:18)" (*Mark*, 914). The point of chapter 3, however, is that there is a first-century precedent for a SM who functions as an exalted judge, executing judicial prerogatives of Yahweh, to say nothing of the unstated correspondences between Ps 110:1/Dan 7:13 and Mark 14:62. Evans supports such a reversal paradigm: "The high priest and his priestly colleagues at the moment sit in judgement on Jesus, but the day will come when they will see his coming with the clouds as 'the son of man' [for the purpose of judgement]" (*Mark*, 451). See also Hooker, *Son of Man*, 166.

132. Evans also takes seriously the negative literary contexts of Dan 7:13 and Ps 110:1 to arrive at the same conclusion that the charge of blasphemy arises from Jesus' implicit claim that he will judge the high priest when he shares God's throne ("Blasphemy," 222).

133. Bock, *Blasphemy*, 208.

it is pointed out to him that he has indeed done so, Paul responds with a slightly modified quotation of Exod 22:27 LXX: "I did not realize, brothers, that he was high priest; for it is written, 'You shall not speak evil of a leader of your people'" (Acts 23:5).[134]

The term βλασφημία is used in 1 Macc 2:6 to describe the defilement and profanation of the temple and the faithful priests by Antiochus IV Epiphanes: "He [the priest Mattathias] saw the blasphemies (βλασφημίας) being committed in Judah and Jerusalem."[135] After a relatively detailed description of these atrocities, "Matthias and his sons tore (διέρρηξεν) their clothes, put on sackcloth, and mourned greatly" (2:14). This narrative is preceded by an account of Antiochus's order to paganize Judah and Jerusalem that includes the mandate "to defile the sanctuary and priests" (1:46). Even though the term "blasphemy" is not used technically by Mattathias, 1 Macc 2 provides a helpful background for the high priest's charge of blasphemy in Mark. Jesus has not denied the charge of 14:58, has committed violent activity in the temple (11:15-17), identified its leaders as rebellious (12:12), predicted the temple's demise (13:2), and now, moreover, asserts that he, as the exalted SM will judge the high priest and his cohorts from Yahweh's heavenly dwelling for their rebellion. Just as Mattathias and his sons witness the sacrilege of the temple and the defilement of faithful priests almost two centuries before, the high priest in Mark rends (διαρρήξας) his garments declaring Jesus guilty of "blasphemy" (v. 64).

A. Y. Collins discusses two important cultural sources, Philo and Josephus, for an understanding of Mark's use of blasphemy, which support the argument above.[136] For Josephus and many Jews, the second temple is the most holy place on earth (Exod 40:34-38; Num 9:15-23) and is overseen by the most holy people, the priests (Lev 21-22). In one text, Josephus discusses the priesthood:

> We have but one temple for the one God (for like ever loveth like), common to all as God is common to all. The priests are continually engaged in his worship, under the leadership of him who for the time is head of the line. With his colleagues he will sacrifice to God, safeguard the laws, adjudicate in cases of dispute, punish those convicted of crime. Any who disobey him will pay the

---

134. Marshall, "Acts," 598.
135. Collins, "Blasphemy," 386.
136. See the discussion in Collins, "Blasphemy," 386-95.

Chapter 6: The Coming of the Son of Man in the Heavenly Temple

penalty *as impiety towards God himself* (*Ag. Ap.* 2.193-94 [LCL Thackeray]).

Philo also holds the priests in high regard as the most holy of Israel:

> Right in the middle stands the sanctuary itself with a beauty baffling description, to judge from what is exposed to view. For all inside is unseen except by the high priest alone, and indeed he, though charged with the duty of entering once a year, gets no view of anything. For he takes with him a brazier full of lighted coals and incense, and the quantity of vapor which this naturally gives forth covers everything around it, beclouds the eyesight and prevents it from being able to penetrate any distance (Philo, *Spec. Laws* 1.72).

These ancient authors esteem the priesthood and the temple as the most holy people and place respectively. To speak against them is to speak against God himself. The prediction that Jesus as the SM will judge the high priest and Sanhedrin when he comes in the heavenly temple certainly constitutes a defamatory message. It is no surprise that they accuse him of blasphemy.

Initial Fulfilment: The Rending of the Temple Veil and Going to Galilee

As shown above, the so-called false accusation in 14:58 appears to reflect more truth than falsehood. To reiterate, Jesus has enacted a parable of judgement against the temple (11:12–21), predicted its destruction (13:2), and has not denied his alleged association with its destruction (14:58a). In keeping with these things, when the SM is finally "killed" (8:31; 9:31; 10:34), or as Mark describes it in 15:37, when Jesus "breathed his last," the veil of the sanctuary is torn from top to bottom (v. 38). Coupled with the darkness that comes ἐφ' ὅλην τὴν γῆν at noon, which in itself symbolizes Yahweh's judgement, e.g., Amos 8:9; Jer 15:9, the rending of the veil at the moment Jesus dies marks a climactic moment of judgement in Mark and functions as the initial fulfilment of all that Jesus said and did against the temple. In keeping with the narrative sequence of Mark's third section, that is the words and/or deeds recorded in 11:12–21 and 13:2, along with the first half of the false accusation which rightly associates Jesus as a threat to the temple, God now manifests his judgement proleptically by rending the veil to open the holy sanctuary, which sends a much more forceful message than Jesus did in 11:12–17.[137] The end of the corrupt and oppressive regime that was responsible for the crucifixion of Jesus has been set in motion in a very dramatic way.

The rending of the veil in the present also anticipates the SM's future coming in his celestial dwelling to execute final judgement centered on the temple structure and its leadership. This judgement, for Mark's readers, will be demonstrated, if it hasn't been already, through the Roman siege of Jerusalem beginning in 66 CE culminating with the burning of the temple in 70. However, the events of 70 CE also point to the vindication of the redemptive effects of the suffering and death of the SM which, as argued earlier, leads to the redundancy of the temple's cult and the formation of a new covenant community. On this Martin Hengel comments, "Jesus' death opens the way into the holy of holies, the place of atonement for the sins of Israel and of the presence of God, and robs the cult of its old force."[138] In light of the redemptive and sacrificial significance of the SM's suffering, rejection, and death, the locus of God's dwelling is shifting to the new covenant community founded on the SM. This is evident in Mark 13:27. After the SM has judged the temple, manifested in its destruction, he will then send his angels from the heavenly temple drawing the elect to himself which signals that in the exalted SM the locus of Yahweh's presence is centred to whom both Israel and the nations alike are gathered and not to the Jerusalem temple as was once thought (see Mic 4:1–5).

This relates to the positive side of the false accusation, a temple "made without hands," which begins to take shape on the day of Jesus' resurrection, both of which occur "after/in three days." Toward the beginning of Mark's passion narrative, Jesus makes a prediction to his disciples which associates the formation of a new covenant community with the SM's resurrection: "But after I am raised up, I will go before you to Galilee" (14:28). Prior to this, Jesus claims that they will all desert him in fulfilment of a line from Zech 13:7: "I will strike the shepherd, and the sheep will be scattered."[139]

---

137. Brown, *Death*, 1100–102; Brower, "Reader," 131.

138. Hengel, *Atonement*, 43.

139. Mark's quotation is closer to the MT than the LXX with the first-person form πατάξω in v. 27 drawing out the implicit meaning of Zech 13:7a that Yahweh is indeed the one who is responsible for striking the sheperd: "'Awake, O sword, against my shepherd, against the man who stands next to me,' declares the LORD of hosts." France suggests that it is "a grammatical adaptation necessitated by the abbreviated quotation, which does not include the explicit mention of the 'sword' in the opening line of the oracle"

Chapter 6: The Coming of the Son of Man in the Heavenly Temple

Together vv. 27–28 express a symmetry in which the resurrection of Jesus is the remedy to the "scattering" of the disciples.[140] This symmetry is actually evident in the wider context of Zech 13:7.[141] The following verses speak of Yahweh sparing one third of the nation who will endure hardship and trial but then as a purified remnant "they will call on my name, and I will answer them. I will say, 'They are my people'; and they will say, 'The LORD is our God'" (v. 9b). Given the *thematic coherence* that the quotation of 13:7 creates in vv. 27–28 which involves an evocation of that which is not stated in Zech 13:9b by means of v. 28, this OT passage is a formative background by which we realize that the gathering of the disciples in Galilee is a gathering around the presence of Yahweh centered in his Son, Jesus. This gathering is indeed a temple "made without hands" whose capstone is the rejected son.

The reference to Jesus' resurrection in v. 28 and then in 16:8 calls to mind the passion-resurrection predictions in which Jesus promises that "after three days" the SM will rise from the dead.[142] Upon finding an empty tomb, a young man tells the women that Jesus is not here, but in fact has been raised (ἠγέρθη) and then commands them "to go, tell his disciples and Peter that he is going ahead of you to Galilee; there you will see him just as he told you" (16:7).[143] The redemptive effects of the SM's suffering, rejection and death are *beginning* to be realized now that he has indeed risen. The command to re-gather on the resurrection day is a visual first step in the formation of the new covenant community, paralleling a purified remnant gathered around Yahweh in Zechariah 13. Just as the rending of the temple veil begins to vindicate the notion that redemption is found no longer in the temple but through the suffering and death of the SM, the call to go to Galilee to reunite with Jesus after the SM's resurrection begins to vindicate the covenant-forming effects of that same suffering and death. The dwelling

---

(*Mark*, 575).

140. France, *Mark*, 577.

141. Marcus, *Way*, 155.

142. The use of the verb ἐγείρω in both 14:28 and 16:6 still alludes to 8:31, 9:31 and 10:33–34 where ἀνίστημι is employed simply because both verbs describe the same event—the resurrection of Jesus, the Son of Man. In support of this, France claims that "in connection with the resurrection of Jesus the two verbs are to all intents and purposes synonyms" (*Mark*, 576).

143. To question that the disciples reunited with Jesus because the women did not tell anyone due to fear (16:8) misses the literary function of v. 8 which is to continue the tension between Jesus and his obtuse followers evident particularly throughout the second half of Mark (8:17–21, 32; 9:10, 18, 32; etc.). Further, as Brower rightfully points out, "Mark and his readers, of course, know that the story continues" ("Reader," 134).

of God is now with his faithful followers, a temple made without hands, through the SM's death and resurrection. From this point on, "this new people, the new covenant community, the dwelling place of God in Christ through the Spirit, are on God's mission, announcing and effecting his mission, and acting in his way."[144]

Conclusion

In the first section of this chapter, I have argued that the Gospel author depicts the coming of the SM in the heavenly temple to judge those who are ashamed of him and his words by being ashamed of would-be followers that leads to a separation between them and the SM. While Yahweh is never portrayed as being ashamed of those who are unfaithful to him, the same term is used to describe Israel being ashamed or being put to shame when Yahweh judges them because of covenantal unfaithfulness, e.g., Isa 1:29. This is an illuminating background for Mark's use of ἐπαισχύνομαι because the result of "being ashamed" is the same—separation and estrangement—which is in coherence with Mark's portrayal of the SM as an exalted judge dealing with those who have chosen to align themselves with "this adulterous and sinful generation." Because of terminological correspondences between 8:38—9:1 and Dan 7:13–14, a strong case can be made for the evocation of the latter, namely, the heavenly temple scene at the center of which is judicial activity, which is the larger context of vv. 13–14. This proposal is strengthened when we realize that specific terms in the phrases ἐν τῇ δόξῃ τοῦ πατρὸς αὐτοῦ μετὰ τῶν ἀγγέλων τῶν ἁγίων appear in both biblical and extra-biblical literature to describe Yahweh in his celestial dwelling. Just as the markan SM executed prerogatives of Yahweh when he forgave sins and reigned over sabbath at the beginning of the Gospel, he will deal with those ones who cannot accept the costly call of the gospel from the heavenly dwelling this time exercising judicial prerogatives of Yahweh, similar to the enochic SM in the *Parables*. I concluded that discussion with the claim that while we cannot identify with any precision the historical event which reflects that the Kingdom will have come with power during the lifetime of some of the disciples, the promise of Jesus in 9:1 sounds an ominous note because of the literary and thematic relationship that this passage has with 13:26 and 14:62 coupled with the militaristic/judicial uses of "power" which describes the manner in which the Kingdom will come.

144. Brower, "Able," 191.

Chapter 6: The Coming of the Son of Man in the Heavenly Temple

To understand the full significance of the function of the exalted SM in Mark 13:26, one needs to begin in Mark 11 in which Jesus, in a proleptic and symbolic manner, judges the temple for not being a house prayer but rather a haven for those unfaithful to Yahweh, which is reflected in the jeremianic portrayal of the λῃσταί. Jesus then condemns the temple leaders themselves by means of his parable about wicked tenants in Mark 12:1–12 who hoard the owner's vineyard for themselves to the point of killing the owner's son sent to collect the harvest. This parable answers the temple leaders's question in 11:28 on what authority entitles Jesus to disrupt temple activities and condemn the structure—he is sent by Yahweh! Based on the allusion to Jeremiah in the parable, Jesus is but one of many prophets sent to the leaders of Israel and, like the prophets of old, has been resisted by them. However, his rejection will lead to the formation of a new community that replaces the temple institution (12:10). Another important moment leading up to Mark 13 is the discourse between the scribe and Jesus about the greatest commandment from which we concluded that loving Yahweh and neighbor takes priority over sacrificial ritual and, given this story's narrative placement, it is an implicit denunciation of one of the major functions of the temple.

Jesus' prediction of the temple's destruction in Mark 13:2 appears to flow out of the anti-temple theme evident at points in the preceding two chapters. The content of his discourse beginning in Mark 13:5 comes in response to questions posed by the disciples as to the timing of the temple's destruction and signs associated with its demise. Vigilance is the order of the day until they *see* "the abomination that causes desolation standing where it/he should not be" (v. 14). Concentrating on the jeremianic background of τὸ βδέλυγμα τῆς ἐρημώσεως, the abomination that desolates is the corruption of the temple leaders with whom Jesus' followers should not align themselves in any way, hence the exhortation to distance themselves from the temple as much as possible (vv.14b–23). He then uses cosmic imagery to describe the temple's destruction (vv. 24–25) inspired by two texts in Isaiah that depict the destruction of Edom and Babylon. Whereas in Isaiah it is Yahweh who oversees the downfall of these pagan empires, for Mark it is the exalted SM who comes with judicial authority in the heavenly temple. I have appealed to several of Hays's criteria in my argument to establish that Mark evokes the larger context of Dan 7:13–14 of the heavenly temple, which is augmented by the use of the term "glory" in other heavenly temple contexts as well as by the terminological and thematic connection that 13:26 has with 8:38. Those who see his coming, the "out-group," are in an unenviable position, which arguably includes the temple leaders. They will witness the SM coming "with great power" which stresses the judicial force with which he comes to judge an institution that is the center of hostility toward Jesus' messiahship. On the positive side, the SM will then gather his elect from his heavenly dwelling which will mark the full vindication of this new covenant community established by his death outside of the temple's sacrificial system. At the temple's destruction, the SM gathers these ones into Yahweh's presence that is now centered in him, a movement that is commensurate with the danielic figure whose presentation in the heavenly temple marks the restoration of faithful Israel into the presence of Yahweh as well.

In the Jewish trial scene, conflict between Jesus and the temple leaders comes to a climax. He is clearly a threat to the temple establishment and its leaders as seen in Mark 11–13 which comes through in the first half of the false charge associating Jesus with the temple's destruction. The falsity of the charge might stem from the explicit identification that Jesus is the one who will destroy the temple "made with hands" and in three days build another "without hands." The second half of the charge connecting Jesus with the rebuilding of a temple of a different order coheres well with 12:10 in which he becomes the capstone of a new temple. Mark is by no means the first to apply temple architectural language to a person as it is evident in both Qumran and Paul. Not hearing a response to this false charge, the high priest questions Jesus: "Are you the Messiah, the Son of the Blessed One" (v. 61b)? Jesus affirms this and predicts that the high priest and his cohorts will see the SM seated at the right hand of God coming with the clouds of heaven (v. 62). The evocations of Ps 110:1 and Dan 7:13 in this passage depict Jesus as Yahweh's anointed who is seated at his right and will judge those who have been opposed to him. The contexts of both texts share an unstated correspondence with Mark's trial scene and, beyond this, underscore the hostile reception Jesus receives from the temple leaders upon entering Jerusalem: these ones are the enemies of Yahweh of Ps 110 and will be judged as such by the exalted SM, paralleling the adversarial fourth beast which was judged by Yahweh for its rebellion in Dan 7. I have also argued that Mark evokes the setting of Dan 7:13 in 14:62 as well: it is in the heavenly temple that the enthroned SM, not Yahweh, will exercise his judgement against those opposed to him and his followers. This proposal

Chapter 6: The Coming of the Son of Man in the Heavenly Temple

finds *historical probability* on the basis of the enochic SM who judges the adversaries of faithful Israel on a throne from Yahweh's heavenly dwelling.

At the moment Jesus dies, the temple veil is rent which anticipates its final destruction and judgement orchestrated by the future coming of the SM. This preliminary act of judgement also provides concrete support for the irrelevance of the temple's sacrificial system in light of the redemptive effects of the SM's suffering and death that forms the disciples into a new covenant community. After the SM has suffered and died, this new community begins to take shape on the resurrection day when the angel commands the women to tell the disciples to go to Galilee, "just as he told you" (16:7; see 14:28) and will be fully vindicated at the temple's destruction at which point the SM will gather his faithful followers to the heavenly temple (13:27) signaling unequivocally that the presence of Yahweh is centered in him and his elect, a theme expressed in Mark's use of Zechariah 13 in 14:27–28.

Chapter 7: Conclusion

As I have indicated at the beginning, this study attempts to build upon Morna Hooker's monograph, which she published almost fifty years ago, on the SM in Mark. She concluded that "the authority, necessity for suffering, and confidence in final vindication, which are all expressed in the Markan SM sayings, can all be traced to Daniel 7."[1] I have attempted to develop this conclusion through a narrative and intertextual analysis of Mark's SM and have discovered that Mark communicates more than just the theme of authority, the rejection of that authority, and its eventual vindication. Although this pattern still remains, the markan SM, when examined in light of Dan 7 and other relevant OT texts as they emerge along the way, advances one of the Gospel's major themes: the redefinition of the Jerusalem temple and the formation of a new covenant community.

I began this study with a thorough analysis of Dan 7, in particular the heavenly scene depicted in vv. 9–14 and relevant parts of its interpretation (vv. 17–27). A consideration of the vision's historical world reveals that faithful Israel or "the holy ones of the Most High" have been estranged from Yahweh's dwelling due to the profanating actions of Antiochus IV Epiphanes in the Jerusalem temple with the help of a corrupt priesthood. The net result is that the temple no longer functions as the dwelling of Yahweh which is reinforced by the cessation of the daily burnt offering (8:11). However, Yahweh does have something to say about this, and it takes the form of a vision in which he is enthroned in his heavenly temple for the purpose of vindicating faithful Israel not only by judging their pagan adversary but also by restoring them to his presence through the symbol of the SM. I have argued that the celestial parallels between *1 En.* 14 and Dan 7, in addition to temple language in the vision itself, suggest that the latter is more than a celestial courtroom. In keeping with other instances in which Yahweh is surrounded by heavenly beings in biblical and extra-biblical texts, Daniel's

1. Hooker, *Son of Man*, 192.

Chapter 7: Conclusion

vision depicts Yahweh enthroned in his heavenly temple for the purpose of judgement coming in response to terrestrial temple corruption.

Before determining Mark's interpretative rendering of the danielic SM, I examined the ways in which the figure is reused and developed in the *Parables* and *4 Ezra*. Although I do not advocate that these texts inform Mark's portrayal of the SM but, rather, as first-century texts composed around the time of his Gospel, they provide a good degree of *historical probability* for my proposed interpretations. In the former text, the SM is seated upon Yahweh's throne in the heavenly temple executing prerogatives of Yahweh, such as judgement, and is associated with the deliverance of faithful Israel. His judicial actions will not only signal the end of "the kings and the mighty" who have oppressed the faithful (46:4–8; 48:9–10; 62:11) but also will lead to the deliverance of those who endured such oppression (48:4; 62:8). The vision of Ezra in chapter 13 is likely an older piece of tradition, which gives us another example of Jewish interpretation of the danielic SM that predates the fall of Jerusalem. Here, the SM executes a prerogative of Yahweh when he destroys his adversaries through a "stream of fire" from an other-worldly mountain, which is imagery traditionally associated with Yahweh's abode. This action makes it possible for others who are peaceable to come to him.

Turning to Mark, I have argued in chapter 4 that the SM manifests Yahweh's authority do that which only Yahweh can: forgive sins and exercise dominion over the sabbath, which is clearly a development of the passive "one like a son of man" who merely receives authority. This is not unlike the SM in the *Parables* and *4 Ezra* in which he judges sinners, saves the faithful, and destroys his adversaries, all of which are prerogatives of Yahweh. There is one significant dissimilarity, however, and that is Mark's SM acts like Yahweh "on earth" and not, as of yet, in heaven. This close association between the SM and Yahweh does not start in Mark 2:10 but is already evident in three moments in Mark 1. As for the implications of this for Mark's theology, I have suggested that the demonstrations of the SM's authority, to do that which only Yahweh can, appear to encroach upon the temple which is in coherence with Mark's portrayal of this figure who will suffer rejection and death at the hands of the temple leaders but yet through this death will form a new covenant community. The SM who offers forgiveness of sins in Galilee is quite related to the SM who will give his own life for many (10:45) and by whose blood a new covenant is formed (14:24). In the second appearance of the SM in 2:23–28, Mark appears to be teasing out a redefinition of the temple's sacred space around him since work on the sabbath, heretofore permitted only for temple priests serving in the temple, is now permissible for those under his authority. So while Hooker is quite right that the SM manifests authority in these first two sayings, it is specifically Yahweh's authority, which in light of the next series of SM sayings, the passion-resurrection predictions, is an authority which the temple leaders are quite eager to reject, but this, ironically, leads to the undoing of the redemptive, covenant-sustaining temple cult.

When it comes to the intertextual background of the passion-resurrection predictions and the brief explanation of the SM's sacrificial service in 10:45 and 14:24, interpreters must consider a variety of figures and texts, such as Dan 7, Isa 53 and the maccabean martyrs. From my analysis, I have concluded that the sacrificial service of the SM establishes Jesus' faithful followers as a new people of God outside of the temple cult. Of all the proposed backgrounds for the suffering SM, only in Daniel is the SM figure associated with a group of faithful ones who are likewise oppressed by a hostile adversary. In light of this, Jesus calls his disciples to join the SM in being handed over to the hands of men, just as faithful Israel was handed over to their pagan oppressor. But the disciples would have none of it. The corporate significance of Daniel's SM remains in 10:45, in which the markan SM will serve by giving his life to redeem "many" which Jesus describes in more detail in 14:24 highlighting the covenant-forming effects of his death for his followers. So, despite the misguided attempts of Hooker and others who argue that Mark is inspired by an allegedly suffering danielic SM, this background still plays a formative role communicating that the SM is all about others. By means of his sacrificial death, Jesus' followers become a new covenant community making them the direct beneficiaries of the SM's service.

In chapter 6, I have examined Mark's future sayings that depict the coming of the SM in the heavenly temple to judge those who are ashamed of him and his words (8:38), the Jerusalem temple (13:26), and those in charge of this institution (14:62). In my study of 8:38, I have argued that the SM comes in Yahweh's celestial dwelling because of lexical correspondences between 8:38—9:1 and Dan 7:13–14, by which Mark evokes the larger context of vv. 13–14. This is supported by specific terms in the phrases ἐν τῇ δόξῃ τοῦ πατρὸς αὐτοῦ μετὰ τῶν ἀγγέλων τῶν ἁγίων that appear in both biblical and extra-biblical literature to describe Yahweh in his heavenly abode. Whereas in Daniel Yahweh judged those opposed to him and his

Chapter 7: Conclusion

kingdom from the heavenly temple, for Mark it is the exalted SM who will now do so. Mark depicts the SM's judicial action through being ashamed of prospective followers who refuse to embrace his call to live cruciform lives. While Yahweh is not described as ashamed of those who are unfaithful to him elsewhere, the same term is used to describe Israel being ashamed or being put to shame when Yahweh judges and, therefore, is still relevant for Mark's understanding of ἐπαισχύνομαι because one of the consequences of "being ashamed" is separation. Those who reject the cross will not have a place in the future Kingdom. Just as the SM executed prerogatives of Yahweh "on earth" when he forgave sins and reigned over sabbath in his first two appearances, he will one day exercise Yahweh's judicial action from the heavenly temple against those who refused to suffer as he suffered as the SM. As I have indicated earlier, this finds a good deal of *historical probability* in the *Parables* in which the enochic SM in Yahweh's celestial dwelling judges those opposed to the Lord of Spirits and his faithful followers. The SM in late second-temple thinking is a judicial figure.

In order to get a full understanding of the significance of 13:26–27 for Mark's narrative, one needs to begin in chapter 11 in which Mark introduces what becomes a pronounced anti-temple theme. Here Jesus condemns the temple for not being a house prayer but rather a den for those unfaithful to Yahweh. He then turns to the temple leaders identifying them as wicked tenants in 12:1–12, and, in light of the allusion to Jeremiah, underscores their participation in the continued rejection of Yahweh which now demonstrates itself in the murder of Yahweh's own son. However, Jesus hints that his rejection will lead to a vindication that will take the form of a new temple for which he is the capstone that replaces the current one (12:10). We also saw that the discussion between the scribe and Jesus about the greatest commandment highlights that the double love command takes precedence over sacrificial ritual and, due to this story's location, functions as an implicit critique of the temple's sacrificial system. Needless to say, Jesus' prediction of the temple's destruction in Mark 13:2 does not come as a complete surprise. He orders the disciples to be watchful until they *see* "the abomination that causes desolation standing where it/he should not be" (v. 14). Considering the background of τὸ βδέλυγμα τῆς ἐρημώσεως that I trace to Jeremiah 7, the abomination that desolates is the corruption of the temple leaders with whom Jesus' followers should not align themselves, hence the following call, among other things, to flee Jerusalem (vv. 14b–23). Jesus then employs cosmic imagery to describe the temple's destruction in

vv. 24–25 based on two texts in Isaiah that describe the downfall of pagan kingdoms. In v. 26, Mark then describes the coming of the exalted SM "with great glory and power" in the heavenly temple not for the purpose of judging a pagan empire but, rather, the central symbol of the Jewish nation, the temple, which represents a persistent rejection of Yahweh's messiah and prophets. An application of Hays's criteria reveals that Mark evokes the larger context of Dan 7:13–14 as he did in 8:38 in which the SM is now the judge in the heavenly temple. This evocation is strengthened by the use of the term "glory," which occurs in other heavenly temple contexts, as well as by the linguistic and thematic correspondence that this passage has with 8:38. The narrative placement of 13:26 with its depiction of the judicial SM suits the context as he will deal with a temple institution characterized by its hostility toward him that has become a den of insurrectionists whose destruction Jesus forecasts with very dramatic language. But following this, the SM will gather his faithful from his heavenly dwelling (13:27) which points to the full vindication of the new covenant community now that the Jerusalem temple is no more reaffirming that the locus of Yahweh's presence is now centered in him and his elect which finds embodiment in this new community, a temple made without hands.

In the last SM saying I have examined, the one found in the Jewish trial scene, Jesus directs the judicial action of the SM directly at the temple leadership. This scene constitutes a climax of conflict between Jesus and the temple leaders. An important moment is the false charge levelled at Jesus. I have suggested that the falsity of the charge is related to agency: that Jesus allegedly said *he* will destroy the temple "made with hands" and in three days *he* will build another "without hands." There is just too much coherence with preceding narratives to write the whole thing off. Further, Mark's insertion of the unusual terms χειροποίητον and ἀχειροποίητον suggests that there is more to this than a mere trumped up charge. In keeping with the first half of the accusation, it is quite evident in Mark 11–13 that Jesus is a threat to the Jerusalem temple. Meanwhile, the second half associates him with the rebuilding of a temple of a different order that corresponds with 12:10 in which he becomes the capstone of a new temple, which will be realized at the SM's resurrection.

When the high priest does not hear a response to the charge, he questions Jesus: "Are you the Messiah, the Son of the Blessed One" (v. 61b)? This question, following the false accusation, reflects the strong connection between messiah and temple in Jewish literature. Jesus answers in the

Chapter 7: Conclusion

affirmative implying that he has authority over the temple as messiah, over the one "made with hands," which he demonstrated earlier, and the one "made without hands," and then he goes on to predict that the high priest and his compatriots will see the SM seated at the right hand of God coming with the clouds of heaven (v. 62). The evocations of Ps 110:1 and Dan 7:13 in this passage depict Jesus as Yahweh's anointed seated at his right hand exercising Yahweh's authority to judge those who have been opposed to him. Further, the contexts of these passages have an unstated correspondence with Mark's trial scene that in fact encapsulates the hostility that the temple leaders have demonstrated toward Jesus since he arrived in Jerusalem. These ones are the enemies of Yahweh from Dan 7 and Psalm 110 for their resistance to the saving purposes revealed through Yahweh's messiah and will be consequently judged by the exalted SM. I have also argued that Mark evokes the celestial setting of Dan 7:13 in 14:62 as well: similar to Yahweh, the SM is seated upon a throne and will judge those opposed to him and his followers from his heavenly temple. This proposal finds *historical probability* on the basis of the enochic SM who likewise judges the adversaries of faithful Israel on a throne from Yahweh's celestial abode. Further, the throne in both *1 En.* 14 and Dan 7 is one outfitted with wheels, which might be the throne from which the SM judges and hence explains both his concurrent sitting and coming.

In Mark 15, the temple veil is torn in two at the moment Jesus dies which is a proleptic moment pointing to its final destruction and judgement that will be overseen by the future coming of the SM. At the same time, this temporal act also marks the transition of the locus of Yahweh's saving presence from temple cult to the SM's sacrificial death on the cross. Mark's Jesus is clear in the last supper scene that his death or, more specifically, his poured out blood, forms the disciples into a new covenant community. However, the SM's death is not the end of the story. Just as he predicted three times, the SM was raised from the dead in three days at which point this new community does take shape. This is clearly seen in the reassuring words of the angel that Jesus is now in Galilee "just as he told you" and that the disciples need to go and meet him there (16:7; see 14:28). Finally, this newly formed community, a temple made without hands, will find full vindication at the Jerusalem temple's destruction, a temple made with hands, which marks the SM's gathering of his faithful followers (13:27) and affirms that which has been the case since the call to go to Galilee: Yahweh's presence is located in this community.

Bibliography

Ådna, Jostein. "Jesus' Symbolic Act in the Temple (Mark 11:15-17)." In *Gemeinde ohne Tempel: zur Substituierung und Transformation des Jerusalemer Tempels und seines Kults im Alten Testament, antiken Judentum und frühen Christentum*, edited by B. Ego et al., 461-75. Tübingen: Mohr Siebeck, 1999.

Aland, Kurt, et al., eds. *Novum testamentum Graece*. Instituto Studiorum Textus Novi Testamenti Monasteriensi Westphaliae. 27th ed. Stuttgart: Deutsche Bibelsgesellschaft, 1993.

Alexander, Philip S. "From Son of Adam to Second God: Transformations of the Biblical Enoch." In *Biblical Figures Outside the Bible*, edited by M. E. Stone and T. A. Bergren, 87-122. Harrisburg, PA: Trinity International, 1998.

———. "Retelling the Old Testament." In *It is Written: Scripture Citing Scripture*, edited by D. A. Carson and H. G. M. Williamson, 99-121. Cambridge: Cambridge University Press, 1988.

Allen, Leslie C. *Psalms 101-150 revised*. Word Biblical Commentary 21. Nashville: Thomas Nelson, 2002.

Baldwin, Joyce G. *Daniel: An Introduction and Commentary*. Downers Grove, IL: InterVarsity, 1978.

Barrett, Charles K. "The Background of Mark 10:45." In *New Testament Essays: Studies in Memory of T. W. Manson*, edited by A. J. B. Higgins, 1-18. Manchester: Manchester University Press, 1959.

Bauckham, Richard. *God Crucified: Monotheism and Christology in the New Testament*. Carlisle, UK: Paternoster, 1998.

Bauer, Walter, et al., eds. *A Greek-English Lexicon of the New Testament and Other Early Christian Literature*. 2nd ed. Chicago: University of Chicago Press, 1979.

Beale, G. K. "The Problem of the Man from the Sea in 4 Ezra 13 and Its Relation to the Messianic Concept in John's Apocalypse." *Novum Testamentum* 25 (1983) 182-8.

———. *The Temple and the Church's Mission: A Biblical Theology of the Dwelling Place of God*. New Studies in Biblical Theology 17. Downers Grove, IL: InterVarsity, 2004.

Beasley-Murray, George R. "The Interpretation of Daniel 7." *Catholic Biblical Quarterly* 45 (1983) 44-58.

———. *Jesus and the Future*. London: MacMillan, 1954.

Bertram, G. "σαλεύω, σάλος." In *Theological Dictionary of the New Testament* 7:65-70.

Beyerle, Stefan. "'One Like a Son of Man': Innuendoes of a Heavenly Individual." In *Enoch and Qumran Origins: New Light on a Forgotten Connection*, edited by G. Boccaccini, 54-8. Grand Rapids: Eerdmans, 2005.

Bibliography

Bird, Michael. "The Crucifixion of Jesus as the Fulfilment of Mark 9:1." *Trinity Journal* 24 (2003) 23–36.
Bittner, Wolfgang. "Gott—Menschensohn—Davidsohn: eine Untersuchung zur Traditionsgeschichte von Daniel 7:13f." *Freiburger Zeitschrift für Philosophie und Theologie* 32 (1985) 343–72.
Black, Matthew. "Die Apotheose Israels: eine neue Interpretation des danielischen Menschensohn." In *Jesus und der Menschensohn: für Anton Vögtle*, edited by R. Pesch and R. Schnackenburg, 92–99. Freiburg: Herder, 1975.
———. "The Composition, Character, and Date of the 'Second Vision of Enoch.'" In *Text—Wort—Glaube: Studien zu Uberlieferung, Interpretation und Autorisierung biblischer Texte—Kurt Aland gewidmet Berlin, 1980*, edited by M. Brecht, 19–30. Berlin: de Gruyter, 1980.
———. "The Eschatology of the Similitudes of Enoch." *Journal of Theological Studies* 3 (1952) 1–10.
———. "The Messianism of the Parables of Enoch: Their Date and Contributions to Christological Origins." In *The Messiah: Developments in Earliest Judaism and Christianity*, edited by J. H. Charlesworth et al., 145–68. Minneapolis: Fortress, 1992.
———. "The 'Parables' of Enoch (1 En 37–71) and the 'Son of Man.'" *Expository Times* 88 (1976) 5–8.
———. "The Throne-Theophany Prophetic Commission of the 'Son of Man': A Study in Tradition-History." In *Jews, Greeks and Christians: Religious Cultures in Late Antiquity*, edited by R. Hamerton-Kelly and R. Scroggs, 57–73. Studies in Judaism in Late Antiquity 21. Leiden: Brill, 1976.
Blass, Friedrich, et al. *A Greek Grammar of the New Testament and Other Early Christian Literature. A Translation and Revision of the 9th German Edition.* Chicago: University of Chicago Press, 1961.
Blenkinsopp, Joseph. *Isaiah 1–39: A New Translation with Introduction and Commentary*. Anchor Bible. New York: Doubleday, 2000.
Boccaccini, Gabriele. *Beyond the Essene Hypothesis: The Parting of the Ways between Qumran and Enochic Judaism*. Grand Rapids: Eerdmans, 1998.
———. The Covenantal Theology of the Apocalyptic Book of Daniel." In *Enoch and Qumran Origins: New Light on a Forgotten Connection*, edited by G. Boccaccini, 39–44. Grand Rapids: Eerdmans, 2005.
Bock, Darrell L. *Blasphemy and Exaltation in Judaism: The Charge against Jesus in Mark 14:53–65*. Tübingen: J. C. B. Mohr (Paul Siebeck), 1998. Reprint, Grand Rapids: Baker Books, 2000.
———. "The Son of Man and the Debate over Jesus' 'Blasphemy.'" In *Jesus of Nazareth: Lord and Christ*, edited by J. B. Green, 181–91. Grand Rapids: Eerdmans, 1994.
———. "The Use of Daniel 7 in Jesus' Trial, with Implications for His Self-understanding." In *'Who is This Son of Man?': The Latest Scholarship on a Puzzling Expression of the Historical Jesus*, edited by L. W. Hurtado and P. L. Owen, 78–100. Library of New Testament Studies 390. London: T. & T. Clark, 2011.
Bolt, Peter G. *The Cross from a Distance: Atonement in Mark's Gospel*. New Studies in Biblical Theology 18. Downers Grove, IL: InterVarsity, 2004.
———. "Mark 13: An Apocalyptic Precursor to the Passion Narrative." *Reformed Theological Review* 54 (1995) 10–32.
Bond, Helen K. *Caiaphas: High Priest and Friend of Rome*. Louisville, KY: Westminster, 2004.

Bibliography

———. "Caiaphas: Reflections on a High Priest." *Expository Times* 113 (2002) 183-7.
Borsch, Frederick H. *The Son of Man in Myth and History*. London: SCM, 1967.
Bowker, J. "The Son of Man." *Journal of Theological Studies* 28 (1977) 19-48.
Brower, Kent. "Elijah in the Markan Passion Narrative." *Journal for the Study of the New Testament* 18 (1983) 85-101.
———. *Holiness in the Gospels*. Kansas City: Beacon Hill of Kansas City, 2005.
———. "'Let the Reader Understand': Temple and Eschatology in Mark." In *Eschatology in Bible and Theology*, edited by Kent E. Brower and M. W. Elliot, 119-43. Downers Grove, IL: InterVarsity, 1997.
———. "Seeing the Kingdom in Power." *Journal for the Study of the New Testament* 6 (1980) 17-41.
———. "'We are able': Cross-bearing Discipleship and the Way of the Lord in Mark." *Horizons in Biblical Theology* 29 (2007) 177-201.
Brown, Francis, et al. *The New Brown, Driver, Briggs, Gesenius Hebrew and English Lexicon*. Peabody, MA: Hendrickson, 1979.
Brown, Raymond E. *The Death of the Messiah: From Gethsemane to the Grave*. 2 vols. New York: Doubleday, 1994.
Broyles, Craig. *Psalms*. New International Biblical Commentary 11. Peabody, MA: Hendrickson, 1999.
Bruce, F. F. "The Background to the Son of Man Sayings." In *Christ the Lord: Studies Presented to Donald Guthrie*, edited by H. H. Rowdon, 50-70. Leicester: InterVarsity, 1982.
Bryan, David J. *Cosmos, Chaos, and the Kosher Mentality: The Roots and Rationale of Zoomorphic Imagery in the Animal Apocalypse, the Testament of Naphtali, and Daniel 7*. Oxford: Oxford University Press, 1989.
Bryan, Steven M. *Jesus and Israel's Traditions of Judgement and Restoration*. Society for New Testament Studies Monograph Series 117. Cambridge: Cambridge University Press, 2002.
Bultmann, Rudolf. "αἰσχύνω, ἐπαισχύνω, et al." In *Theological Dictionary of the New Testament* 1:189-91.
———. *Theology of the New Testament*. Translated by K. Grobel. 2 vols. New York: Scribner, 1951-55.
Burkett, Delbert. *The Son of Man Debate: A History and Evaluation*. Society for New Testament Studies Monograph Series 107. Cambridge: Cambridge University Press, 1999.
Caquot, André. "Remarques sur les Chapters 70 et 71 du Livre Éthiopien d'Hénoch." In *Apocalypses et théologie de l'espérance*, edited by Louis Monloubou, 111-22. Paris: Editions du Cerf, 1977.
Caragounis, Chrys C. "Greek Culture and Jewish Piety: The Clash and the Fourth Beast of Daniel 7." *Ephemerides theologicae Lovanienses* 65 (1989) 280-308.
———. "History and Supra-History: Daniel and The Four Empires." In *The Book of Daniel in the Light of New Findings*, edited by A. S. van der Woude, 387-97. Bibliotheca ephemeridum theologicarum Lovaniensium 106. Leuven: Leuven University Press, 1993.
———. "The Interpretation of the Ten Horns of Daniel 7." *Ephemerides theologicae Lovanienses* 63 (1987) 106-13.
———. *The Son of Man: Vision and Interpretation*. Wissenschaftliche Untersuchungen zum Neuen Testament 38. Tübingen: J. C. B. Mohr, 1986.

Bibliography

Casey Maurice P. "Culture and Historicity: The Plucking of the Grain (Mark 2:23–28)." *New Testament Studies* 34 (1988) 1–23.

———. "General, Generic, and Indefinite: The Use of the Term 'Son of Man' in Aramaic Sources and in the Teaching of Jesus." *Journal for the Study of the New Testament* 29 (1987) 21–56.

———. "Method in Our Madness and Madness in Their Methods: Some Approaches to the Son of Man Problem in Recent Scholarship." *Journal for the Study of the New Testament* 42 (1991) 17–43.

———. *The Solution to the "Son of Man" Problem*. Library of New Testament Studies. London: T. & T. Clark, 2007.

———. "The Son of Man Problem." *Zeitschrift für die neutestamentliche Wissenschaft und die Kunde der älteren Kirche* 67 (1976) 147–54.

———. *Son of Man: The Interpretation and Influence of Daniel 7*. London: SPCK, 1979.

———. "The Use of the Term 'Son of Man' in the Similitudes of Enoch." *Journal for the Study of Religion of Judaism in the Persian, Hellenistic, and Roman Periods* 7 (1976) 11–29.

Catchpole, David R. *The Trial of Jesus: A Study in the Gospels and Jewish Historiography from 1770 to the Present Day*. Studia post-Biblica 18. Leiden: Brill, 1971.

———. "You Have Heard His Blasphemy." *Tyndale Bulletin* 16 (1965) 10–18.

Charles, R. H. *The Apocrypha and Pseudepigrapha of the Old Testament in English*. Oxford: Clarendon, 1963–64.

———. *The Book of Enoch or 1 Enoch*. Oxford: Clarendon, 1912.

———. *The Ethiopic Version of the Book of Enoch*. Anecdota Oxoniensia 11. Oxford: Clarendon, 1906.

Chialà, Sabino. "The Son of Man: The Evolution of an Expression." In *Enoch and the Messiah Son of Man: Revisiting the Book of Parables*, edited by G. Boccaccini, 153–178. Grand Rapids: Eerdmans, 2007.

Childs, Brevard. *Exodus*. London: SCM, 1974.

Chilton, Bruce D. *Jesus' Baptism and Jesus' Healing*. Harrisburg, PA: Trinity International, 1998.

———. *Judaism in the New Testament*. London: Routledge, 1995.

———. "The Son of Man: Human and Heavenly." In *The Four Gospels 1992: Festschrift für Frans Neirynck*, edited by F. Van Segbroeck et al., 203–18. vol. 1. Leuven: Leuven University Press, 1992.

———. "(The) Son of (the) Man, and Jesus." In *Authenticating the Words of Jesus*, edited by C. A. Evans and B. D. Chilton, 259–87. Leiden: Brill, 1999.

———. "The Transfiguration: Dominical Assurance and Apostolic Vision." *New Testament Studies* 27 (1980) 115–24.

Chronis, Harry L. "To Reveal and to Conceal: A Literary-Critical Perspective on 'the Son of Man' in Mark." *New Testament Studies* 51 (2005) 459–81.

Clines, David J. A. *Job 1–20*. Word Biblical Commentary 17. Waco, TX: Word Books, 1989.

Cohen, J. *Be Fertile and Increase, Fill the Earth and Master It: The Ancient and Medieval Career of the Biblical Text*. Ithaca, NY: Cornell University Press, 1989.

Collins, Adela Yarbro. "The Apocalyptic Rhetoric of Mark 13 in Historical Context." *Biblical Research* 41 (1996) 5–36

Bibliography

———. "The Apocalyptic Son of Man Sayings." In *The Future of Christianity: Essays in Honor of Helmut Koester*, edited by B. A. Pearson et al., 220-28. Minneapolis: Fortress, 1991.

———. "The Charge of Blasphemy in Mark 14:64." *Journal for the Study of the New Testament* 26 (2004) 379-401.

———. "Daniel 7 and the Historical Jesus." In *Of Scribes and Scrolls: Studies in the Hebrew Bible, Intertestamental Judaism and Christian Origins Presented to John Strugnell on the Occasion of his Sixtieth Birthday*, edited by Harold W. Attridge et al., 187-93. Lanham, MD: University Press of America, 1990.

———. "Daniel 7 and Jesus." *Journal of Theology* 93 (1989) 5-19.

———. "The Eschatological Discourse of Mark 13." In *The Four Gospels: Festschrift für Frans Neirynck*, edited by F. van Segbroeck et al., 1125-40. Louvain: Peeters, 1992.

———. *Mark: A Commentary*. Hermeneia. Minneapolis: Fortress, 2007.

———. "The Origin of the Designation of Jesus as 'Son of Man.'" *Harvard Theological Review* 80 (1987) 391-407.

Collins, John J. *The Apocalyptic Imagination: An Introduction to Jewish Apocalyptic Literature*. 2nd ed. Grand Rapids: Eerdmans, 1998.

———. *The Apocalyptic Vision of the Book of Daniel*. Harvard Semitic Monographs 16. Missoula, MT: Scholars, 1977.

———. "The Heavenly Representative: The 'Son of Man' in the Similitudes of Enoch." In *Ideal Figures in Ancient Judaism: Profiles and Paradigms*, edited by J. J. Collins and G. W. E. Nickelsburg, 111-33. Septuagint and Cognate Studies 12. Chico, CA: Scholars, 1980.

———. "Response: The Apocalyptic Worldview of Daniel." In *Enoch and Qumran Origins: New Light on a Forgotten Connection*, edited by G. Boccaccini, 59-66. Grand Rapids: Eerdmans, 2005.

———. "The Son of Man in First-Century Judaism." *New Testament Studies* 38 (1992) 448-66.

———. "Son of Man and the Saints of the Most High in the Book of Daniel." *Journal of Biblical Literature* 93 (1974): 50-66.

———. "Stirring Up the Great Sea: The Religio-Historical Background of Daniel 7." In *The Book of Daniel in the Light of New Findings*, edited by A. S. van der Woude, 121-136. Bibliotheca ephemeridum theologicarum Lovaniensium 106. Leuven: Leuven University Press, 1993.

Colpe, C. "ὁ υἱὸς τοῦ ἀνθρώπου." In *Theological Dictionary of the New Testament* 8:400-77.

Colson, F. H., et al., trans. *Philo*. 12 vols. Loeb Classical Library. Cambridge: Harvard University Press, 1929-94.

Cook, Joan E. "Creation in 4 Ezra: The Biblical Theme in Support of Theodicy." In *Creation in the Biblical Traditions*, edited by R. J. Clifford and J. J. Collins, 129-39. Catholic Biblical Quarterly Monograph Series 24. Washington, DC: Catholic Biblical Association of America, 1992.

Cook, John G. *The Structure and Persuasive Power of Mark: A Linguistic Approach*. Society of Biblical Literature Semeia Series. Atlanta: Scholars, 1995.

Cook, Michael E. *Mark's Treatment of the Jewish Leaders*. Supplements to Novum Testamentum 51. Leiden: Brill, 1978.

Daube, D. "Responsibilities of Master and Disciples in the Gospels." *New Testament Studies* 19 (1972-73) 1-15.

Bibliography

Davenport, G. L. *The Eschatology of the Book of Jubilees*. Leiden: Brill, 1971.
Davies, Philip R. *Daniel*. Old Testament Guides. Sheffield: JSOT, 1985.
———. "Eschatology in the Book of Daniel." *Journal for the Study of the Old Testament* 17 (1980) 33-53.
———. "Reading Daniel Sociologically." In *The Book of Daniel in the Light of New Findings*, edited by A. S. van der Woude, 345-57. Bibliotheca ephemeridum theologicarum Lovaniensium 106. Leuven: Leuven University Press, 1993.
Déaut, R. Le. "Targumic Literature and New Testament Interpretation." *Biblical Theology Bulletin* 4 (1974) 243-45.
Deissler, Alfons. "Der Menschensohn und das Volk der Heiligen des Höchsten in Dan 7." In *Jesus und der Menschensohn: für Anton Vögtle*, edited by R. Pesch and R. Schnackenburg, 81-91. Freiburg: Herder, 1975.
Delcor. M. *Le Livre de Daniel*. Sources bibliques. Paris: Gabalda, 1971.
Dequeker, L. "Daniel 7 et les Saints du Très Haut." *Ephemerides theologicae Lovanienses* 36 (1960) 353-92.
Dewey, Joanna. "Mark as Aural Narrative: Structures as Clues to Understanding." *Sewanee Theological Review* 36 (1992) 45-65.
———. "Mark as Interwoven Tapestry: Forecasts and Echoes for a Listening Audience." *Catholic Biblical Quarterly* 52 (1991) 221-236.
———. *Markan Public Debate: Literary Technique, Concentric Structure, and Theology in Mark 2:1—3:6*. Society of Biblical Literature Dissertation Series 48. Chico, CA: Scholars Press, 1979.
Di Lella, Alexander A. "One in Human Likeness and the Holy Ones of the Most High in Daniel 7." *Catholic Biblical Quarterly* 39 (1977) 1-19.
DiTommaso, Lorenzo. "Dating the Eagle Vision of *4 Ezra*: A New Look at an Old Theory." *Journal for the Study of the Pseudepigrapha* 20 (1999) 3-38.
Dodd, C. H. *According to the Scriptures: The Sub-structure of New Testament Theology*. London: Nisbet, 1952.
———. *The Founder of Christianity*. London: Collins, 1970.
Donahue, J. R. *Are You the Christ? The Trial Narrative in the Gospel of Mark*. Society of Biblical Literature Dissertation Series 10. Missoula, MT: Society of Biblical Literature, 1973.
Donaldson, Terence L. *Jesus on the Mountain: A Study in Matthean Theology*. Journal for the Study of the New Testament Supplement Series 8. Sheffield: JSOT Press, 1985.
Douglas, Mary. *Purity and Danger: An Analysis of the Concepts of Pollution and Taboo*. London: Ark Paperbacks, 1966.
Doukhan, Jacques B. "Allusions à la Création dans le Livre de Daniel: Dépistage et Significations." In *The Book of Daniel in the Light of New Findings*, edited by A. S. van der Woude, 285-92. Bibliotheca ephemeridum theologicarum Lovaniensium 106. Leuven: Leuven University Press, 1993.
Dumbrell, William J. "Daniel 7." *Stimulus* 2 (1994) 26-31.
Dunn, James D. G. "'Are You the Messiah?': Is the crux of Mark 14:61-62 Resolvable?" In *Christology, Controversy, and Community: New Testament Essays in Honour of David R. Catchpole*, edited by David G. Horrell and Christopher M. Tuckett, 1-22. Supplements to Novum Testamentum 99. Leiden: Brill, 2000.
———. "'Son of God' as 'Son of man' in the Dead Sea Scrolls: A Response to John Collins on 4Q246." In *The Scrolls and the Scriptures: Qumran Fifty Years After*, edited by Stanley E. Porter and Craig A. Evans, 198-210. Sheffield: Sheffield University, 1997.

Bibliography

———. *Unity and Diversity in the New Testament: An Inquiry into the Character of Earliest Christianity*. 2nd ed. London: SCM, 1990.

Dupont, Jacques. "La Ruine du temple et la fin des temps dans le discourse de Mark 13." In *Apocalypses et théologie de l'espérance*, edited by Louis Monloubou, 207-69. Paris: Éditions du Cerf, 1977.

Durham, John I. *Exodus*. Word Biblical Commentary 3. Waco, TX: Word Books, 1987.

Elliger, K. and W. Rudolph, eds. *Biblia Hebraica Stuttgartensia*. Stuttgart: Deutsche Bibelgesellschaft, 1967-77.

Ellingworth, P. "Forgiveness of Sins." In *Dictionary of Jesus and the Gospels*, 241-43.

Esler, Philip Francis. "The Social Function of 4 Ezra." *Journal for the Study of the Old Testament* 54 (1994) 99-123.

Evans, Craig A. "Daniel in the New Testament: Visions of God's Kingdom." In *The Book of Daniel: Composition and Reception*, edited by J. J. Collins and P. W. Flint, 490-527. Supplements to Vetus Testamentum 83. vol. 2. Leiden: Brill, 2001.

———. "In What Sense Blasphemy? Jesus Before Caiaphas in Mark 14:61-64." In the *Society of Biblical Literature 1991 Seminar Papers*, 215-34. Society of Biblical Literature Seminar Papers 30. Chico, CA: Scholars, 1991.

———. *Mark 8:27—16:20*. Word Biblical Commentary 34b. Nashville: Thomas Nelson, 2001.

Ferch, Arthur. "Daniel 7 and Ugarit: A Reconsideration." *Journal of Biblical Literature* 99 (1980) 75-86.

Fitzmyer, Joseph A. "Another Approach to the 'Son of Man' Debate." *Journal for the Study of the New Testament* 4 (1979) 58-68.

———. "The Implications of the New Enoch Literature from Qumran." *Theological Studies* 38 (1977) 332-45

———. "The New Testament Title 'Son of Man' Philologically Considered." In *A Wandering Aramean: Collected Aramaic Essays*, 143-60. Society of Biblical Literature Manuscript Series 25. Missoula, MT: Scholars, 1979.

———. Review of *An Aramaic Approach to the Gospels and Acts* 3rd ed., by M. Black. *Catholic Biblical Quarterly* 30 (1968) 417-28.

Fletcher-Louis, Crispin H. T. *All of the Glory of Adam: Liturgical Anthropology in the Dead Sea Scrolls*. Studies on the Texts of the Desert of Judah 42. Leiden: Brill, 2002.

———. "The High Priest as Divine Mediator in the Hebrew Bible: Dan 7:13 as a Test Case." In *Society of Biblical Literature 1997 Seminar Papers*, 161-93. Society Biblical Literature Seminar Papers 36. Atlanta: Scholars, 1997.

———. "Jesus and the High Priest." Paper presented at the British New Testament Conference. University of Birmingham, September 4-6, 2004.

———. "Jesus, the Temple and the Dissolution of Heaven and Earth." In *Apocalyptic in History and Tradition*, edited by C. H. Rowland and J. Barton, 117-41. Journal for the Study of the Pseudepigrapha Supplement Series 43. London: Sheffield Academic, 2002.

———. "Revelation of the Sacral Son of Man." In *Auferstehung: the Fourth Durham-Tübingen Research Symposium—Resurrection, Transfiguration and Exaltation in Old Testament, Ancient Judaism, and Early Christianity*, edited by F. Avemarie and H. Lichtenberger, 247-98. Tübingen: Mohr Siebeck, 2001.

Florentino, García Martínez, and Eibert J. C. Tigchelaar, eds. *The Dead Sea Scrolls Study Edition*. 2 vols. Grand Rapids: Eerdmans, 1997-1998.

Bibliography

Foster, George M. "The Anatomy of Envy: A Study in Symbolic Behavior." *Convivium assisiense* 13 (1972) 165–86.

France, R. T. *The Gospel of Mark*. New International Greek Testament Commentary. Grand Rapids: Eerdmans, 2002.

———. *Jesus and the Old Testament: His Application of Old Testament Passages to Himself and his Mission*. London: SCM, 1971. Reprint, Vancouver: Regent College, 1998.

Fröhlich, Ida. "The Symbolical Language of the Animal Apocalypse of Enoch (1 Enoch 85–90)." *Revue de Qumran* 14 (1990) 629–36.

Fuellet, A. 'Le Fils de l'Homme de Daniel et la Tradition Biblique." *Revue biblique* (1953) 170–202.

Fuller, H. *The Foundations of New Testament Christology*. New York: Scribner, 1965.

Gane, Roy. "'Bread of the Presence' and Creator-in-Residence." *Vetus Testamentum* 42 (1992) 179–203.

Gardner, Anne E. "Daniel 7:2–14: Another Look at Its Mythic Pattern." *Biblica* 82 (2001) 244–52.

———. "The Great Sea of Dan VII 2." *Vetus Testamentum* 49 (1999) 412–15.

Gärtner, Bertil. *The Temple and the Community in the Qumran School and the New Testament*. Society for New Testament Studies Monograph Series 1. Cambridge: Cambridge University, 1965.

Gathercole, Simon. *The Pre-existent Son: Recovering the Christologies of Matthew, Mark and Luke*. Grand Rapids: Eerdmans, 2006.

———. "The Son of Man in Mark's Gospel." *Expository Times* 115 (2004) 366–72.

Geddart, T. J. *Watchwords: Mark 13 in Markan Eschatology*. Journal for the Study of the New Testament Supplement Series 26. Sheffield: JSOT, 1989.

Glasson, Thomas F. "The Reply to Caiaphas (Mark xiv 62)." *New Testament Studies* 7 (1961) 88–93.

———. "Son of Man Imagery: Enoch XIV and Daniel VII." *New Testament Studies* 23 (1976) 82–90.

Gnilka, Joachim. *Das Evangelium Nach Markus: Mk 1—8,26*. Evangelisch-katholischer Kommentar zum Neuen Testament 2. vol. 1. Zürich: Benziger Verlag, 1978.

———. *Das Evangelium Nach Markus: Mk 8,27—16,20*. Evangelisch-katholischer Kommentar zum Neuen Testament 2. vol. 2. Zürich: Benziger Verlag, 1979.

Goldingay, John. *Daniel*. Word Biblical Commentary 30. Dallas: Word Books, 1989.

———. "'Holy Ones on High' in Daniel 7:18." *Journal of Biblical Literature* 107 (1988) 495–97.

Goulder, Michael. "Psalm 8 and the Son of Man." *New Testament Studies* 48 (2002) 18–29.

Grabbe, Lester L. "Chronology in 4 Ezra and 2 Baruch." In *Society of Biblical Literature 1981 Seminar Papers*, 49–63. Society of Biblical Literature Seminar Papers 20. Atlanta: Scholars, 1981.

Gray, Timothy C. *The Temple in the Gospel of Mark: A Study in Its Narrative Role*. Tübingen: Mohr Siebeck, 2008. Reprint, Grand Rapids: Baker Academic, 2010.

Greenfield, Jonas C. and Michael E. Stone. "The Enochic Pentateuch and the Date of the Similitudes." *Harvard Theological Review* 70 (1977) 51–65.

Grundmann, Walter. *Das Evangelium nach Markus*. Theologischer Handkommentar zum Neuen Testament 2. Berlin: Evangelische Verlagsanstalt, 1973.

———. "δύναμαι, δύναμις." In *Theological Dictionary of the New Testament* 2:284-317.

Guelich, Robert A. *Mark 1—8:26*. Word Biblical Commentary 34a. Dallas: Word Books, 1989.

BIBLIOGRAPHY

Gundry, Robert H. *Mark: A Commentary on His Apology for the Cross*. Grand Rapids: Eerdmans, 1993.

Gurney, Robert J. M. "The Four Kingdoms of Daniel 2 and 7." *Themelios* 2 (1977) 39-45.

Haag, Ernst. "Der Menschensohn und die Heiligen (des) Höchsten: eine literar-, form- und traditionsgeschichtliche Untersuchung zu Daniel 7." In *The Book of Daniel in the Light of New Findings*, edited by A. S. van der Woude, 137-85. Bibliotheca ephemeridum theologicarum Lovaniensium 106. Leuven: Leuven University, 1993.

Haenchen, Ernst. *Der Weg Jesu: Eine Erklärung des Markus-Evangeliums und der kanonischen Parallelen*. Berlin: Töpelmann, 1966.

Hagedorn, Anselm C. and Jerome H. Neyrey. "'It Was Out of Envy That They Handed Jesus Over' (Mark 15:10): The Anatomy of Envy and the Gospel of Mark." *Journal for the Study of the New Testament* 69 (1998) 15-56.

Hahn, Ferdinand. *The Titles of Jesus in Christology: Their History in Early Christianity*. Translated by H. Knight and G. Ogg. London: Lutterworth, 1969.

Hampel, V. *Menschensohn und historischer Jesus. Ein Rätselwort als Schlüssel zum messianischen Selbstverständnis Jesu*. Neukirchen: Neukirchener, 1990.

Hannah, Darrell D. "The Elect Son of Man of the *Parables of Enoch*." In *'Who Is This Son of Man?' The Latest Scholarship on a Puzzling Expression of the Historical Jesus*, edited by L. W. Hurtado and P. L. Owen, 130-58. London: T. & T. Clark, 2011.

Hare, Douglas. *The Son of Man Tradition*. Minneapolis: Fortress, 1990.

Harnisch, W. "Die Ironie der Offenbarung: Exegetische Erwägungen zur Zionvision im 4. Buch Ezra." In *Society of Biblical Literature 1981 Seminar Papers*, 79-104. Society of Biblical Literature Seminar Papers 20. Atlanta: Scholars, 1981.

Harrington, Daniel J. "The 'Holy Land' in Pseudo-Philo, 4 Ezra, and 2 Baruch." In *Emanuel: Studies in Hebrew Bible, Septuagint, and Dead Sea Scrolls in Honor of Emanuel Tov*, edited by Shalom M. Paul et al., 661-72. Supplements to Vetus Testamentum 94. Leiden: Brill, 2003.

Hartley, J. E. *Genesis*. New International Bible Commentary. Peabody, MA: Hendrickson, 2000.

Hartman, Louis F. and Alexander A. Di Lella. *The Book of Daniel*. Anchor Bible 23. New York: Doubleday, 1978.

Hasel, Gerhard F. "The Identity of 'The Saints of the Most High' in Daniel 7." *Biblica* 56 (1975) 173-92.

Hatch, E., and H. Redpath. *A Concordance to the Septuagint and Other Greek Versions of the Old Testament (Including the Apocryphal Books)*. Graz, Austria: Akademische Druck- u. Verlagsanstalt, 1975.

Hatina, Thomas R. "The Focus of Mark 13:24-27: The Parousia, or the Destruction of the Temple?" *Bulletin for Biblical Research* 6 (1996) 43-66.

———. *In Search of a Context: The Function of Scripture in Mark's Narrative*. Journal for the Study of the New Testament 232. London: Sheffield Academic, 2002.

———. "Who Will See 'The Kingdom of God Coming with Power' in Mark 9,1 — Protagonists or Antagonists?" *Biblica* 86 (2005) 20-34.

Hay, Lewis H. "The Son of Man in Mark 2:10 and 2:28." *Journal of Biblical Literature* 89 (1970) 69-75.

Hays, Richard B. *Echoes of Scripture in the Letters of Paul*. New Haven, CT: Yale University Press, 1989.

Heaton, Eric W. *The Book of Daniel: Introduction and Commentary*. London: SCM, 1956.

Bibliography

Heil, John Paul. "The Narrative Strategy and Pragmatics of the Temple Theme in Mark." *Catholic Biblical Quarterly* 59 (1997) 76-100.

Hengel, Martin. *The Atonement: The Origins of the Doctrine in the New Testament.* Translated by J. Bowden. London: SCM, 1981.

———. *Judaism and Hellenism: Studies in their Encounter in Palestine during the Early Hellenistic Period.* 2 vols. Translated by J. Bowden. London: SCM, 1974.

———. "Psalm 110 und die Erhöhung des Auferstanden zur Rechten." In *Anfänge der Christologie: Festschrift für Ferdinand Hahn zum 65. Geburstag,* edited by C. Breytenbach and H. Paulsen, 43-73. Göttingen: Vandenhoeck & Ruprecht, 1991.

———. *Studies in Early Christology.* Edinburgh: T. & T. Clark, 1995.

Henten, Jan W. Van. "Antiochus IV as a Typhonic Figure in Daniel 7." In *The Book of Daniel in the Light of New Findings.* Bibliotheca ephemeridum theologicarum Lovaniensium 106, edited by A. S. van der Woude, 223-43. Leuven: Leuven University Press, 1993.

Henze, Matthias. "Enoch's Dream Visions and the Visions of Daniel Reexamined." In *Enoch and Qumran Origins: New Light on a Forgotten Connection,* edited by G. Boccaccini, 17-38. Grand Rapids: Eerdmans, 2005.

Higgins, A. J. B. *Jesus and the Son of Man.* Philadelphia: Fortress, 1964.

Himmelfarb, Martha J. "Apocalyptic Ascent and the Heavenly Temple." In *Society of Biblical Literature 1987 Seminar Papers,* 210-17. Society of Biblical Literature Seminar Papers 26. Missoula, MT: Scholars, 1987.

———. *Ascent to Heaven in Jewish and Christian Apocalypses.* New York: Oxford University Press, 1993.

———. "From Prophecy to Apocalypse: The *Book of Watchers* and the Tours of Heaven." In *Jewish Spirituality,* edited by A. Green, 145-65. Vol. 1. New York: Crossroad, 1986.

Hofius, Otfried. "Vergebungszuspruch und Vollmachtsfrage: Mk 2,1—12 und das Problem priesterlicher Absolution im antiken Judentum." In *Wenn nicht jetzt, wann dann: Aufsätze für Hans-Joachim Kraus zum 65 Geburstag,* edited by H. G. Geyer, 115-27. Neukirchen-Vluyn: Neukirchener Verlag, 1983.

Hooker, Morna D. *The Gospel According to Saint Mark.* Black's New Testament Commentaries 2. Peabody, MA: Hendrickson Publishers, 1991.

———. *Jesus and the Servant.* London: SPCK, 1959.

———. "Mark." In *It is Written: Scripture Citing Scripture,* edited by D. A. Carson and H. G. M. Williamson, 220-30. Cambridge: Cambridge University Press, 1988.

———. *Not Ashamed of the Gospel: New Testament Interpretations of the Death of Christ.* Grand Rapids: Eerdmans, 1995. Reprint, Carlisle, UK: Paternoster, 1994.

———. *The Son of Man in Mark: A Study of the Background of the Term 'Son of Man' and Its Use in St. Mark's Gospel.* London: SPCK, 1967.

Horbury, William. "The Messianic Associations of 'The Son of Man.'" *Journal of Theological Studies* 36 (1985) 34-55.

Hurtado, Larry W. *How on Earth Did Jesus Become a God?* Grand Rapids: Eerdmans, 2005.

———. *Lord Jesus Christ: Devotion to Jesus in Earliest Christianity.* Grand Rapids: Eerdmans, 2003.

———. *Mark.* New International Biblical Commentary 2. Peabody: Hendrickson, 1989.

———. *One God, One Lord: Early Christian Devotion and Ancient Jewish Monotheism.* Philadelphia: Fortress, 1988.

———. "Summary and Concluding Observations." In *'Who is This Son of Man?': The Latest Scholarship on a Puzzling Expression of the Historical Jesus,* edited by L. W.

Bibliography

Hurtado and P. L. Owen, 159-77. Library of New Testament Studies 390. London: T. & T. Clark, 2011.

Iersel, B. M. F. van. "The Sun, Moon, and Stars of Mark 13:24-25 in a Greco-Roman Reading." *Biblica* 77 (1996) 84-92.

Janowski, Bernd. "He Bore Our Sins: Isaiah 53 and the Drama of Taking Another's Place." In *The Suffering Servant: Isaiah 53 in Jewish and Christian Sources*, edited by B. Janowski and P. Stuhlmacher, 48-74. Translated by D. P. Bailey. Grand Rapids: Eerdmans, 2004.

Jenni, Ersnt, and Claus Westermann, eds. *Theological Lexicon of the Old Testament*. Translated by M. E. Biddle. 3 vols. Peabody, MA: Hendrickson, 1997.

Jennings, Theodore W. "The Martyrdom of the Son of Man." In *Text and Logos: The Humanistic Interpretation of the New Testament*, edited by T. Jennings, 229-43. Atlanta: Scholars, 1990.

Jeremias, J. "Die älteste Schicht der Menschensohn-Logien." *Zeitschrift für die neutestamentliche Wissenschaft und die Kunde der älteren Kirche* 58 (1967) 159-72.

Josephus. Translated by H. St. J. Thackeray et al. 10 vols. Loeb Classical Library. Cambridge: Harvard University Press, 1976-1981.

Judisch, Douglas M. L. "The Saints of the Most High." *Concordia Theological Quarterly* 53 (1989) 96-103.

Juel, Donald. *Messiah and Temple: The Trial of Jesus in the Gospel of Mark*. Society of Biblical Literature Dissertation Series 31. Missoula, MT: Scholars, 1977.

Kaufman, Stephan A., et al. *A Key-Word-In-Context Concordance to Targum Neofiti: A Guide to the Complete Palestinian Aramaic Text of the Torah*. Publications of the Comprehensive Aramaic Lexicon Project 2. Baltimore: John Hopkins University Press, 1993.

Kee, Howard C. "The Function of Scripture Quotations and Allusions in Mark 11—16." In *Jesus und Paulus: Festschrift für Werner Georg Kümmel zum 70. Geburtstag*, edited by E. E. Ellis and E. Gräßer, 165-88. Göttingen: Vandenhoeck & Ruprecht, 1978.

———. "'The Man' in Fourth Ezra: Growth of a Tradition." In *Society of Biblical Literature 1981 Seminar Papers*, 199-208. Society of Biblical Literature Seminar Papers 20. Atlanta: Scholars, 1981.

———. "Messiah and the People of God." In *Understanding the Word: Essays in Honour of Bernhard W. Anderson*, edited by J. T. Butler, et al., 341-58. Journal for the Study of the Old Testament Supplement Series 37. Sheffield: JSOT, 1985.

———. "The Transfiguration in Mark: Epiphany or Apocalyptic Vision?" In *Understanding the Sacred Text: Essays in Honor of Morton S. Enslin on the Hebrew Bible and Christian Beginnings*, edited by J. Reumann, 137-52. Valley Forge, PA: Judson, 1972.

Kelber, W. H. *The Kingdom in Mark: A New Place and a New Time*. Philadelphia: Fortress, 1974.

Kellner, Wendelin. *Der Traum vom Menschensohn: Die politisch-theologische Botschaft Jesu*. Münich: Kösel, 1985.

Kilgallen, John J. "Mk 9,1—the Conclusion of a Pericope." *Biblica* 63 (1982) 81-83.

Kim, Seyoon. "Jesus—The Son of God, the Stone, the Son of Man, and the Servant: The Role of Zechariah in the Self-Identification of Jesus." In *Tradition and Interpretation in the New Testament: Essays in Honor of Earle E. Ellis for his 60th Birthday*, edited by G. F. Hawthorne and O. Betz, 134-48. Grand Rapids: Eerdmans, 1987.

———. *The 'Son of Man' as the Son of God*. Wissenschaftliche Untersuchungen zum Neuen Testament 30. Tübingen: Mohr, 1983.

Bibliography

Kingsbury, Jack Dean. *The Christology of Mark's Gospel*. Philadelphia: Fortress, 1983.

———. *Conflict in Mark: Jesus, Authorities, Disciples*. Minneapolis: Fortress, 1989.

———. "Observations on 'the Son of Man' in the Gospel According to Luke." *Currents in Theology and Mission* 17 (1990) 283-90.

———. "The Religious Authorities in the Gospel of Mark." *New Testament Studies* 36 (1990) 42-65.

Kittel, G., and G. von Rad. "δοκέω, δόξα, etc." In *Theological Dictionary of the New Testament* 2:232-255.

Klauck, Hans-Josef. "Die Frage der Sündenvergebung in der Perikope von der Heilung des Gelähmten (Mk 2, 1-12 parr)." *Biblische Zeitschrift* 25 (1981) 223-48.

Kmiecik, Ulrich. *Der Menschensohn im Markusevangelium*. Forschung zur bibel 81. Würzburg: Echter Verlag, 1997.

Knibb, Michael A. "Apocalyptic and Wisdom in 4 Ezra." *Journal for the Study of Judaism in the Persian, Hellenistic, and Roman Period* 13 (1982) 56-74.

———. "The Date of the Parables of Enoch: A Critical Review." *New Testament Studies* 25 (1979) 345-59.

———, and Edward Ullendorff. *Ethiopic Book of Enoch*. 2 vols. Oxford: Clarendon, 1978.

Koch, Klaus. "Messias und Menschensohn." In *Der Messias*, 73-102. Jahrbuch für biblische Theologie 8. Neukirchen-Vluyn: Neukirchener Verlag, 1993.

———. "Sühne und Sündenvergebung um die Wende von der exilischen zur nachexilischen Zeit." *Evangelische Theologie* 26 (1966) 217-39.

Kooij, Arie van der. "The Concept of Covenant (*BERÎT*) in the Book of Daniel." In *The Book of Daniel in the Light of New Findings*, edited by A. S. van der Woude, 495-501. Bibliotheca ephemeridum theologicarum Lovaniensium 106. Leuven: Leuven University Press, 1993.

Kraus, Hans-Joachim. *Psalms 60—150: A Commentary*. Minneapolis: Augsburg, 1989.

Kuhn, Heinz-Wolfgang. Ältere Sammlungen im Markusevangelium. Studien zur Umwelt des Neuen Testaments 8. Göttingen: Vandenhoeck & Ruprecht, 1971.

Kvanvig, Heldge S. "Henoch und der Menschensohn: das Verhältnis von Hen 14 zu Dan 7." *Studia theologica* 38 (1984) 101-33.

———. "The Son of Man in the Parables of Enoch." In *Enoch and the Messiah Son of Man: Revisiting the Book of Parables*, edited by G. Boccaccini, 179-215. Grand Rapids: Eerdmans, 2007.

Lacocque, André. "Allusions to Creation in Daniel 7." In *The Book of Daniel: Composition and Reception*, edited by J. J. Collins and P. W. Flint, 114-31. Supplements to Vetus Testamentum 83. vol. 2. Leiden: Brill, 2001.

———. *The Book of Daniel*. Translated by D. Pellauer. Atlanta: John Knox, 1979.

———. "The Socio-Spiritual Formative Milieu of the Daniel Apocalypse." In *The Book of Daniel in the Light of New Findings*, edited by A. S. van der Woude, 315-43. Bibliotheca ephemeridum theologicarum Lovaniensium 106. Leuven: Leuven University, 1993.

Lane, William. *The Gospel According to Mark*. The New International Commentary on the New Testament. Grand Rapids: Eerdmans, 1974.

Lebram, J. C. H. "Apokalyptik und Hellenismus im Buche Daniel." *Vetus Testamentum* 20 (1970) 503-24.

Leivestad, Ragnar. "Exit the Apocalyptic Son of Man." *New Testament Studies* 18 (1972) 243-67.

Lenglet, A. "La structure littéraire de Dan 2—7." *Biblica* 53 (1972) 169-90.

Bibliography

Levenson, Jon D. *Sinai and Zion: An Entry into the Jewish Bible*. New Voices in Biblical Studies. Edited by A. Y. Collins and J. J. Collins. Minneapolis: Winston, 1985.

Lichtenberger, Hermann. "Zion and the Destruction of the Temple in 4 Ezra 9—10." In *Gemeinde ohne Tempel: zur Substituierung und Transformation des Jerusalemer Tempels und seines Kults im Alten Testament, antiken Judentum und frühen Christentum*, edited by B. Ego et al., 239-49. Wissenschaftliche Untersuchungen zum Neuen Testament 118. Tübingen: Mohr, 1999.

Lindars, Barnabas. "Jesus as Advocate: A Contribution to the Christology Debate." *Bulletin of the John Rylands University Library of Manchester* 62 (1980) 476-97.

———. *Jesus the Son of Man: A Fresh Examination of the Son of Man Sayings in the Gospels*. London: SPCK, 1983.

———. "The New Look on the Son of Man." *Bulletin of the John Rylands University Library of Manchester* 63 (1981) 437-62.

Lindenberger, James M. "Daniel 7:13-14." *Interpretation* 39 (1985) 181-86.

Lioy, Dan. *Axis of Glory: A Biblical and Theological Analysis of the Temple Motif in Scripture*. Studies in Biblical Literature 138. New York: Peter Lang, 2010.

Lohmeyer, Ernst. *Das Evangelium des Markus*. Kritisch-exegetischer Kommentar über das Neue Testament 2. Göttingen: Vandenhoeck & Ruprecht, 1963.

Lohse, E. "σάββατον." In *Theological Dictionary of the New Testament* 7:12-14.

———. "χειροποίητον." In *Theological Dictionary of the New Testament* 9:436-37.

Longenecker, Bruce W. "Locating 4 Ezra: A Consideration of Its Social Setting and Functions." *Journal for the Study of Judaism in the Persian, Hellenistic and Roman Periods* 28 (1997) 271-93.

———. "'Son of Man' as a Self-Designation of Jesus." *Journal of the Evangelical Theological Society* 12 (1969) 151-58.

Lucas, Ernest C. "The Origin of Daniel's Four Empires Scheme Re-examined." *Tyndale Bulletin* 40 (1989) 185-202.

———. "The Source of Daniel's Animal Imagery." *Tyndale Bulletin* 41 (1990) 161-85.

Lührmann, Dieter. *Das Markusevangelium*. Handbuch Neuen Testament 3. Tübingen: J. C. B. Mohr (Paul Siebeck), 1987.

Maddox, R. "The Function of the Son of Man according to the Synoptic Gospels." *New Testament Studies* 15 (1968) 45-74.

Maier, J. *Vom Kultus zur Gnosis: Studien zur Vor- und Frühgeschichte der 'jüdischen Gnosis'*. Religionswissenschaftliche Studien 1. Salzburg: O. Müller, 1964.

Malbon, Elizabeth Struthers. "The Jewish Leaders in the Gospel of Mark: A Literary Study of Marcan Characterization." *Journal of Biblical Literature* 108 (1989) 259-81.

———. "Literary Contexts of Mark 13." In *Biblical and Humane: A Festschrift for John F. Priest*, edited by L. B. Elder and J. L. Barr, 105-24. Scholars Press Homage Series 20. Atlanta: Scholars, 1996.

———. "Narrative Christology and the Son of Man: What the Markan Jesus Says Instead." *Biblical Interpretation* 11 (2003) 373-85.

Manson, T. W. "The Son of Man in Daniel, Enoch, and the Gospels." In *Studies in the Gospels and Epistles*, edited by M. Black, 123-45. Manchester: Manchester University Press, 1962.

———. *The Teaching of Jesus: Studies of Its Form and Content*. Cambridge: Cambridge University Press, 1951.

Marcus, Joel. "Authority to Forgive Sins Upon the Earth: The *Shema* in the Gospel of Mark." In *The Gospels and the Scriptures of Israel*, edited by C. A. Evans and W. R.

Bibliography

Stegner, 196–211. Journal for the Study of the New Testament Supplement Series 104. Sheffield: Sheffield Academic Press, 1994.

———. *Mark 1—8: A New Translation with Introduction and Commentary*. Anchor Bible 27. New York: Doubleday, 2000.

———. *Mark 8—16: A New Translation with Introduction and Commentary*. Anchor Yale Bible 27. New Haven: Yale University, 2009.

———. "Mark 14:61: 'Are You the Messiah-Son-of-God?'" *Novum Testamentum* 31 (1989) 125–41.

———. "Son of Man as Son of Adam. Part I." *Revue Biblique* 110 (2003) 38–61.

———. "Son of Man as Son of Adam. Part II." *Revue Biblique* 110 (2003) 370–86.

———. *The Way of the Lord: Christological Exegesis of the Old Testament in the Gospel of Mark*. Louisville: Westminster, 1992.

Marlow, R. "The Son of Man in Recent Journal Literature." *Catholic Biblical Quarterly* (1966) 20–30.

Marshall, C. D. *Faith as a Theme in Mark's Narrative*. Society for New Testament Studies Monograph Series 64. Cambridge: Cambridge University Press, 1989.

Marshall, I. H. "Acts." In *Commentary on the New Testament Use of the Old Testament*, edited by G. K. Beale and D. A. Carson, 513–606. Grand Rapids: Baker, 2007.

———. *Last Supper and Lord's Supper*. Exeter: Paternoster, 1980.

———. "The Synoptic Son of Man Sayings in Recent Discussion." *New Testament Studies* 12 (1965) 327–51.

Martínez, Florentino García. "Comparing the Groups Behind Dream Visions and Daniel: A Brief Note." In *Enoch and Qumran Origins: New Light on a Forgotten Connection*, edited by G. Boccaccini, 45–46. Grand Rapids: Eerdmans, 2005.

McConville, J. G. *Deuteronomy*. Apollos Old Testament Commentary 5. Downers Grove IL: InterVarsity, 2002.

McKelvey, R. J. *The New Temple: The Church in the New Testament*. London: Oxford University Press, 1969.

Mearns, Christopher L. "Dating the Similitudes of Enoch." *New Testament Studies* 25 (1979) 360–69.

Meier, John P. "The Historical Jesus and the Plucking of the Grain on the Sabbath." *Catholic Biblical Quarterly* 66 (2004) 561–81.

Mendels, D. "Hecataeus of Abdera and a Jewish 'patrios politeia' of the Persian Period (Diodorus Siculus XL, 3)." *Zeitschrift für die neutestamentliche Wissenschaft und die Kunde der älteren Kirche* 95 (1983) 96–110.

Metzger, Bruce M., ed. *A Textual Commentary on the New Testament*. 2nd ed. Stuttgart: Biblia-Druck, 1994.

Milgrom, Jacob. *Leviticus 1—16: A New Translation with Introduction and Commentary*. The Anchor Bible 3A. New York: Doubleday, 1991.

———. *Leviticus 23—27: A New Translation with Introduction and Commentary*. Anchor Bible 3C. New York: Doubleday, 2001.

Milik, J. T. *The Books of Enoch: Aramaic Fragments of Qumrân Cave 4*. Oxford: Clarendon, 1976.

Mkole, J. C. Loba. "Mark 14:62: Substantial Compendium of New Testament Christology." *Hervormde Teologiese Studies* 56 (2000) 1119–45.

Moloney, Francis J. *The Gospel of Mark: A Commentary*. Peabody, MA: Hendrickson, 2002.

Bibliography

Montgomery, James M. *A Critical and Exegetical Commentary on the Book of Daniel.* International Critical Commentary. Edinburgh: T. & T. Clark, 1927.

Moo, Douglas J. *The Old Testament in the Gospel Passion Narratives.* Sheffield: Almond, 1983.

Mosca, Paul G. "Ugarit and Daniel 7: A Missing Link." *Biblica* 67 (1986) 496–517.

Moule, C. F. D. "Neglected Features in the Problem of 'the Son of Man.'" In *Neuen Testament und Kirche. Festschrift für Rudolf Schnackenburg,* edited by J. Gnilka, 413–28. Freiburg: Herder, 1974.

———. *The Origin of Christology.* Cambridge: Cambridge University Press, 1977.

———. "The Son of Man: Some of the Facts." *New Testament Studies* 41 (1995) 277–79.

Müller, Mogens. *Der Ausdruck 'Menschensohn' in den Evangelien: Vorassetzungen und Bedeutung.* Acta theological danica 17. Leiden: Brill, 1984.

———. "Betydningen af bar 'enas i Dan 7:13: en anmeldelsesartikel." *Dansk theologisk tidsskrift* 47 (1984) 177–86.

———. "Have You Faith in the Son of Man? (John 9.35)." *New Testament Studies* 37 (1991) 291–94.

———. "The Source of Daniel's Animal Imagery." *Tyndale Bulletin* 41 (1990) 161–85.

Müller, U. B. *Messias und Menschensohn in jüdischen Apokalypsen und in der Offenbarung des Johannes.* Studien zum Neuen Testament 6. Gütersloh: Mohn, 1972.

Myers, Jacob M. *1 and 11 Esdras: Introduction, Translation and Commentary.* Anchor Bible 42. Garden City, NY: Doubleday, 1974.

Nardoni, Enrique. "A Redactional Interpretation of Mark 9:1." *Catholic Biblical Quarterly* 43 (1981) 365–84.

Neusner, Jacob. "Money-Changers in the Temple: The Mishnah's Explanation." *New Testament Studies* 35 (1989) 287–90.

Neyrey, Jerome H. "The Idea of Purity in Mark's Gospel." *Semeia* 35 (1986) 91–128.

Nicholson, E. W. "The Covenant Ritual in Exodus XXIV 3–8." *Vetus Testamentum* 32 (1982) 74–86.

Nickelsburg, George W. E. "Apocalyptic and Myth in 1 Enoch 6–11." *Journal of Biblical Literature* 96 (1977) 383–405.

———. "The Bible Rewritten and Expanded." In *Jewish Writings of the Second Temple Period: Apocrypha, Pseudepigrapha, Qumran sectarian writings, Philo, Josephus,* edited by M. E. Stone, 89–156. Philadelphia: Fortress, 1984.

———. "Enoch, Levi, and Peter: Recipients of Revelation in Upper Galilee." *Journal of Biblical Literature* 100 (1981) 575–600.

———, and James C. VanderKam. *1 Enoch: A New Translation.* Minneapolis: Fortress, 2004.

———. *Jewish Literature between the Bible and the Mishnah: A Historical and Literary Introduction.* 2nd ed. Minneapolis: Fortress, 2005.

Noth, M. *The Laws in the Pentateuch, and Other Studies.* Translated by D. R. Ap-Thomas. Edinburgh: Oliver & Boyd, 1966.

O'Brien, Kelli S. *The Use of Scripture in the Markan Passion Narrative.* Library of New Testament Studies 384. London: T. & T. Clark, 2010.

Öhler, Markus. *Elia im Neuen Testament: Untersuchungen zur Bedeutung des alttestamentlichen Propheten im frühen Christentum.* Beihefte zur Zeitschrift für die neutestamentliche 88. Berlin: Walter de Gruyter, 1997.

Olson, Daniel C. "Enoch and the Son of Man in the Epilogue of the Parables." *Journal for the Study of the Pseudepigrapha* 18 (1998) 27–38.

Bibliography

O'Neill, John C. "The Desolate House and the New Kingdom of Jerusalem: Jewish Oracles of Ezra in 2 Esdras 1—2." In *Templum Amicitiae: Essays on the Second Temple Presented to Ernst Bammel*, edited by W. Horbury, 226-36. Sheffield: JSOT, 1991.

Owen, Paul, and David Shepherd. "Speaking Up for Qumran, Dalman, and the Son of Man: Was *Bar Enasha* a Common Term for 'Man' in the Time of Jesus?" *Journal for the Study of the New Testament* 81 (2001) 81-122.

Parlier, Isabelle. "L'Autorité Qui Révèle La Foi et L'Incrédulité: Marc 2/1-12." *Etudes théologiques et religieuses* 67 (1992) 243-47.

Patterson, Richard D. "The Key Role of Daniel 7." *Grace Theological Journal* 12 (1991) 245-61.

Perrin, Norman. "The Composition of Mark ix i." *Novum Testamentum* 11 (1969) 67-70.

———. *The Kingdom of God in the Teaching of Jesus*. London: SCM, 1963.

———. *A Modern Pilgrimage in New Testament Christology*. Minneapolis: Fortress, 1974.

———. *Rediscovering the Teachings of Jesus*. London: SCM, 1967.

Pesch, Rudolf. *Das Abendmal und Jesu Todesverständnis*. Freiburg: Herder, 1978.

———. *Das Markusevangelium: Einleitung und Kommentar zu Kap. 1,1-8,26*. Herders theologischer Kommentar zum Neuen Testament 2. vol. 1. Freiburg: Herder, 1977.

———. *Das Markusevangelium: Einleitung und Kommentar zu Kap. 8,27-16,20*. Herders theologischer Kommentar zum Neuen Testament 2. vol. 2. Freiburg: Herder, 1980.

Porteous, Norman W. *Daniel: A Commentary*. Old Testament Library. Philadelphia: Westminster, 1965.

Porter, P. A. *Metaphors and Monsters: A Literary-Critical Study of Daniel 7 and 8*. Lund: Gleerup, 1983.

Poythress, V. S. "The Holy Ones of the Most High in Daniel 7." *Vetus Testamentum* 26 (1976) 208-13.

Raabe, Paul R. "Daniel 7: Its Structure and Role in the Book." *Hebrew Annual Review* 9 (1985) 267-75.

Rahlfs, Alfred. *Septuaginta*. 2 vols. Stuttgart: Württembergische Bibelanstalt, 1935.

Reif, S. C. *Judaism and Hebrew Prayer: New Perspectives on Jewish Liturgical History*. Cambridge: Cambridge University Press, 1993.

Reynolds, Benjamin E. *The Apocalyptic Son of Man in the Gospel of John*. Wissenschaftliche Untersuchungen zum Neuen Testament 249. Tübingen: Mohr Siebeck, 2008.

———. "The Use of the Son of Man Idiom in the Gospel of John." In *'Who is This Son of Man?': The Latest Scholarship on a Puzzling Expression of the Historical Jesus*, edited by L. W. Hurtado and P. L. Owen, 101-29. Library of New Testament Studies 390. London: T. & T. Clark, 2011.

Rhoads, David, et al. *Mark as Story: An Introduction to the Narrative of a Gospel*. 2nd ed. Minneapolis: Fortress, 1999.

Riesenfeld, Harold. *Jésus transfigure: L'Arrière-plan du récit évangelique de la Transfiguration de Nôtre Seigneur*. Acta seminarii neotestamentici upsaliensis 16. Lund: Gleerup, 1944.

Robbins, V. K. "Summons and Outline in Mark: The Three Step Progression." In *New Boundaries in Old Territory: Form and Social Rhetoric in Mark*, edited by David B. Gowler, 119-36. New York: Peter Lang, 1994.

Roure, Damià. "La Figure de David dans L'Évangile de Marc: Des Traditions Juives aux Interprétations Évangéliques." In *Jesus aux Origines de la Christologie*, edited by P. Benoit and Jacques Dupont, 397-412. Louvain: Louvain University Press, 1975.

Bibliography

Rowe, Robert D. "Is Daniel's 'Son of Man' Messianic?" In *Christ the Lord: Studies in Christology Presented to Donald Guthrie*, edited by H. H. Rowdon, 71-96. Leicester: InterVarsity, 1982.

Rowland, Christopher. "Apocalyptic Literature." In *It is Written: Scripture Citing Scripture*, edited by D. A. Carson and H. G. M. Williamson, 170-89. Cambridge: Cambridge University Press, 1988.

Sanders, E. P. *Judaism: Practice and Belief, 63 BCE—66 CE*. Philadelphia: Trinity International, 1992.

Schaberg, Jane. "Daniel 7, 12 and the New Testament Passion-Resurrection." *New Testament Studies* 31 (1985) 208-22.

Schottroff, Luise, and Wolfgang Stegemann. "The Sabbath was Made for Man: The Interpretation of Mark 2:23-28." In *God of the Lowly: Socio-historical Interpretations of the Bible*, edited by W. Schottroff and W. Stegemann, 118-28. Translated by M. J. O'Connell. Maryknoll, NY: Orbis, 1984.

Schreiber, Stefan. "Henoch als Menschensohn: Zur problematischen Schlußidentifikation in den Bilderreden des äthiopischen Henochbuches (äthHen 71,14)." *Zeitschrift für die neutestamentliche Wissenschaft und die Kunde der älteren Kirche* 91 (2000) 1-17.

Schröter, Jens. "The Son of Man as the Representative of God's Kingdom: On the Interpretation of Jesus in Mark and Q." In *Jesus, Mark and Q: The Teaching of Jesus and Its Earliest Records*, edited by M. Labahn and A. Schmidt, 34-68. Journal for the Study of the New Testament Supplement Series 214. Sheffield: Sheffield Academic, 2001.

Schürer, Emil. *The History of the Jewish People in the Age of Jesus Christ (175 BC—135 AD)*. Edited by G. Vermes and F. Millar. Vol. 1. Edinburgh: T. & T. Clark, 1973.

Schweizer, Eduard. "The Son of Man." *Journal of Biblical Literature* 79 (1960) 119-29.

Seitz, O. J. F. "The Future Coming of the Son of Man: Three Midrashic Formulations in the Gospel of Mark." *Studia evangelica* 6 (1973) 478-94.

Shea, William H. "The Neo-Babylonian Historical Setting for Daniel 7." *Andrews University Seminary Studies* 24 (1986) 31-36.

Shepherd, Michael B. "Daniel 7:13 and the New Testament Son of Man." *Westminster Theological Journal* 68 (2006) 99-111.

Slater, Thomas B. "One Like a Son of Man in First-Century CE Judaism." *New Testament Studies* 41 (1995) 183-98.

Smith, R. H. "Darkness at Noon: Mark's Passion Narrative." *Concordia Theological Monthly* 44 (1973) 325-38.

Snow, Robert S. "Let the Reader Understand: Mark's Use of Jeremiah 7 in Mark 13:14." *Bulletin for Biblical Research* 21 (2011) 467-77.

Staley, Jeffrey L. Review of *The Apocalyptic Son of Man in the Gospel of John*, by Benjamin E. Reynolds. *Catholic Biblical Quarterly* (2010) 160-61.

Stanley, Christopher D. *Paul and the Language of Scripture: Citation Technique in the Pauline Epistles and Contemporary Literature*. Society for New Testament Study Manuscript Series 69. Cambridge: Cambridge University Press, 1992.

Stauffer, E. *Jesus and His Story*. Translated by R. & C. Winston. London: SCM, 1960.

Stegemann, Ekkehard W. "From Criticism to Enmity: An Interpretation of Mark 2:1—3:6." In *God of the Lowly*, edited by W. Schottroff and W. Stegemann, 104-17. Translated by M. J. O'Connell. Maryknoll, NY: Orbis, 1984.

Stokes, R. E. "The Throne Visions of Daniel 7, 1 Enoch 14, and the Qumran *Book of Giants* (4Q530): An Analysis of Their Literary Relationship." *Dead Sea Discoveries* 15 (2008) 340-58.

Bibliography

Stone, Michael E. "The Book of Enoch and Judaism in the Third Century BCE." *Catholic Biblical Quarterly* 40 (1978) 479-92.

———. "The Concept of the Messiah in IV Ezra." In *Religions in Antiquity: Essays in Memory of Erwin Ramsdell Goodenough*, edited by J. Neusner, 295-312. Leiden: Brill, 1968.

———. *Fourth Ezra: A Commentary on the Book of Fourth Ezra*. Hermeneia. Minneapolis: Fortress, 1990.

———. "Reactions to the Destruction of the Second Temple: Theology, Perception and Conversion." *Journal for the Study of Judaism in the Persian, Hellenistic and Roman Period* 12 (1981) 195-204.

Stott, W. "'Son of Man'– A Title of Abasement." *Expository Times* 83 (1971/2) 278-81.

Stowasser, M. "Mk 13,26f und die urchristliche Rezeption des Menschensohns. Eine Anfrage an Anton Vögtle." *Biblische Zeitschrift* 39 (1995) 246-52.

Stuckenbruck, Loren T. "Daniel and Early Enoch Traditions in the Dead Sea Scrolls." In *The Book of Daniel: Composition and Reception*, edited by J. J. Collins and P. W. Flint, 369-86. vol. 2. Supplements to Vetus Testamentum 83. Boston: Brill, 2001.

———. "The Throne-Theophany of the Book of Giants: Some New Light on the Background of Daniel 7." In *The Scrolls and the Scriptures: Qumran after Fifty Years*, edited by S. E. Porter and C. A. Evans, 211-20. Journal for the Study of the Pseudepigrapha Supplement Series 26. Sheffield: Sheffield Academic, 1997.

Such, W. A. "The Crux Critecorum of Mark 13:14." *Römische Quartalschrift für christliche Altertumskunde und Kirchengeschichte* 38 (1996) 93-108.

Suter, David. "Enoch in Sheol: Updating the Dating of the Book of Parables." In *Enoch and the Messiah Son of Man: Revisiting the Book of Parables*, edited by G. Boccaccini, 415-43. Grand Rapids: Eerdmans, 2007.

———. "Fallen Angel, Fallen Priest: The Problem of Family Purity in 1 Enoch 6—16." *Hebrew Union College Annual* 50 (1979) 115-35.

———. *Tradition and Composition in the Parables of Enoch*. Society of Biblical Literature Dissertation Series 47. Missoula, MT: Scholars, 1979.

Sweet, J. P. M. "A House Not Made with Hands." In *Templum Amicitiae: Essays on the Second Temple*, edited by W. Horbury, 368-71. Sheffield: Sheffield University Press, 1991.

Taylor, Nicholas H. "The Destruction of Jerusalem and the Transmission of the Synoptic Eschatological Discourse." *Hervormde teologiese studies* 59 (2003) 283-311.

Telford, William R. *The Barren Fig Tree and the Withered Temple*. Journal for the Study of the New Testament Supplement Series 1. Sheffield: JSOT, 1980.

———. *The Theology of the Gospel of Mark*. New Testament Theology. Cambridge: Cambridge University Press, 1999.

Terrien, Samuel. *The Psalms: Strophic Structure and Theological Commentary*. Eerdmans Critical Commentary. Grand Rapids: Eerdmans, 2003.

Theisohn, Johannes. *Der auserwählte Richter: Untersuchungen zum traditionsgeschichtlichen Bilderreden des Äthiopischen Henoch*. Studien zur Umwelt des Neuen Testaments 12. Göttingen: Vandenhoeck & Ruprecht, 1975.

Thrall, M. E. "Elijah and Moses in Mark's Account of the Transfiguration." *New Testament Studies* 16 (1970) 305-17.

Tiller, Patrick A. *A Commentary on the Animal Apocalypse of 1 Enoch*. Society of Biblical Literature Early Judaism and Its Literature 4. Atlanta: Scholars, 1993.

Tödt, Heinz E. *The Son of Man in the Synoptic Tradition*. Translated by D. M. Barton. London: SCM, 1965.

Bibliography

Trevor, John C. "The Book of Daniel and the Origin of the Qumran Community." *Biblical Archeologist* 48 (1985) 89-102.

Trocmé, Etienne. "Marc 9,1: prédiction ou réprimande?" *Studia evangelica* 2 (1964) 259-65.

Tuckett, C. M. "The Son of Man and Daniel 7: Inclusive Aspects of Early Christologies." In *Christian Origins*, edited by Kieran O'Mahony, 164-90. London: Sheffield Academic, 2003.

———. "The Son of Man in Daniel 7: Q and Jesus." In *The Sayings Source Q and the Historical Jesus*, edited by A. Lindemann, 371-94. Bibliotheca Ephemeridum theologicarum Lovaniensium 158. Sterling, VA: Peeters, 2001.

VanderKam, James C. "Biblical Interpretation in 1 Enoch and Jubilees." In *The Pseudepigrapha and Early Biblical Interpretation*, edited by J. H. Charlesworth and C. A. Evans, 96-125. Journal for the Study of the Pseudepigrapha: Supplement Series 14. Sheffield: JSOT, 1993.

———. *From Joshua to Caiaphas: High Priests after the Exile*. Assen: Van Gorcum, 2004.

———. "Righteous One, Messiah, Chosen One, and Son of Man in 1 Enoch." In *The Messiah: Developments in Earliest Judaism and Christianity*, edited by J. H. Charlesworth et al., 169-91. Minneapolis: Fortress, 1992.

Venter, P. M. "Daniel and Enoch: Two Different Reactions." *Hervormde Teologiese Studies* 53 (1997) 68-91.

———. "Spatiality in the Second Parable of Enoch." In *Enoch and the Messiah Son of Man: Revisiting the Book of Parables*, edited by G. Boccaccini, 403-412. Grand Rapids: Eerdmans, 2007.

Verheyden, Jozef. "Describing the Parousia: The Cosmic Phenomena in Mark 13:24-25." In *The Scriptures in the Gospels*, edited by C. M. Tuckett, 525-50. Bibliotheca ephemeridum theologicarum Lovaniensium 131. Leuven: Leuven University Press, 1997.

Vermes, Geza. "Appendix E: The Use of בר נשא/בר נש in Jewish Aramaic." In *An Aramaic Approach to the Gospels and Acts: with an Appendix on the Son of Man*, 310-30. 3rd ed. Oxford: Clarendon, 1967.

———. *Jesus the Jew: A Historian's Reading of the Gospels*. London: SCM, 1973.

———. *Scripture and Tradition in Judaism: Haggadic Studies*. Studia Post-Biblica 4. Leiden: Brill, 1973.

Vielhauer, Philipp. "Gottesreich und Menschensohn in der Verkündigung Jesu." In *Festschrift für Günther Dehn*, edited by W. Schneemelcher, 51-79. Neukirchen: Moers, 1957.

Walker, William O. "Daniel 7:13-14." *Interpretation* 39 (1985) 176-81.

Wallace, Daniel B. *Greek Grammar Beyond the Basics: An Exegetical Syntax of the New Testament*. Grand Rapids: Zondervan, 1996.

Walton, John H. *Genesis*. The NIV Application Commentary. Grand Rapids: Zondervan, 2001.

Wardle, Timothy. *The Jerusalem Temple and Early Christian Identity*. Wissenschaftliche Untersuchungen zum Neuen Testament II. 291. Tübingen: Mohr Siebeck, 2010.

Watts, John D. *Isaiah 1-33*. Word Biblical Commentary 24. Waco, TX: Word Books, 1985.

Watts, Rikki E. "The Influence of the Isaianic New Exodus on the Gospel of Mark." PhD diss., University of Cambridge, 1990.

———. *Isaiah's New Exodus and Mark*. Grand Rapids: Baker, 1997.

Bibliography

———. "Jesus' Death, Isaiah 53, and Mark 10:45." In *Jesus and the Suffering Servant: Isaiah 53 and Christian Origins*, edited by W. H. Bellinger, Jr., and W. R. Farmer, 125–51. Harrisburg, PA: Trinity International, 1998.

———. "Mark." In *Commentary on the New Testament Use of the Old Testament*, edited by G. K. Beale and D. A. Carson, 111–249. Grand Rapids: Baker, 2007.

Weiser, Artur. *The Psalms: A Commentary*. Philadelphia: Westminster, 1962.

Wenham, David. "The Kingdom of God and Daniel." *Expository Times* 98 (1987) 132–4.

———. *The Rediscovery of Jesus' Eschatological Discourse*. Gospel Perspectives 4. Sheffield: JSOT, 1984.

Wenham, Gordon. *The Book of Leviticus*. London: Hodder & Stoughton, 1979.

Westerholm, S. "Sabbath." In *Dictionary of Jesus and the Gospels* 716–9.

Wildberger, Hans. *Isaiah 1—12*. Translated by T. H. Trapp. Minneapolis: Fortress, 1991.

Williamson, H. G. M. "History." In *It is Written: Scripture Citing Scripture*, edited by D. A. Carson and H. G. M. Williamson, 25–38. Cambridge: Cambridge University Press, 1988.

Wilson, Robert R. "Creation and New Creation: The Role of Creation Imagery in the Book of Daniel." In *God Who Creates: Essays in Honour of W. Sibley Towner*, edited by W. P. Brown and S. D. McBride, 190–203. Grand Rapids: Eerdmans, 2000.

Wink, Walter. *The Human Being: Jesus and the Enigma of the Son of Man*. Minneapolis: Fortress, 2002.

Wintermute, O. S. "Jubilees: A New Translation and Introduction." In *The Old Testament Pseudepigrapha*, edited by J. H. Charlesworth, 35–142. vol. 2. New York: Doubleday, 1985.

Wolff, W. M. *Jesaja 53 im Urchristentum*. Berlin: Evangelische Verlagsanstalt, 1952.

Wright, N. T. *The Challenge of Jesus: Rediscovering Who Jesus Was and Is*. Downers Grove, IL: InterVarsity, 1999.

———. *Jesus and the Victory of God*. Vol. 2 of Christian Origins and the Question of God. Minneapolis: Fortress, 1996.

———. *The New Testament and the People of God*. Vol. 1 of Christian Origins and the Question of God. Minneapolis: Fortress, 1992.

———. *The Resurrection of the Son of God*. Vol. 3 of Christian Origins and the Question of God. Minneapolis: Fortress, 2003.

Yadin, Y. *The Scroll of the War of the Sons of Light against the Sons of Darkness*. Translated by B. and C. Rabin. London: Oxford University Press, 1962.

Zeller, Dieter. "Bedeutung und Religionsgeschichtlicher Hintergrund der Verwandlung Jesu (Markus 9:2–8)." In *Authenticating the Words of Jesus*, edited by B. Chilton and C. A. Evans, 303–21. Leiden: Brill, 1999.

Zevit, Z. "The Structure and Individual Elements of Daniel 7." *Zeitschrift für die alttestamentliche Wissenschaft* 80 (1968) 385–96.

Zimmerman, Frank. "The Language, the Date, and the Portrayal of the Messiah in 4 Ezra." *Hebrew Studies* 26 (1985) 203–18.

Author Index

Adams, Edward, 129–30n12, 132
Alexander, Philip S., 49n23

Barrett, C.K., 115–18, 123
Beale, Gregory, 59, 61
Beasley-Murray, George R., 29n69, 37n102, 143–44
Black, Matthew, 31n79, 32, 34n84, 38n104, 46, 48–49n16, 163
Boccaccini, Gabriele, 31n78, 48
Bock, Darrell L., 1, 160–61, 160n117
Bolt, Peter G., 103, 139n40
Brower, Kent, 127–28n4, 155n97, 169n143
Brown, Raymond E., 155n99, 160, 164n128
Bultmann, Rudolf, 134
Burkett, Delbert, 2n7, 4n16

Caquot, André, 49
Caragounis, Chrys C., 2n8, 24
Casey, Maurice, 1–4, 49n17, 74, 74n25, 86–87
Charles, R.H., 45, 45n2, 53n29
Chialà, Sabino, 44n1, 51
Chilton, Bruce, 71n14, 89, 128n7
Chronis, Harry L., 5
Collins, Adela Yarbro, 73, 84, 86n78, 123, 151, 156n102, 165n131, 166
Collins, John J., 25, 25n50, 28n63, 29n69, 30–31n76, 37–40, 37n102, 38n108, 39n114, 47–48n12
Cook, Michael J., 92n1, 93, 93n5

Davenport, G.I., 19n14
Davies, Philip R., 24–25, 24n44

Dewey, Joanna, 81n57, 82
Di Lella, Alexander A., 26–27, 38n108
Dillmann, August, 21n28
DiTommaso, Lorenzo, 57n39
Dodd, C.H., 7n33
Dunn, James D.G., 143n58, 154
Dupont, Jacques, 139n41, 142, 145

Ellingworth, P., 76n33
Evans, Craig A., 105, 107n53, 114, 114n77, 118n98, 165nn130–32

Fishbane, Michael, 8
Fitzmeyer, Joseph A., 45n4
Fletcher-Louis, Crispin, 35, 70–71, 77, 145n70
France, Richard, 69n6, 71–72n17, 81, 84, 85n74, 95–96, 96n14, 111n70, 129–30nn11–12, 140n48, 146nn72–73, 150–51n83, 153n92, 168–69n139, 169n142
Fuellet, A., 42

Gardner, Anne E., 26, 26n53, 26n55
Gathercole, Simon, 6
Geddart, T.W., 153
Glasson, Thomas F., 164n128
Gnilka, Joachim, 70n8
Goldingay, John, 16n1, 29–30, 39–40, 39n111, 41n125
Grabbe, Lester, 57–58, 58n41
Gray, Timothy, 6–7n31, 11n48
Gray, Timothy C., 143n60, 158
Greenfield, Jonas C., 45n4
Guelich, Robert, 78

Author Index

Gundry, Robert H., 84n71, 85n74, 88n83, 95n10, 108n57, 109n62, 110, 144, 146n73, 147n76, 155, 165n131

Haenchen, Ernst, 75–76
Hampel, V., 27n60
Hannah, Darrell D., 49n23, 50
Hare, Douglas, 6
Hartley, J.E., 41
Hartman, Louis F., 26–27, 38n108
Hatina, Tom, 102, 128, 135–37, 136n29, 144nn66–67
Hayman, Peter, 60, 60n54
Hays, Richard B., 6–10, 12, 14, 82, 130, 171, 178
Heaton, Eric W., 42
Heil, John Paul, 142
Hengel, Martin, 102n32, 118n96, 168
Henten, Jan W. Van, 27n62
Himmelfarb, Martha J., 18, 30n72, 32, 56n34
Hofius, Otfried, 75n28, 77
Hooker, Morna, 4–5, 11, 13, 40–41, 79n48, 80, 83n67, 84, 87n80, 93, 96, 101, 101n30, 116–17, 119–20, 123–24, 139, 152n89, 153n94, 160, 162n125, 176
Hurtado, Larry W., 1, 5, 73n20, 84

Iersel, Bas M.F. van, 144, 150, 150n81

Juel, Donald, 155n98, 156n101

Kee, Howard C., 107n55, 152n88
Kellner, Wendelin, 26n57, 28n64
Kilgallen, John J., 128n5
Kingsbury, Jack Dean, 93n3
Kittel, G., 133n20
Kmiecik, Ulrich, 5–6
Knibb, Michael A., 47–48n12, 53n29, 56n36, 59n50, 60
Kooij, Arie van der, 22
Kraus, Hans-Joachim, 76n36, 161n124
Kvanvig, Heldge S., 30–31, 54, 97

Lacocque, André, 21n31, 23n39, 42n126
Lane, William, 139n40

Lebram, J.C.H., 22n32
Leivestad, Ragnar, 2n8
Lichtenberger, Hermann, 62n61
Lindars, Barnabas, 3–4
Lindenberger, James M., 25n52
Lohmeyer, Ernst, 75–76, 76n32
Lohse, E., 158
Longnecker, Bruce W., 57n40, 58
Lührmann, Dieter, 129n10

Malbon, Elizabeth Struthers, 5n25, 137, 164
Manson, T.W., 1, 97n19, 100, 100n27, 100n29
Marcus, Joel, 74n24, 77–78n42, 78–80, 79n49, 84, 106n52, 109n63
Mearns, Christopher L., 46n10
Meier, John P., 81–83
Milgrom, Jacob, 77
Milik, J.T., 31n79, 45–46
Moloney, Francis J., 84, 106
Mosca, Paul G., 26n56
Moule, C.F.D., 25n52, 73n18
Myers, Jacob M., 61–62, 63n68

Nardoni, Enrique, 127n3
Neusner, Jacob, 89, 156–57
Nicholson, E.W., 119–20
Nickelsberg, George W.E., 18, 18n8, 19, 20n25, 32n80, 32n82, 36, 49n21, 56n36, 102n32

O'Brien, Kelli S., 7–9, 12
Öhler, Marcus, 107–8
Olson, Daniel C., 49
O'Neill, John C., 58n45

Perrin, Norman, 2n8, 5, 127
Pesch, Rudolf, 121n115, 147

Reynolds, Benjamin E., 4n21, 41n124
Robbins, V.K., 136n28

Schaberg, Jane, 111–12
Schottroff, Luise, 81–82n60
Schreiber, Stefan, 48–49n16
Schröter, Jens, 11

Author Index

Schürer, Emil, 22
Seitz, O.J.F., 110n66
Stanley, Christopher, 10n45
Stegermann, Wolfgang, 81–82n60
Stokes, R.E., 30–31n76
Stone, Michael E., 58–59, 60n51, 61, 62n63, 63, 63n68, 98n23
Stowasser, M., 150–51n83
Stuckenbruck, Loren T., 34n83
Suter, David, 46n10, 47–48n12

Theisohn, Johannes, 45n6
Tiller, Patrick A., 20–21, 20n25, 21n28
Tuckett, C.M., 11n47

Ullendorff, Edward, 53n29, 56n36

VanderKam, James C., 20n25, 48–49, 49n21, 51n26, 56, 56n36

Verheyden, Jozef, 144n66, 145n70, 149–50
Vermes, Geza, 2n8, 3
Vielhauser, Philipp, 129n10
von Rad, G., 131

Wardle, Timothy, 37, 106n50, 122n119, 158n110
Watts, Rikk, 68n3, 84, 96, 101, 103, 115–18, 115n80, 115n83, 120–21, 123
Wenham, Gordon, 81n57
Westerholm, S., 84n68
Wildberger, Hans, 30
Wright, N.T., 10–11, 37n102, 40, 71, 104, 133, 153n94

Yadin, Y., 38n108

Zimmerman, Frank, 57n38

Subject Index

Aaron, 42, 69–70, 77
Abiathar, 85, 85n74
Adam, 40
Ahab, 30
Ahimelech, 85
allusion
   overview, 9–12
   availability, 10
   coming of Son of Man in Heavenly Temple, regarding, 126–38, 146–50, 158–65
   divine authority of Son of Man, regarding, 73–75
   historical probability (*See* Historical probability, allusion and)
   history of interpretation, 12
   recurrence, 11, 115, 141, 148
   satisfaction, 12
   suffering and death of Son of Man, regarding, 94–114
   thematic coherence (*See* Thematic coherence, allusion and)
   volume, 10–11, 146, 160
angelic nature of Son of Man, 37–39
Animal Apocalypse, Son of Man and, 20–23
Antiochus IV Epiphanes (Seleucid), 16–17, 19, 21–23, 37–42, 112–14, 118, 135, 148, 161, 166, 174
apocalyptic nature of Son of Man, 2–3
Apollonius, 102n32
Aramaic background of Son of Man, 1–4
availability, allusion and, 10

Ba'al (Canaanite deity), 60

Babylon
   in *Daniel*, 26
   destruction of, 144–45
baptism, 68, 78, 90
Bartimaeus, 114n77
beast imagery, 24–28
blood imagery, 120–21, 124–25
Book of Watchers, Son of Man and, 17–18, 31–32, 36, 43, 47, 54–56, 64–65

Caesarea Philippi, prediction of suffering and death of Jesus at, 94–107
Caligula (Rome), 140
Callirrhoe (healing waters), 46–47, 64
capstone imagery, 105–6, 125
circumcision, 159
cloud imagery, 143–44, 147
coming of Son of Man in Heavenly Temple
   overview, 15, 126, 170–73
   angels and, 145–47, 150–53
   being "ashamed" of Son of Man and, 127–37
   cloud imagery and, 143–44, 147
   construction of new Temple, prediction of, 154–59
   Daniel, allusion to, 126–38, 146–50, 158–65
   destruction of Temple, prediction of, 137–43, 148–49
   1 Enoch, allusion to, 130–31
   Galilee, and journey to, 167–70
   literary context of, 128–30
   Mark 8:38, in, 127–37

Subject Index

coming of Son of Man in Heavenly
Temple *(continued)*
   Mark 13:26-27, in, 137-53
   Mark 14:62, in, 153-67
   rending of Temple veil and, 167-70
   signs in sky regarding, 145-47, 150
   throne imagery and, 163-64,
     164n128
   trial of Son of Man and, 153-67
   wicked tenants, and parable of, 141

Damascus Document, Son of Man and, 18
Daniel, Son of Man in. *See also Index of Scriptural References*
   overview, 1-2, 14, 16, 42-43, 174-75
   angelic nature of Son of Man, 37-39
   Babylon in, 26
   beast imagery in, 24-28
   coming of Son of Man in Heavenly Temple, allusion regarding, 126-38, 146-50, 158-65
   dreams in, 25-26
   1 Enoch compared, 33
   faithful Israel and, 37-42
   fire imagery in, 29, 35
   Greece in, 26
   Greek influence on, 17-23
   Hellenistic influence on, 17-23
   historical context, 17-23
   intertextual approach to, 6-13
   judgment from Heavenly Temple and, 28-32, 34-37, 43
   kingdoms in, 24-28
   literary context, 24-28
   Mark, allusions to in, 73-75, 94-114, 126-38, 146-50, 158-65
   Media in, 26
   messianic nature of Son of Man, 37
   narrative approach to, 6-13
   Persia in, 26
   research, survey of, 2-6
   sea imagery in, 26
   Seleucid influence on, 17-23
   suffering and death of Son of Man, allusion regarding, 94-114
David, 76, 81, 83-85, 83n67, 90, 154, 162

death of Son of Man. *See* suffering and death of Son of Man
divine authority of Son of Man
   overview, 7, 14-15, 67, 90-91
   Disciples and, 82-85
   exorcism, 68-70, 90
   leper, cleansing of, 70-72, 91
   literary context of, 68-72
   Sabbath, over, 80-90, 91
   sins, authority to forgive, 72-80, 91

echo, 9
Edom, destruction of, 144-45
Eleazar, 77, 102
Elijah, 108-9nn61-63, 108-10, 128n7
Eliphaz, 132-33
Elisha, 70
Enoch, 46-48, 51n26, 54-56, 64-65
1 Enoch, Son of Man in. *See also Index of Scriptural References*
   overview, 14, 174-75
   coming of Son of Man in Heavenly Temple, allusion regarding, 130-31
   Daniel compared, 33
   judgment from Heavenly Temple in, 30-32, 34-36
   exorcism, 68-70, 90
4 Ezra, Son of Man in. *See also Index of Scriptural References*
   overview, 14, 44, 64-66, 175
   apocalyptic nature of, 57-58
   Danielic imagery in, 59-61
   date of composition, 57-58
   dreams in, 58-63, 65-66
   fire imagery in, 60, 63-66
   literary structure of, 58-59
   Mark compared, 96-99, 124, 133
   messianic nature of Son of Man, 63-64
   older tradition of, 63-64
   provenance of, 57-58
   sea imagery in, 60-61
   temple-mountain and, 61-63, 79
   visions in, 58-63, 65-66
   wind imagery in, 59-60

Subject Index

fire imagery, 29, 35, 55–56, 60, 63–66
forgiveness of sins. *See* sins, forgiveness of

Galilee, journey to, 167–70
Gentiles, Son of Man and, 52, 62, 97, 111–14, 151, 159
Greece in *Daniel*, 26
Greek influence on *Daniel*, 17–23

Hasis (Canaanite deity), 60
Heavenly Temple
    coming of Son of Man in, 127–67
    (*See also* Coming of Son of Man in Heavenly Temple)
    4 Ezra, temple-mountain in, 61–63, 79
    judgment from, 28–37
    in *Parables*, 50–57, 65, 79
Hellenistic influence on *Daniel*, 17–23
Herod, 46–47, 64, 109
Herodians, 92–93, 109
historical probability, allusion and
    overview, 11–12
    coming of Son of Man in Heavenly Temple, 130, 148, 151, 163, 172–73
    suffering and death of Son of Man, 97, 124
history of interpretation, allusion and, 12

intertextual approach, 6–13
Ithamar, 77

Jacob, 19
Jason (High Priest), 20–21
Jerusalem, prediction of suffering and
    death of Jesus before journey to, 113–14
Jesus
    atoning purpose of, 115–23
    baptism of, 68, 78, 90
    being "ashamed" of, 127–37
    betrayal of, 110–11

blasphemy, charge of, 159–61, 165–67, 165n132
blood imagery and, 120–21, 124–25
Caesarea Philippi, prediction at, 94–107
capstone imagery and, 105–6, 125
cleansing of Temple by, 106
condemnation of, 113–14
construction of new Temple, prediction of, 155
destruction of Temple, prediction of, 137–43, 148–49
Disciples and, 82–85
exorcism by, 68–70, 90
Galilee, journey to, 167–70
Jerusalem, prediction before journey to, 113–14
leper, cleansing of, 70–72, 91
redemptive purpose of, 115–23
rejection of, 103–5
rending of Temple veil and, 167–70
Sabbath and, 81–82n60, 82–85, 91
sins, forgiveness of, 72–75, 91
Temple imagery and, 122–23, 125
throne imagery and, 163–64
transfiguration, prediction during, 107–13
trial of, 153–67
wicked tenants, parable of, 103–5, 110, 141
Job, 132–33
John the Baptist, 109–10, 109nn62–63
Josephus, 22, 46–47, 166–67
Judas (Iscariot), 111, 111n69, 113
Judas Maccabeus, 17, 21

Kothar (Canaanite deity), 60

leper, cleansing of, 70–72, 91
Levi, 19
Leviathan, 26, 60

Maccabean martyrs, 101–3, 109, 116n88, 118, 123

Subject Index

Mark, Son of Man in. *See also Index of Scriptural References*
overview, 1-2, 14-15, 67, 90-91, 92-94, 123-25, 126, 170-73, 175-79
angels in, 145-47, 150-53
atonement in, 115-23
baptism in, 68, 78, 90
betrayal of Son of Man, 110-11
blood imagery in, 120-21, 124-25
Caesarea Philippi, prediction at, 94-107
capstone imagery in, 105-6, 125
cleansing of Temple in, 106
cloud imagery in, 143-44, 147
coming of Son of Man in Heavenly Temple, 127-67
condemnation of Son of Man, 113-14
construction of new Temple, prediction of, 154-59
Daniel, allusions to, 73-75, 94-114, 126-38, 146-50, 158-65
destruction of Temple, prediction of, 137-43, 148-49
Disciples in, 82-85
exorcism in, 68-70, 90
4 *Ezra* compared, 96-99, 124, 133
Galilee, journey to in, 167-70
intertextual approach to, 6-13
Jerusalem, prediction before journey to, 113-14
leper, cleansing of, 70-72, 91
literary context of, 68-72
Mark 8:38, coming of Son of Man in Heavenly Temple, 127-37
Mark 13:26-27, coming of Son of Man in Heavenly Temple, 137-53
Mark 14:62, coming of Son of Man in Heavenly Temple, 153-67
narrative approach to, 6-13
Parables compared, 96-99, 124, 133
redemption in, 115-23
rejection of Son of Man, 103-5
rending of Temple veil in, 167-70
research, survey of, 2-6
Resurrection, predictions of, 94-114
Sabbath, authority over, 80-90, 91
signs in sky regarding coming of Son of Man in, 145-47, 150
sins, authority to forgive, 72-80, 91
Temple imagery in, 122-23, 125
throne imagery in, 163-64, 164n128
transfiguration, prediction during, 107-13
trial of Jesus in, 153-67
media (empire)
in *Daniel*, 26
in *Parables*, 45-46
Menelaus (High Priest), 20-22
Messianic nature of Son of Man, 2-3
Micaiah, 30, 149
Michael (archangel), 38-39
Moses, 35, 42, 107n55, 119, 121, 128n7

narrative approach, 6-13
Nathan, 76
Nebuchadnezzar, 62

Old Testament significance of Son of Man, 4-6
"One like a Son of Man." *See Daniel*, Son of Man in
Onias III (High Priest), 21

Parables, Son of Man in. *See also Index of Scriptural References*
overview, 44, 64-66, 175
angelic nature of Son of Man, 50-57
ascent of *Enoch* in, 54-56, 64-65
date of composition, 45-48, 47-48n12
Enoch as Son of Man in, 46-48, 51n26
fire imagery in, 55-56
Head of Days in, 50-53, 55-57
Heavenly Temple, reign of Son of Man in, 50-57, 65, 79
literary structure of, 48-50
Mark compared, 96-99, 124, 133
Media in, 45-46

208

Subject Index

messianic nature of Son of Man, 52–53
Parthia in, 45–46, 64
Qumran fragments and, 45
whirlwind imagery in, 54, 56
Parousia, 127, 132, 143, 162n125
Parthia in *Parables*, 45–46, 64
passion of Son of Man. *See* Suffering and death of Son of Man
Passover, 156–57
Paul, 6–7, 9, 122, 159, 166, 172
Persia in *Daniel*, 26
Peter, 127, 137
Pharisees, 47, 80–83, 88–89, 91, 92–93, 125
Philo, 166–67
Pontius Pilate, 113, 154, 165n130

Qumran fragments, 45, 137, 154, 172

Rahab, 26
recurrence, allusion and, 11, 115, 141, 148
rending of Temple veil, 167–70
research, survey of, 2–6
resurrection of Son of Man. *See* Suffering and death of Son of Man

Sabbath
 overview, 80–82
 Disciples and, 82–85
 Jesus and, 81–82n60, 82–85, 91
 in *Mark*, 80–90, 91
 Son of Man, authority of, 85–90
Sadducees, 93
Sanhedrin, 153, 159–60, 162, 165, 167
satisfaction, allusion and, 12
Scriptural References. *See Index of Scriptural References*
sea imagery, 26, 60–61
Second Coming of Son of Man. *See* Coming of Son of Man in Heavenly Temple

Seleucid influence on *Daniel*, 17–23
Simon, 76–77
sins, forgiveness of
 authority of Son of Man, 75–80
 by Jesus, 72–75, 91
 in *Mark*, 72–80, 91
suffering and death of Son of Man
 overview, 15, 92–94, 123–25
 atoning purpose of, 115–23
 betrayal of Son of Man, 110–11
 blood imagery and, 120–21, 124–25
 Caesarea Philippi, prediction at, 94–107
 capstone imagery and, 105–6, 125
 cleansing of Temple and, 106
 condemnation of Son of Man, 113–14
 Daniel, allusion to, 94–114
 Jerusalem, prediction before journey to, 113–14
 predictions of, 94–114
 purpose of, 115–23
 redemptive purpose of, 115–23
 rejection of Son of Man, 103–5
 Resurrection, predictions of, 94–114, 155–57, 169–70
 Temple imagery and, 122–23, 125
 transfiguration, prediction during, 107–13
survey of research, 2–6

Temple imagery, 122–23, 125
Testament of Levi, Son of Man and, 18–19
thematic coherence, allusion and
 overview, 11
 coming of Son of Man in Heavenly Temple, 130, 132, 148, 164, 169
 divine authority of Son of Man, 74
 suffering and death of Son of Man, 99–100, 124
Theodotion, 112–13, 144, 160
throne imagery, 163–64, 164n128
transfiguration, prediction of suffering and death of Jesus during, 107–13

Subject Index

Vaticanus, 144
volume, allusion and, 10–11, 146, 160

whirlwind imagery, 54, 56

wicked tenants, parable of, 103–5, 110, 141
wind imagery, 59–60

Yam (Canaanite deity), 60

Ancient Document Index

Old Testament

Genesis

1:1—2:4a	86	19:18	29
1:11	27	20:10	86–87
1:21	27	20:12	86n76
1:26	41	20:23	109
1:28	41	21:30	117
5:24	71	22:27	165–66
6:1–4	17, 31, 31n79	24	120–21, 124
9:6	120	24:3–8	119, 124
9:13	36	24:4c	120
14:18	161	24:6b	119
28	30	24:7–8	121n115
28:22	62	24:8	119–21
34	19	24:8a	119
41:1–8	26n56	24:11	120
49	120	24:15–17	107n55
49:5–7	19	25:30	81n57
		28:1	35n92
		28:4	35n92

Exodus

		28:35	35
		28:36–38	77
3:2	29	28:38	77
15:17–18	154	28:43	35
16:23a	81	29–44	35n92
16:25	87	29:4	35
16:26	81	29:8	35
16:29a	85	29:12	120
19–20	99, 120	29:20	119
19–24	121	29:21	119n104, 120
19:3b–8	119	29:38	23
19:6	23, 42, 119, 124–25	29:38–42	23

Exodus (continued)

29:39–41	23
29:42	23
30:12	117
30:20	35
31:13	86
31:17	86
33:14–16	23
34:6–7	72, 77
34:7	76
34:21	80, 80n54
34:29	107n55
40:34–35	36
40:34–58	166
42:14	35
45:4–5	35
46:24	35

Leviticus

4:18	120
4:20	75n28, 76
4:20b	75–76
4:25	120
4:26	75n28
4:30	120
4:31	75n28
4:34	120
4:35	75n28
5:6	75n28
5:10	75n28
5:13	75n28
5:16	75n28
5:18	75n28
5:26	75n28
7:35	35
8:6	35
8:13	35
8:15	120
8:22–30	119
8:24	35
10:17	77
13:6	70
13:13	70
13:17	70
13:46	70–71
14	71
19:22	75n28
20:2	19
21–22	166
21:9	19
23:3	80, 87, 89
23:3b	89
24:5–9	89, 89n85
24:8	89
26:1	158
26:14–16	75n27

Numbers

5:1–4	71
8:9	35
8:10	35
9:15–23	166
14:18–20	76
16:5	35
16:7	70
23:19	73n20
28:3–10	89
34:7	26n55

Deuteronomy

4:19	149
4:24	29
5:14	87
6:4	78
10:17a	38n108
17:3	149
17:12	35n92
19:10	120
23:25	80
30:4	151

Joshua

1:4	26n55
9:1	26n55
15:12	26n55
15:47	26n55
23:4	26n55

Ancient Document Index

Judges

5:20	39
16:17	70

1 Samuel

21	84
21:1	84
21:1–6	81, 84, 84n68, 91
21:2b	85
21:4b-5	85
21:6b	89
23:6–11	85n74

2 Samuel

6:13–14	161n124
6:18	161n124
7:10	154
7:12–14	154
8:11	41
8:17	85n74
12:13	76
15:24	85n74
15:35	85n74
17:15	85n74
19:11	85n74
20:25	85n74
24:25	161n124

1 Kings

2:19	161
6:3	32
8:10–11	36
8:11b	131, 147
8:14	161n124
8:30–50	76n33
8:62–64	161n124
19:2–14	108–9n61
22	30
22:19	29–30, 36, 55, 131, 149, 163

2 Kings

1:8	109
4:9	70
5:18	76n33
10:24	117n93
17:16	149
21:1–9	149
21:3	149
21:5	149
23:4	149
23:5	149

1 Chronicles

24:6	85n74

2 Chronicles

5:13–14	36
6:21–39	76n33
20:19	34
21:18–19	75n27
30:27	34

Ezra

6:18	34n89
9:1–4	18

Nehemiah

9:3	34
9:4	34
9:6	149
9:17	76

Judith

16:15	61, 150n80

1 Maccabees

1:11–15	21
1:46	38, 166

1 Maccabees (continued)

1:54	140
1:57–64	23n37
2	166
2:6	166
2:14	166
3:10–26	21
3:38–4:27	21

2 Maccabees

4:14	22
5:15	22
7:18	101, 103
7:32	102
7:34–38	165n131
7:37	118

4 Maccabees

4:2	102n32
4:25	102
6:16–30	116n88
6:27–29	118
6:28–29	102
6:29b	116n88
10:10	102
10:21	165n131
12:18	165n131
17:21–22	116n88
17:21–23	102

Job

5:1	147
38:7	39

Psalms

8:5	73n20
12:3	28
17:8	150
18:6–7	150
18:9–14	29
18:12	143
20:9–14	147
21:8–13	136
21:10	29
25:11	76n33
25:18b	77
29	30
32	75n27
32:1b	77
32:5c	77
34:10	38
48:8	117
50:3	29
74:12–17	60
74:13–14	26
79:16	73n20
79:92	76n33
82	30
82:1	29, 36, 131
82:1a	30
82:1b	30
82:8	30
88:8	147
89	52, 133
89:9–11	60
96:4–5	150
96:10–13	29
97:3	29, 29n68
101:5	28
102:19–20	147
103:19–20	132
104	61
104:25–26	26
106:16	69
106:38	120
107:20	76n36
109:1	159
110	53, 162, 172
110:1	74n24, 126, 136, 159–61, 163–65, 165nn131–32, 179
110:2a	161
110:2b	161
110:3a	161
110:4	161
110:4b	161
110:5–6	161
110:5a	161
114	76n36

Ancient Document Index

117:22	103–4, 110
118	103
118:5–18	104
118:9b	104
118:19	104
118:19–27	104
118:22	103n37, 104, 106n49, 107n53
118:22–23	103–4
119:6	134
119:21	134
119:31	134
119:75	134
119:81–82	76n36
119:84–85	134
122:5	29
130	76
130:4	76
130:5c	76
138:4	76n36
146:2	151n87
147	76n36
148:1–2	132

Proverbs

1:16	120
8	52

Isaiah

1:11	138
1:28–31	134
1:29	134, 170
1:34–35	134
2:11	28
5:1–7	104, 141
5:7	105
5:15	28
6	30, 36, 54, 131, 146
6:1	55, 131n15
6:1b-2a	30, 163
6:3b	131, 147
6:7	76
6:8–13	30
13:10	144–145, 144n66, 145n70
19:1	143
27:12	152n88
27:13	152n88
28:16	62
33:24	75n27
34:4	144–145, 144n67, 145n70, 149
34:4a	144
37:23	28
42:1b-4	115n83
42:6b	115n83
43:25	72, 77
44:22	72, 77
46:6	158
49:5–6	99
49:6	115n83
51	111n70
51:9–10	26
52	117
52:3	116
53	101–103, 111, 111n70, 115–117, 115n80, 116n86, 116n88, 117–118, 121, 124–125
53:3	101
53:3b	103
53:4	101, 103
53:10	116, 120
53:10–12	101, 116n85
53:11	102, 115
53:12	116, 120–21
54	117
54:11–12	122
56:7	138, 152
59:7	120
63	68
63:10	68
63:15	68
63:19	68
64:1	68
64:1–2a	150
64:2	68
65:17–25	68
66:15–16	61
66:20	62
66:21	62

Ancient Document Index

Jeremiah

7	140–42, 148, 157, 177
7:9–10	142
7:10	142
7:10b–11a	142
7:11	138, 140
7:21–22	140–41
7:22	138
7:22–23	139
7:30	141–42
7:34	142
8:2	149
15:9	167
16:3–4	75n27
16:16–18	136
16:21	136, 146
19:13	149
26:18	62
44:22	141
49:38	29

Ezekiel

1	131
1:1	30
1:15–21	34n84, 163
1:27	34n84, 163
8:6	142n52
8:9	142n52
8:13	142n52
8:15	142n52
8:17	142n52
16	35n95
20:12	86
22:3–12	120
32:7	144
39:27	152n88
39:29	152n88
43:1	131
43:1–5	131
43:4	131, 147
44:4	131
44:15	35n95
45:4	35n95
47:10	26n55
47:15	26n55
47:19	26n55
47:20	26n55
48:28	26n55

Daniel

1–6	17, 24, 40
1:1—2:42	25n52
1:6–8	24
1:12–13	24
2	24, 59, 62, 158
2–6	25, 25n50
2–7	24n43, 25
2:34	24, 158
2:35b	62
2:40–43	24–25
2:44–45	62
2:47	38n108
3	38
3:16–18	24
6:11–12	25
7	1–2, 4, 4n18, 5–8, 10–11, 11n47, 14–17, 24, 24n44, 25, 25n50, 29–31n76, 36, 38–40, 42–43, 51–53, 55–56, 59, 60n52, 61, 65, 67, 73, 74nn24–25, 78, 80, 88, 90–91, 95–100, 110–11, 126, 128–30n12, 132–35, 146–50, 161–63, 172, 174, 179
7–8	40
7–12	25
7:1	59
7:1–14	16
7:1c	39
7:2	59, 59n50
7:2–3	26, 26n53
7:2–8	26
7:2–14	25
7:3	26, 39, 59, 60n51
7:3b	26
7:4a	27
7:5	27
7:6	27, 59n50
7:7	24, 27, 59n50
7:7–8	24
7:7a	27n60

Ancient Document Index

7:7b	27	8–12	25, 40
7:7b-8	27n60	8:1–12:13	25n52
7:8a	27	8:11	22–23, 27, 174
7:8b	27	8:11b	28
7:9	32	8:14	42
7:9–10	14, 26, 30–31n76, 32–33, 34n83, 43, 53, 129–30	8:15	16n1
		8:24–25	40
7:9–14	29, 40, 174	8:24b-25a	39
7:9a	28, 34	8:24c	39–40
7:9b	57	8:25b	39–40
7:9b-c	29, 34	9	22
7:9c	29, 34, 163	9:9	74n24, 76
7:10	34, 60, 129n11, 132	9:24	42
7:10–11	60	9:26	21n31
7:10a	34	9:27	140, 140n47, 142
7:10b	34–35	9:27a	21
7:11	60	10	51
7:11–12	26	10–12	38, 40
7:13	10, 10n44, 11, 15, 24, 29, 59n50, 60, 73n21, 74n24, 96, 126, 136, 146, 152n89, 159–61, 163–65, 165nn131–32, 172, 179	10:16	16n1
		10:18	16n1
		11	21–22, 38–39
		11:22b	21
		11:28b	22
7:13–14	14, 26, 32, 42–43, 53, 73, 74n24, 95, 129–30, 170–71, 176, 178	11:30	21–22
		11:31	22, 140n47
		11:32a	22
7:13c	35	11:35	102
7:14	16n1, 40, 73–74, 96, 131, 150–51n83	11:35a	102
		11:36	38, 39n114
7:14a	40, 146	11:36a	38
7:15–27	25	11:38	38
7:17	27	12	102
7:17–27	174	12:1–3	39n111
7:18	37	12:1a	38
7:21	25, 28, 37, 41	12:3	39
7:21–22	56n37, 96, 164	12:10	102
7:22	37, 40, 135	12:11	140, 140n47
7:23–24	27		
7:25	19, 27n62, 28, 37, 40–41, 111–13, 123	**Hosea**	
7:25b	112	6:2	112
7:25c	112	6:6	138
7:26–27	135		
7:27	39–40, 74, 96	**Joel**	
7:27a	37, 40		
7:40	27	2:10	145, 145n70
8	148		

Ancient Document Index

Amos

5:2	138
8:9	144–45, 167

Micah

1:2–4	150
1:4a	61
4:1	62
4:1–5	63, 168
7:18	76

Nahum

1:2–5	150n80

Habakkuk

3:6	150n80

Zephaniah

1:5	149

Haggai

2:11–13	71

Zechariah

1:18–21	28
2:1–4	28n63
2:6	152n88
2:6b	151
2:10	151, 152n88
2:14	151
4:7–10	62
13	169, 173
13:7	168–69
13:7a	168–69n139
13:9b	169
14:1–5	29
14:3–5a	132
14:5	132, 152n88
14:5b	132
14:6–11	132

Malachi

3:1	109
3:3	108
4:6	108

NEW TESTAMENT

Matthew

8:20	3n14
9:8	78n44
11:19	3n14
12:5	89
12:32	3n14
16:27b	134
17:23	112
18:18	79
24:37–39	2
26:61	155, 158

Mark

1	14, 67–68, 90
1:2	109
1:2–3	95
1:2–5	109n63
1:4	72
1:4–5	109
1:5	72, 109n62
1:6	72, 109
1:7	72
1:7–8	109n62
1:8	72
1:9–11	90
1:10	72

Ancient Document Index

1:12b	72	2:23–28	67, 91, 94, 99, 175
1:14–8:21	92n1	2:23a	82
1:21–27	72	2:23b	82
1:21–28	78, 90	2:24	69, 82, 92
1:22	69, 99	2:25	81n57, 83, 83n66
1:24	68n3	2:25–26	81–83, 85, 85n75, 88–90
1:25	99	2:26	69, 83, 85, 90
1:27	99	2:26b	84–85, 90
1:28	72	2:27	69, 81–82n60, 81n57, 85–88, 86n78, 88n83, 91
1:32–34	72, 74		
1:34	99		
1:37	72	2:27–28	81–82n60, 85, 88, 90
1:39	99	2:27a	128n5
1:40–45	71n15, 78, 91	2:28	3, 3n14, 5, 14, 69, 81–82n60, 82, 86–88, 88n84, 91, 94–95, 98
1:42	70		
1:45	72		
2	15, 68, 74, 78, 92, 125	2:31	86
2:1	92	2:31–35	158
2:1–3:67	67	2:32	86
2:1–10	91	2:40–45	68–70
2:1–12	7, 67, 70, 77–78, 94	2:44	71
2:3–4	74	2:44b	71
2:5	75, 75n28, 91	2:45a	71
2:5a	74	2:48–49	133n20
2:5b-10	74n26, 75	3	69n7
2:6	78	3:1	108
2:6–7	92–93	3:1–6	81–82n60, 90
2:7	69, 75n28, 77	3:3	108
2:7b	78	3:4	108
2:9–11	68	3:5	108
2:10	3, 3n14, 5, 14, 69, 73–74, 73n21, 74–75, 77–78n42, 78n44, 79, 82, 87–88, 88n84, 94–95, 98–99, 105, 175	3:6	92
		3:7	108
		3:11	70
		3:11–12	99
2:10–13	79	3:13	99–100
2:12	79	3:13–15	120
2:13–19	77	3:15	69n7, 99–100
2:15	83, 94	3:22	93–94, 114
2:17	86, 94, 103	3:23	108
2:18	83	3:27	68n3
2:18–20	83	3:28–29	4n16
2:19	86	4:2b	128n5
2:21–28	68	4:11	128n5
2:22b	68	4:18	133
2:23	69, 85	4:21	128n5
2:23–24	83	4:24	128n5
2:23–26	90	4:41	114n77

Mark *(continued)*

5:1	133
5:15	114n77
6:4	128n5
6:7	69n7, 99–100
6:10	128n5
6:11	71
6:17–29	109
6:30	103
7:1	93–94
7:1–5	114
7:9	128n5
7:24	141
7:25	141
7:26	141
7:27	99
7:29	103
8:17–21	169n143
8:21	128n5
8:27	92n1
8:27–10:45	92n1
8:27–28	94
8:28	159
8:29a	94
8:29b	95
8:30	95
8:31	6, 69, 92–93, 94n8, 95, 101, 103–4, 106–7, 107n53, 108–10, 123, 127, 138, 153, 155, 156n102, 159, 167, 169n142
8:31–38	162
8:32–33	95n10, 98, 101, 169n143
8:33	127
8:34	113
8:34–9:1	128n5
8:34–37	92, 100–101, 127
8:34a–37	98
8:35	127–28
8:35–38	128n5
8:36	127
8:36–38	128
8:38	2, 3n14, 5n25, 6, 12, 15, 126–28n4, 129–30n12, 130–35, 137, 146–48, 152n89, 153, 162–63, 172, 176, 178
8:38–9:1	127–30, 135–37, 136n28, 148, 170, 176
8:38a	135
8:38b	129–30
9:1	127–28nn3–4, 133, 135, 137, 170
9:2b–7	107
9:6	110
9:7	107, 107n55
9:9	107, 110
9:10	108, 169n143
9:11	108
9:11–12a	93n5
9:11–13	109n63
9:12	3n14, 93, 95, 107–9, 109n62, 110
9:12a	109
9:12b	95, 109
9:13	109
9:13a	93n5
9:18	169n143
9:27	140
9:31	6, 92–93, 101, 107–8, 110–12, 111n70, 113–14, 123–24, 128n5, 138, 153, 155, 156n102, 167, 169n142
9:32	101, 114, 169n143
9:35	113
9:35–37	100–101
10:33	94n8, 111, 111n70, 113–14, 124
10:33–34	6, 92–93, 101, 107–8, 110, 113, 138, 153, 169n142
10:34	155, 156n102, 167
10:35–41	101
10:39	113
10:39b–44	100–101
10:43	119
10:45	3n14, 6, 15, 93, 93n4, 94–95, 101, 103–4, 111, 113, 115, 115n83, 117–19, 121, 124, 175–76
10:45–52	114n77
10:45a	115–16

Ancient Document Index

10:45b	115–16	12:7	138
11	106, 142, 148, 171, 177	12:9	138
11–12	137, 144	12:10	103–4, 106, 107n53, 125, 138, 157, 171–72, 177–78
11–13	121, 172, 178		
11:1	92n1	12:11	140
11:1–16:8	92n1	12:12	93n3, 164, 166
11:9b-10	154	12:12a	141
11:10	106n52	12:12b	141
11:12–14	137	12:28–34	141
11:12–17	139, 168	12:28–34a	93n5
11:12–21	106, 167	12:33	141
11:12–24	68n3, 138	12:33b	157
11:12a	106	12:35–45	93n5
11:12b	106	12:61b	172
11:13–14	106	12:62	172
11:14	177	13	136n29, 137, 139, 142–43, 143n58, 171
11:14b-23	177		
11:15	148	13:1	144, 155
11:15–17	137, 154, 156–57, 166	13:2	139, 139n40, 155, 166–67, 171, 177
11:15–18	106n50		
11:17	128n5, 140–42, 152	13:4	139, 144
11:18	93n3, 94n8, 164	13:5	136, 139, 171
11:20–21	106	13:7	136, 139, 169
11:20–24	137	13:9	71–72n17, 114, 136, 139, 153
11:22–25	106		
11:23	138	13:9b	169
11:24–25	178	13:14	139, 141–42, 153, 171
11:27	93n3, 94n8, 106n52, 138, 164	13:14–23	143
		13:14b-23	143, 171
11:27–33	138	13:20	150–51n83
11:28	154, 171	13:21	136
11:28b	138	13:22	150–51n83
11:29–31	138	13:24	143, 144n66
11:31	139	13:24–25	143–44, 145n70, 150n82, 153n92, 171
11:33b	138		
11:38–40	139	13:24–26	153, 162
11:40b	139	13:24–27	143
11:41–44	139	13:24b-25a	143–44
11:61b	178	13:25	144nn66–67, 149
11:62	179	13:25b	143–44
12	103, 106, 142, 148	13:26	5n25, 6, 10, 10n44, 12, 126, 135–37, 136n28, 145–46, 147n76, 148–51n83, 153n92, 160, 162–63, 165, 170–72, 176, 178
12:1	157		
12:1–8	104		
12:1–9	141		
12:1–10	106n52, 141		
12:1–12	138, 171, 177	13:26–27	15, 152n89, 177
12:6	138		

Ancient Document Index

Mark (continued)

13:27	15, 145–47, 150–51n83, 152n88, 153, 168–69n139, 173, 178–79
13:27–28	169
13:28	168
13:39–50	98n23
13:64	166
14–16	137
14:1	93n3, 94n8, 153, 164
14:10	94n8, 111, 111n69, 113, 164
14:10–11	153
14:17	120
14:17–25	120, 124
14:19	103
14:21	3, 3n14, 95, 111, 111n69–11n70, 113
14:21a	95
14:24	15, 94, 101, 103–4, 111, 119, 121, 123–24, 175–76
14:27–28	173
14:28	169n142, 173, 179
14:36	95, 115n83, 118
14:41	93, 111, 111nn69–70, 113
14:41–49	153
14:43	164
14:43–50	101
14:48	157
14:49	95
14:53	153, 164
14:53–65	153
14:53b	153
14:55	94n8, 153–54, 164–65
14:56–59	153
14:58	106, 154, 156, 166–67
14:58a	155, 167
14:58b	157
14:61b	154
14:62	5n25, 6, 10, 12, 15, 74n24, 126, 135–37, 136n28, 147–48, 162–63, 165n131, 170, 172, 176, 179
15	105
15:1	113, 164
15:3	94n8, 164
15:10	94, 94n8
15:10–11	164
15:11	94n8
15:15	113
15:15–20	113
15:26	154
15:31	164
15:34	113
15:37	167
15:38	155, 167
15:39	155
15:56	155
15:57–58	155
15:59	155
15:60	159
15:61b	159
15:62a	159
15:62b	159
15:63–64	160
16:6	169n142
16:7	169, 173, 179
16:8	169, 169n143

Luke

5:15	71
12:8	3n14
17:23–24	2
22:22	3n14

Acts

1:9–11	144
4:11	105, 110
7:48	158
23:5	166

1 Corinthians

3:16	157
3:16–17	122
15:4	112

2 Corinthians

5:1	159
5:4	159

Colossians

2:11	159

1 Thessalonians

4:15–17	144

Revelation

11	112
11:2	147
11:11–12	112

PSEUDEPIGRAPHA

2 Baruch

4:2–7	157
6:6–9	157

1 *Enoch*

5:7–8	151
6–11	18
13:1–3	31
14	30–31n76, 31, 34, 36, 41, 43, 48–49n16, 56, 56n34, 130, 146, 149, 163, 174, 179
14:2	56
14:8	32, 54
14:8–24	30
14:9	32, 56
14:9–10	56
14:10–14	56
14:10a	32
14:10b	32
14:11	56
14:11–12	32
14:13	32
14:15	32
14:15–17	56
14:16	32, 131, 147
14:18	34, 131, 163
14:18–20	55
14:18–23	32–33
14:19	34
14:20	34, 131, 147
14:22	32, 56
14:22–23	34, 163
14:22b	34
14:23	34, 36
15:2	34
15:3–4	36, 149
16:4b	31
37–71	14
37:1	45
37:1–2	49n18
37:1–5	53
37:1a	48
37:2a	54
37:2b	53
37:4	38n108
37:4–5	48
37:5	54
38–44	48
38:1—39:2	54
38:2	38n108, 50
38:6	38n108
39	54
39:3	54–56
39:4	54
39:5	54
39:6	50
39:6–7	151
39:7	54
39:12	54–55
45–57	48, 50
46:1–5	50–51
46:1a	57
46:2–6	51
46:3	51n26
46:4	51n26

Ancient Document Index

1 *Enoch (continued)*

46:4–8	51
46:5	47
46:7b	47
46:8	47
47:1	47
47:1–2	55
47:1–2b	55
47:3	55, 65
47:3—48:6	52
47:4	47
47:4b	52
47:8b	55
48:2	51n26, 52
48:3	52
48:4	52
48:5	53
48:9	52
48:10	50
48:10b	47, 52
52	56n36
53:7	47
54:7—55:2	48
56:5–7	46–47
56:6	47–48n12
56:7a	46
56:7b	46
56:8	46
58–69	48, 51
60	48
61:8	52, 53n29
62	53
62:1–12	53
62:2	52, 53n29
62:3	165n131
62:3–5	12, 147
62:3a	147
62:5	51n26, 53, 165n131
62:5a	147
62:7	51n26
62:8	53
62:9	53
62:10–12	53
62:14	51n26
62:15b	55n33
62:16	55n33
62:16a	55n33
63	47n11
63:10	47
63:11	51n26
64:1–2	47n11
65:1—69:25	48
67:4–5	47
67:8–13	46–47
67:8a	46
67:12	47
67:13	47
69:26	51n26
69:27	51n26
69:29	51n26
70	48
70–71	48–49, 55
70:1	48, 51n26
70:1—71:13	48–49n16
70:2	56
70:2–4	56
70:3	56
71	65
71:1–4	56
71:5	56
71:5–16	56
71:7	56
71:8	133, 147
71:8a	56
71:9–10	55–56
71:10	57
71:11–12	57
71:14	48–49, 51n26, 57
71:14–16	48–49n16
71:17	51n26
79	53n29
85–91	20
89:73	20
89:74	20
90:4	20
90:6	20
90:7	20, 20n25
90:8	20
90:9	28
90:9–10	21
90:12–13	21
90:14–39	20
90:20–37	21

90:28–29	157
93:1–10	151
104:2–6	39
133	20n25

4 Ezra

1–2	58
1:1a	57
1:24–37	58n45
3–14	57–58, 58n45, 65
3:1–5:20	58
5:21–6:34	58
6	60
6:35–9:25	58
6:52b	60
6:54a	60
9:26–10:59	58–59
10:19–24	59
10:25	157
10:25–28	59
10:44	59
10:55	59
11–12	63
11:1–12:51	57–58, 63
12	65
12:11	59
12:48	62n61, 63, 65
13	66–67, 79, 175
13:1	59
13:1–13a	14, 59, 63–64, 63n68
13:1–58	58
13:2	59
13:3	59n50, 60n51
13:3b	59–60
13:3b-4	61
13:5	59n50, 61
13:6	59n50, 62
13:7	61
13:8	59n50
13:9–13	99
13:10	60, 63
13:10–11	60
13:10–11a	61
13:11a	60
13:12	62, 98
13:13a	62, 98
13:13b-24	59
13:25–50	59, 63, 65
13:32a	61
13:35–36	61
13:36	62
13:37–38	63
13:38	64
13:39–50	62n63
13:51–56	59
13:57–58	59
14:1–48	58
15–16	58
17:31a	63
37:3	64

Jubilees

3:31	19
6:17	19n18
6:17–22	19
7:28–33	19
20:7–9	19
22:16–18	19
30	19
30:7–23	19
30:18–20	19

Parables

38:2	96
38:3	96
40:5	96, 151
45:3	96
45:3–5	151
45:4a	96
45:5b	96
46:1–2	79
46:1–5	134
46:4–8	65, 79, 175
47:3—48:6	134
48:4	65, 96, 151, 175
48:7a	97
48:9–10	65, 175
48:10b	134
51:2	96
51:3–5	151

Parables *(continued)*

53:6	97
61:8	134
62:5	79, 134, 163
62:5–6	97
62:8	65, 97, 151, 175
62:11	65, 175
62:14–15	151
62:14b	97

Psalms of Solomon

17:21–32	154

Sirach

5:2	147
36:2	147
36:3	136
48:10	108
48:13	108
50:20–21	76

APOCRYPHA

2 Esdras

1–2	58n45

Testament of Levi

14:4	18
14:5	18
14:6–7	19
16:2	18

www.ingramcontent.com/pod-product-compliance
Lightning Source LLC
Chambersburg PA
CBHW051641230426
43669CB00013B/2387